GU00792141

Office Administr
and Management

MIKE HARVEY
MSc, BSc (Econ), FRSA, FCCA, FCIS, FBIM, MInstM

Professor and Head of Department of Accounting and Finance,
City of London Polytechnic

ICSA Publishing · Cambridge

Published by ICSA Publishing Ltd
Fitzwilliam House, 32 Trumpington Street
Cambridge CB2 1QY, England
and
27 South Main Street, Wolfeboro,
New Hampshire, 03894–2069, USA

First published 1986
Second impression 1988

British Library Cataloguing in Publication Data
Harvey, Mike
   Office administration and management.
   1. Office management
   I. Title
   651.3   HF5547

   ISBN 0-902197-35-5
   ISBN 0-902197-36-3 Pbk

Library of Congress Cataloging in Publication Data
Harvey, Mike
Office administration and management.
   Bibliography: P
   Includes index
   1. Office management.   I. Title
HF5547.H3273   1986   651.3   86–10354
ISBN 0-902197-35-5
ISBN 0-902197-36-3 Pbk

Designed by Geoff Green
Typeset by Hands Fotoset, Leicester
Printed in Great Britain by St Edmundsbury Press Ltd, Bury St Edmunds, Suffolk

Contents

Preface

I understood the importance of good office practices and procedures early in my working life. I joined the small family business, a retail shop, and within a few years a number of outlets were being opened. In those early days as a retailer, the all-important factor to me was to make sales. Yet the ever-increasing amount of paperwork connected with more and more shops proved a rising barrier to this paramount aim. Staff and their wages; orders, purchases, deliveries; occupancy costs (i.e. rents, rates, and the utilities of water, light and heat); correspondence with suppliers and customers, the solicitor, bank manager and accountant; and the arrangement of advertising and promotion – all demanded sound records. It did not take long to realise that without an efficient office system I could drown in a sea of paper.

Some dozen years later, having changed career direction to become a teacher, I was asked during my first week at college to teach office studies for one of the professional bodies' courses. As I prepared for these lectures I soon realised how little I knew about the principles behind good office practices, having previously developed most of the systems used 'on the job'. I learned how beneficial it would have been if I had studied the area rather than finding out the little I knew the hard way. Nevertheless, as the only teacher of the subject at that polytechnic I was still in a vacuum. In another institution I had the advantage of being exposed to debates and discussions on secretarial studies with colleagues in relation to course and curriculum development for the area. Assessing student projects, on consulting assignments and sitting on committees of employers or professional people looking into the area, there was exposure to the sharp end of office practices, which added to my experience.

Through all this I have become more convinced that the manager's knowledge of office administration, office studies, secretarial studies and information services, together with the influence of information technology on that area, provides one of the crucial ingredients of organisational success. Some professional bodies – the Institute of Chartered Secretaries and Administrators is a good example – are active in this area for their potential members by including a study of it as one of their educational requirements.

The aim of this book is to help both the student and those who have to carry out the office function and require some guidance on the principles and practices involved. Of course a book is no substitute for practice. Although it can lay the ground rules, it must be remembered that these should be applied only as appropriate to an entity's circumstances. The administrative system must be designed to fit the work – not the other way round.

This book takes a conceptual approach to a number of aspects of the areas which make up the subject and provides an introduction to the body of knowledge required by those who want to know about office administration and management. This does not mean that it will ignore some of the things required to make an efficient practitioner, such as descriptive knowledge of the area and how to formulate efficient office systems. What it does not do is to describe office machinery and equipment in detail, for developments take place in these on a daily basis, frequently through improvements in technology and experience gained by manufacturers in the design of their products. It will be far better for those interested to find out about the state of the art from manufacturers' or distributors' information bureaux and catalogues.

The conceptual emphasis has the advantage not only of providing the material required by the student for examination purposes, but also of presenting it within a valid framework for the workplace, where it is expected that the reader, if not already doing so, will soon be assuming supervisory responsibilities.

There is no complete agreement as to what body of knowledge covers the area of office work. A wide consensus exists, however, and the book's Contents list is indicative of the subject matter under examination. Some would argue that data processing or the use of computers in the processing of office work must be included in any contemporary study. While these are mentioned *en passant*, it must be remembered that they concern only more sophisticated processing equipment. The emphasis in this book therefore is on the principles, practices and traditional functions of office work, remembering that these can be applied irrespective of equipment used in the processing.

Similarly, the ranking of presentation could be debated, and again there are inevitably differing views. Many approaches would provide a satisfactory solution. What is clear, as in the study of so many areas, is that although subject matter is usually presented in compartmentalised form, each area of study will impinge upon another. A first reading of the book will give a flavour of the material the reader needs to know, but a second reading will undoubtedly be beneficial in order to recognise the important interrelationships between the contents of the various chapters and to strengthen his understanding of them. For example, in Chapter 2 there is a discussion of the benefits and problems associated with centralisation and decentralisation. In Chapter 3, aspects of office work such as the production of copy, the maintenance of records and the provision of copies of text are dealt with, with the question of centralisation or decentralisation under scrutiny once more.

Obviously, the contents of these two chapters and information on this topic from other chapters must be brought together and considered as a whole.

The principles and practices given in this book have a valid application whether the organisation in question is in the commercial, industrial or public sector. They then must be related to a specific area of employment.

Chapter 1 looks at the role of the office in an organisation, and considers managing information, office work as a system, and the internal and external influences that act upon this system. It also discusses the location of offices and the planning of an office environment. Chapter 2 considers the general principles and practices of management which apply to the administration and management of the office, and looks at the role of the supervisor.

Chapter 3 examines office services and methods, considering the best practices to be implemented and the financing of office machinery and equipment. The 'human factor' – for people are the office's most important resource – is dealt with in Chapter 4, where the formulation of a personnel policy and motivation are highlighted.

Many of the problems that the entity faces have their roots in ineffective, or perhaps non-existent, communications. The lack of formal instruction for managers in embryo in the United Kingdom would come as something of a surprise to professionals in many countries, who put a premium on the importance of effective communication in organisations. Chapter 5 looks at this subject, from the fundamentals of the communication of information and relevant problem areas, to an explanation of the principles behind the presentation and communication of information, especially in reports or through forms. As in any branch of business, there must be control over the work carried out; Chapter 6 introduces the control of office work, especially with regard to improving existing processes. Finally, Chapter 7 speculates on the future role of the office.

In order to avoid the clumsy repetition of 'he/she', or worse, 'person', I have adopted the male pronoun throughout to denote the office worker to whom this book is directed.

A book such as this cannot be produced in isolation, and in this case the many colleagues, students and office managers I have talked to have all had an influence on my knowledge, experience and views. Unfortunately, it is impossible to list all who have helped me in the past. However, I would like to thank Neil Wenborn for having initiated the project, and especially for his patience as it progressed, and Janet Stone for her work on the manuscript. Margaret Fraser, who has worked in many capacities, from being at one time my personal assistant through to running an office; Gill Sugden, who has taught the subject for a number of years; and Doug Richardson, a colleague involved in administration: all receive my grateful thanks for reading initial drafts and commenting upon them.

I originally wrote many of the questions and discussion problems for the Institute of Chartered Secretaries and Administrators' examination papers in this subject, and am grateful to the Institute for permission to reproduce them here.

The new technology was used in the production of the typescript for this book, and I am particularly grateful to my daughter, Gill Harvey, who keyed my somewhat messy, initial drafts onto an IBM-XT using Microsoft's WORD, and then painstakingly made numerous corrections to several subsequent drafts. My thanks also go to David Rosebery of the Accountancy Tuition Centre and Ruth Hone from Granada Microcomputers for getting us started with the equipment. The support of my wife Maureen in yet another book is also appreciated.

City of London   Mike Harvey

1
The role of office work – objectives, environment, location

Introduction

The twentieth century has witnessed an 'information explosion' which could be considered as part of the continuing Industrial Revolution. Since the seventeenth century there has been a series of revolutions related to different areas of economic activity. The unprecedented increase in the requirement for and the availability of information in this century is the latest aspect of these developments. It has been suggested in today's world of commerce, industry and government that information is the most important resource available. Thus historians assessing the contribution of 'paper' to the increasing standard of living associated with advances in economic activity might well be justified in referring to an 'information revolution'.

The direct contribution of information is difficult to measure in either economic or social terms. It could be argued that the net 'value added' by the paperwork carried out all over the world is negligible, or perhaps even negative if the resources consumed to process paper were included in the calculations. Equally, there are strong social arguments militating against the information machinery, as it grows both in size and complexity and so requires costly manning – but more importantly because it may cause an abuse of the right to personal privacy.

It is not the purpose of this book to consider philosophical debates about the value of information, although it might deal with this value in passing. It can be accepted as a basic tenet that today vast amounts of information are required and provided to lubricate commerce, industry and government. The purpose of the book will be to examine the different aspects of office work that contribute to this activity. Attention will be paid, at least indirectly, to economic arguments concerning the balance of the costs *vis-à-vis* the benefits of the information provided within and by the office, and the provision of these services with an eye to efficiency. The basic concern will be with the organisation, administration and management of office services and work, and how the function helps an enterprise to collect, process and present infor-

1

mation at all levels – from the routine recording of data to the provision of more sophisticated information for decision-making purposes.

Although the focus is on office work, it is inevitable that ideas from many disciplines will be brought in. These include economics, law, geography (transport and communication), quantitative techniques, and the behavioural sciences, as well as the rapidly developing area of information technology. Today a multidisciplinary approach is being taken in the application of resources for administrative purposes.

Many terms such as office management, office administration, office organisation and office studies are used to describe the study of the services provided and the functions related to office work which are undertaken. These terms are often taken to be synonymous and are used freely and inter-changeably. With the growth in information requirements and developments in processing techniques, which have given the office an increasingly important position in the enterprise, an approach is required which provides a framework within which all aspects can be examined; the phrase office administration and management is a most appropriate one to cover this study.

'Office work' can be considered a catch-all term which embraces an entity's organisation, administration and management relating to the processing of data and information. The process itself involves the many activities in the record life cycle, from its origination, perhaps as text, through the various aspects of working on the information and storing it, to, perhaps, its eventual destruction. A few years ago this chapter might have been entitled 'The office'. However, developments are so rapid because of changes in technology, especially with regard to where the traditional work of the office may be performed in the future, that perhaps it is more appropriate today (and likely even more so in the future) to refer to 'office work'.

This chapter will consider the objectives of such work, with an analysis of how the function is carried out. The location of the work and its processing flows are important aspects, especially in relation to the effect of environmental influences on office work both internally and externally. The two major elements in office work, personnel and technology, will be dealt with in greater depth in later chapters.

The distinction between data and information

The *Concise Oxford Dictionary* provides general definitions for data and information. It defines datum as, among other things:

> . . . facts or information, esp. as basis for inference; quantities or characters operated on by computers etc. and stored or transmitted . . . data bank, place where data are stored in large amounts; data base, quantity of data available for use . . . data sheet, leaflet summarizing information on a subject.[1]

Elsewhere it defines information as:

. . . informing, telling; thing told, knowledge, (desired) items of knowledge, news . . . information retrieval, tracing of information stored in books, computers, etc.; information science, study of processes for storing and retrieving information; information theory, quantitative study of transmission of information by signals, etc. . . .[2]

More specific definitions are provided in other places, for example by Dennis Longley and Michael Shain in the *Dictionary of Information Technology*:

Data (1) In computing, information which is to be input, processed in some way and output by the computer . . . (2) A representation of the facts, concepts, or instructions in a formalized manner in order that it may be communicated, interpreted, or processed by human or automatic means[3];

and

Information (1) Knowledge that was unknown to the receiver prior to its receipt. Information can only be derived from data that is accurate, timely, relevant and unexpected. (2) The meanings assigned to data by the agreed conventions used in its representation. If the content of a message is known prior to its receipt then no new information is conveyed . . .[4]

As far as these definitions are concerned, the former are too general and the latter too specific as related to the study of office work; perhaps the following definitions would be more appropriate to this area of study:

Data is the word used to describe the resources, operations and transactions of an organisation, collected and retained by the office system, with the objective of processing it to provide useful information.

Thus examples of data would be: the number of employees and details of their employment records; the costs associated with a job; records of customers and sales; details of business transactions; and so on.

Information is meaningful data used to represent items of knowledge by the administration and management of the entity to help them in their decision-making, planning and controlling activities.

For example, data and information can be represented in the form of words, figures, symbols, diagrams, or by any other means. It can be seen that they have a close relationship, the 'raw' data being converted into appropriate, usable information. Information and its communication will be dealt with in Chapter 5.

Growth of information requirements

What factors have contributed to the 'information revolution' discussed in the introduction to this chapter? The ways in which information requirements have grown and continue to grow will mould the way in which data are supplied and processed, although purpose, timeliness, quantity and validity must also be considered. These will affect decisions about the relative processing contributions of men, materials and machines. It is relevant to the study of office systems, therefore, to be aware of the background to the development of the growth of information requirements.

General economic growth

The root cause of the growth of the demand for more and more information is to be found in the Industrial Revolution itself. This period witnessed high growth rates which caused expectations for ever-increasing living standards to become the norm. Whatever the economic system, capitalist or socialist, the increasing complexity of the system required a corresponding advance in the sophistication of the planning and control functions within it. These systems use data and information and so an increased provision is also required. At the same time, the technological advances which have provided and continue to provide the increase in productivity to sustain current economic growth have added to the complexity of the production process. The specialisation consequent on this imposes complex demands on organisation, which increases the need for more information to be generated. All these requirements lead to the creation of information systems both within the individual enterprise and within the economy in which the enterprise operates. These systems need to expand to cope with the more demanding situation.

Mergers and diversification

Subsequent to the factors outlined above, 'size' appears to have become the key to industrial advance. Economies of scale are frequently treated as being one of the crucial factors in rising productivity – hence increased living standards. Thus one objective of management is to promote growth of the firm, and one way in which this can be achieved is through mergers. Sometimes this has been to gain necessary monopolies, as in the case of the octopoid industries.[5] In other cases it has been to gain economies through vertical and horizontal integration. Many firms also try to spread business risk through diversification on a product or geographical basis.

Firms which grow, whether by deepening or by broadening[6] their asset structure or through diversification, often create more administrative problems than they solve in the process and soon seem to be sinking in a sea of paper. Another dimension is added when a firm becomes a multinational one and the information it requires for decision-making, planning and controlling purposes is generated on a multinational basis.

Competitive forces

At home and abroad new developments abound on both the demand and supply side for goods and services, sometimes providing a competitive edge to the organisation which can first meet demand with some new technology or product. Thus it is important to collect information about a firm's area of activities. On the demand side, more sophisticated forms of marketing effort have been introduced as enterprises have focused their attention on the necessity of becoming marketing-orientated and to ensure that their marketing mix[7] optimises the resources allocated for this purpose. On the supply side, research and development has become increasingly necessary to ensure that both processes and products are technically viable. This all means that when an enterprise is striving to survive in a competitive environment, information has to be generated in order to facilitate decision-making for survival.

Lower employee/executive ratios
With the increasing complexity of technology and the consequent sophistication in the processes of administration, the span of control – that is, the number of staff an executive has to manage – has had, of necessity, to be reduced. (See Chapter 2, page 46 for an explanation of the term 'span of control'.) Thus the ratio of management to other employees has tended to increase in most organisations. As a result, more information has to be generated to feed the increasing numbers of management units and to co-ordinate the work of the smaller specialised units. A parallel feature to this development has been the trend for executives to have received a better general education, and specifically business-orientated training. This in turn has encouraged today's executive to expect the provision of more sophisticated information to help him in his tasks; more data being generated for executives poses a problem in that they have only a limited amount of time available to assimilate the information they are confronted with. Care must therefore be taken in the selection of the information to be presented to management, as well as in presenting it in a way which will facilitate its assimilation. Failure to do so will result in the executive being overwhelmed by paperwork, which in itself can lead to a paralysis of work.

Office work today includes the production of information from manufacturing, marketing, financial and personnel data, and many administrative staff need to have a knowledge of the developing quantitative and statistical techniques which can be used to analyse and synthesise these. Thus a higher level of education and training than ever before is required.

Inadequate organisational structures and control procedures
When an entity expands, its organisational structure may, like Topsy, just grow and grow. If this happens and the structure remains based upon the original concept, it may become poorly adapted to the new situation – being saved from collapse only through the generation of inordinate amounts of paper. In this case a complete appraisal of the changed circumstances is necessary; the development of a new structure could make much of the paper generated by the old system obsolete. Yet often such change is not forth-

coming, or at best there is either merely the automation of the existing system or too much of a lag in the introduction of a new administrative system – indicating that most entities require better information control systems.

Forces of centralisation
Where there is a tendency towards centralisation, whether within a business enterprise or a State-controlled organisation, there is likely to be an increase in the information requirements of that entity. Where services are being provided at functional level, the needs of any one particular area will be known. With centralisation many of the information requirements of one function may not be applicable to another, although much the same information will often prove to be necessary and may need to be collected from similar sources. With centralisation the increase in information required to exercise control over outlying components of the entity may be justified on grounds of efficiency, but it cannot be justified on grounds of expediency.

Feeding information technology
This is an aspect in the generation of information that is generally overlooked and frequently denied. Yet all too often it exists. Computers make it easier to generate information, yet some of the additional information that they produce may not be required or have any real value in terms of application. When expensive equipment, such as a computer, is introduced in the processing of paper, there is a tendency to use it to produce as much information as possible since this helps to justify its installation, especially if there is unused capacity. Although it is frequently more economical to leave the spare capacity unused, the psychological hurdle thus produced is often too great to jump. So there may be the generation of additional and unnecessary print-outs. From this may come other costs, e.g. because additional users are required to sift through the mountains of paper being created. There is the real danger that the total costs of processing and appraising the original information requirements *plus* the additional information generated will far outweigh the total benefits.

State requirements
Depending upon whether, as far as the commercial and industrial aspects of an economy are concerned, the State is public- or private-sector orientated, or where it lies on the spectrum between the two, there will be certain basic information that must be supplied to the State. This is apart from any paperwork associated with the collection of taxes, customs duties or other revenues. Returns will be required for national planning purposes. Sometimes these must be made on a regular basis, at others on an *ad hoc* basis. Census, and statistics for production, employment and health are a few examples. Then there may be quasi-government bodies, such as national research institutes, which also collect information.

Thus, both the supplying enterprises and the receiving organisations develop the facilities for collecting and processing the necessary data promptly and economically. Information not required for revenue purposes is likely to be needed for the development of plans as the State tries to integrate political strategy for the various sectors of the economy, on a regional or industrial basis, into an overall economic plan for the nation. Using the information collected, the politicians in power will decide upon any changes necessary in the country's economic infrastructure and will direct commercial and industrial enterprises accordingly, through coercion or incentives.

Society's expectations

Changing social and economic values have encouraged most developed countries' populations to expect more comprehensive and sophisticated services from both the State and the private sector. To meet these demands more information is gathered for an increasing number of aspects of life-styles than ever before. Expectations from education, health and other care services, such as those for the aged, are obvious cases where increasingly more information is being gathered to help provide society, as the consumer of such services, with better facilities. The same applies to demands for consumer products and services.

These factors, generated by the Industrial Revolution, today have a parallel in the information revolution, one reinforcing the other. The system that controls office work must take this into account so that all the information requirements of an organisation are integrated into a whole if wasteful duplication of effort is to be avoided.

The management of information

The traditional field of office administration and management has undergone continuous evolution since the 1950s. This process has been accelerating with the trend towards centralisation of information processing in larger organisations, strengthened by the advent of the computer and its application to office work. It has been reinforced through more interest in office automation. Yet it is all too frequently observed, taught and written about as though it were a static area. A major aim of this book is to introduce concepts which will provide practitioners with a flexible outlook on the area they operate in, or move into as their careers develop. This should enable them to readily adapt to the changing environment within which they and their organisations function.

The information services provided within an organisation will include the processing of the information required for routine daily operational purposes, such as correspondence and accounts, and for the production of special reports which provide accurate, up-to-date information to enable management to make decisions in line with organisational policy, based upon the resources committed to promote the achievement of plans.

The best ways of creating, processing, storing and distributing information related to office work, and the way in which this is managed, must be considered carefully. Here the influence of the characteristics of the data and information to be dealt with will be brought into the analysis. The type of equipment to be used and the abilities of personnel selected to operate it and carry out the processing functions must also be examined.

If efficiency is to be achieved management must have clear objectives as to what is required. In the case of office work the major objective will be 'getting the work done'. The most appropriate framework in which to organise the work must therefore be devised. Of course this will depend upon a number of factors, including: the type of work to be performed and its volume; the equipment available to enable the processing; and the personnel the entity employs. Since different people will have different responsibilities and carry out different functions, both the formal lines of communication and any informal relationships that develop between them will have an influence on the way the work is undertaken. Other considerations will include the type of entity, what goods or services it produces and the intricacy of tasks, which will be influenced by the complexity of its production processes and product range, as well as by its consumers and the methods of marketing to them. The entity's management structure, and leadership styles within the organisation, will also bring influences to bear. This means that the centres of office work within different organisations are unlikely to be identical, and sometimes there will be differences between the ways in which similar work is carried out.

The benefits of careful organisation include: a clarification of authority within the entity, which will help avoid misunderstandings about the responsibilities and authority of employees; and the establishment of clear lines for formal communication, which will help develop the channels of communication throughout the entity, and in so doing should avoid wasteful duplication.

There will be constraints of cost and time related to the provision of both routine and specialist office services. Both have to be set off against the benefits received after appraisals of the system providing them are made.

One important aspect which is all too often neglected is the necessity to innovate. It is easy to pay lip service to the idea of innovation and do nothing about it. Senior administrators must be aware of any new developments likely to help in the processing of office work, whether these concern new technology which makes it possible to automate more and more processes, or new systems which enable procedures to become more streamlined. Techniques like organisation and methods (O & M) and work measurement (both described in Chapter 6), a knowledge of the use of the developing techniques for creating text, or for information storage, reproduction, transmission, etc., should be fully investigated. Quality control of output, which is sometimes ignored in an office, must also be considered; and in these days of escalating costs, the introduction of cost control techniques becomes critical.

It is also important to have an understanding of the behavioural aspects of the area, that is, the effect of people's behaviour in relation to performing office work. Furthermore, it should not be overlooked that information can confer status and/or power on those who have access to it; when this happens, the aim must be to make it work for the benefit of the organisation, rather than of the individual.

The office as a system

The analysis of an organisation and its component parts as a system is a useful exercise; this approach has gained increasing popularity during recent years, especially because it enables careful consideration to be given to the inter-actions and relationships of office work both internally and externally. George Terry states that 'The initial effort of the information manager is *to conceptualize the work required in order to supply the information wanted.*'[8] He continues that 'From the information management viewpoint, a system can be looked upon as a vehicle of thought and analysis. It is an attitude or way of viewing projects and problems. A system has been called a *"think process tool"*.'[9] This form of analysis can be developed simply without delving into the intricacies of systems theory, and even when used at an elementary level it will help in the study of office administration and management.

Any organisation, whether in the public or the private sector of the economy, comprises many subsystems within the total system. One of these is the information system, which embraces all other subsystems to provide the most important link between them.

The five features of a system

Although most people are familiar with biological and engineering systems, difficulties arise when they try to conceptualise an abstract system – such as an organisational system. Basically, however, this is a very simple concept; Fig. 1.1 illustrates the five major components or features of a system in general terms.

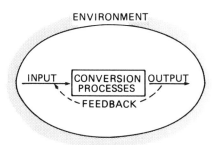

Fig. 1.1 The five major components of a system

The components of the general system depicted in Fig. 1.1 can be explained as follows: *Inputs* into the system are resources and ideas. The *conversion process* will change the inputs into *outputs* and from these there will be a *feedback loop* which enables the performance of the system to be monitored. These four components are bounded by the system's *environment*, which both supplies the input for, and receives the output from, the system.

Systems theory evolved from studies of other sciences, especially biology, where the study of an organism's system in its environment is referred to as ecology. Numerous parallels to a biological organism will become apparent. It also drew some of its concepts from engineering systems, where automatic control mechanisms, which are activated through real-time feedback loops, are often to be found – as in the case of most comprehensive central heating and air-conditioning systems. Similarly, systems may be open or closed: the *open* system has greater links with its environment than does the *closed* system, with boundaries which limit the latter's interchange with its environment.

The general characteristics of a system

It should be noted here that features are not the same as characteristics. Features are the notable characteristics associated with something, whereas characteristics are general distinguishing traits or qualities.

Systems have a number of general characteristics regarding their definition, objectives, communication links and feedback loop. A major characteristic is that systems are *dynamic*.

Definition
All systems must be carefully and clearly defined. Generally, all organisations in the public and private sector are systems with *boundaries*; thus a *bounded* system is being considered. In this book one of the subsystems of such organisations will be considered – the office work system.

Objectives
A system must have an objective. At the simplest level the system's objective may merely be to survive. In the case of business enterprises, as their systems become more complicated they will probably develop multiple objectives, such as those concerning security, stability, success, satisfaction, and so on.

Communications
Systems require a network to enable the communication of information within them. This communications network also needs links with the system's environment so that there can be communication between the system and the environment within which it operates. With the business system this communications network should aim to provide for the optimum, NOT necessarily the maximum, gathering of information to help its management to make decisions, to plan and to control.

Feedback

It is important for all systems to have some form of feedback mechanism, or loop. This will provide information to show whether, in the conversion of resources and ideas, the system is proceeding on the desired course. If not, the feedback mechanism will signal that corrective control action needs to be taken. Thus the system will be regulated through information from the feedback mechanism.

Dynamic

The most problematic characteristic of business systems is that they are dynamic. Yet from the point of view of helping in the study of an organisation, this is probably the most useful characteristic of systems theory. It is this characteristic which impels systems towards their goals and seeks to maintain balance. Constant reappraisal of the operation of the system is required by an entity if it is to maintain its position *vis-à-vis* other systems and in relation to its environment. It will be seen that a business entity can lose 'balance' in many ways, but it is dynamism that provides the required flexibility to enable it to maintain equilibrium. This may operate even to the extent of enabling the entity to reappraise and change its fundamental objectives when it becomes appropriate to do so.

The office work system

The office work to be carried out within an organisation can be considered as a single subsystem of that entity, although it would also be valid to view the individual aspects of office work as even smaller subsystems of the office administration and management system. The approach of analysing office work as a system is shown in Fig. 1.2. This pin-points the five essential features of systems discussed above, namely the systems input, its conversion process, and the output with signals going back to the input through the feedback loop, all of which are within the system's environment. This approach is developed in Fig. 1.2, showing the major components of office work and services together with their interrelationships. At the same time, it sets the complete office work system within the context of the major functional areas of a business's office work. These areas form the *inner* boundary to the office system. Its *outer* boundary is formed by the external business contacts and other components of the business environment. The analysis of the system is simplified if these two environments within which the office functions lie are viewed as a single boundary to the organisation's office work. From this boundary the inputs of data and resources will be fed into the system.

From Fig. 1.2 it can be seen that to understand the conversion process, it is necessary to appreciate both how the office work is organised and what the means of processing the data into information are. When considering the organisation, planning, control and review procedures, careful attention must be given to the way in which people working within the office system behave;

this is where motivation comes in. There must be a thorough understanding of the subsystems associated with the production and collection of data and with its processing, which may include calculation and the production of text, as well as its analysis, before methods of storing, retrieving and perhaps ultimately disposing of the records can usefully be examined. In the organisation of any subsystems, the end product and the total system must be kept clearly in mind to ensure that all outputs of office work are in a usable form. Information may be required for planning or control purposes, as well as for other aspects of long- and short-term decision-making – all for both routine and one-off situations. The objectives behind the production of the information will provide one of the criteria used in decisions such as whether to store the information for future use or to dispose of it when it is no longer relevant.

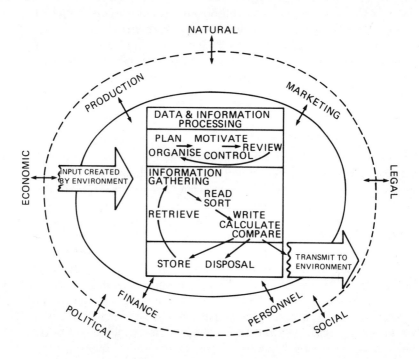

Fig. 1.2 The systems approach to office management

It should be noted that Fig. 1.2 shows the office system as being central in its environment. Of course, in many organisations this will not be the case since there will not be a centralised administrative function; the various line, staff and functional areas will have their own mini-administrative systems, which will have varying degrees of autonomy. Even then, each exists as a subsystem in its own right.

The internal and external environments and their influence on the office system

The office work system shown in Fig. 1.2 depicts areas from which there will be both internal and external forces exerting diverse influences. As well as the *endogenous* or internal influences on an organisation's administrative system from such functional areas as production and marketing, there will also be the *exogenous* or external influences upon it. During recent years the latter have played an increasingly important role in the way in which office work is undertaken. Sometimes they even impose severe constraints upon the system. These encompass the natural, social, economic, political and legal influences acting upon the office work system, especially as far as any output for external users is concerned.

Internal influences

Organisations have a number of functions, and their nature will depend upon the entity concerned. Those in private-sector industry will usually have purchasing and marketing as their main activities, whereas those in the service industries may give different activities prime importance. For example, the firm in retailing is likely to have procurement and selling as the main activities, while many enterprises in banking would consider attracting deposits and making loans as theirs. In the public sector some central and local government authorities, or at least departments within them, will even have administration as one of their major functions – for example, where a local government department administers a rent and rate rebate scheme through a housing rebates department, which 'administers' the reduction of the payment made by the tenant. Or a local authority may provide a service such as the loan of books through libraries, which requires considerable administrative skills.

An entity's functions will have a major influence on the component of its office work and the way in which this is carried out. Thus a manufacturing department may require clerical functions associated with production planning and quality control, the former also being linked in with the marketing area through such functions as the sales forecast. Sales will have its office work requirements linked in with supplying customers and servicing them, including dealing with any complaints. In the public sector there will be administrative demands created by the provision of education, medical and other social services, as well as in the supply of utilities such as water, power, transport, etc. – all of which will have their own particular influences on the nature of office work and the structure developed to perform it.

External influences

No organisation's administrative system is an island. For example, although a commercial enterprise may try to impose upon others the way that it wants paperwork carried out, the firm's customers are unlikely to do this in the way required but rather in one which satisfies their own needs. This may cause conflict between the two organisations' administrative systems, and if either method does not prove to be acceptable to the other party, it could lead to the loss of a customer, or supplier, depending upon the point of view.

As society has moved from a free enterprise orientation into a more controlled and directed position, it is inevitable that the State will try to impose its paperwork requirements on the population at large and on the business community in particular. Thus in the United Kingdom there are legal requirements concerning the completion of census forms, tax returns, etc., with the onus on the entity to make the return.

Many of the external influences on office work have social or economic roots, and have caused sufficient interest to pressure the appropriate politicians of the day. An example of this would be the Health and Safety Act 1974, where social and unionised pressure group influences eventually caused a statutory requirement to be enforced covering working conditions in offices, including a statement about the required office temperature. More recently the Data Protection Act 1984, with its ramifications concerning the holding of data and information about people in computer data banks, and legislation for equal opportunities and the employment of disabled people, have had their influences. Such influences must, inevitably, have an effect on the way in which an entity's office work is carried out as well as on the resulting output and any controls over it. So allowances have to be made for such constraints in the development or modification of the office work processing system.

Location decisions: siting the office

Alan Delgado points out that 'An office is not necessarily in a building; one can be set up anywhere. It can be a room in a house, an hotel bedroom or a cabin on board a ship. It can be a shed in a garden. The firm's representative uses his car as an office, and the executive, as he is driven from appointment to appointment, dictates into a machine while making or taking calls from the telephone at his side.'[10] Harry Richardson writes, 'Industry tends to be agglomerated in a few prosperous regions of an economy, and this process is usually self-sustaining. In the last century basic industry was strongly attracted to sources of raw materials and fuel supplies, but the coming of electric power and changing technology greatly widened the locational choice. The build-up of industry near large high-income population centres indicated an increasing trend towards market orientation.'[11] To some extent the location of office work has followed the location of industry since a considerable proportion of it is carried out where enterprises establish their manufacturing capacity. An adjunct to this is that administration is required to support the infrastructure of industrial and commercial areas. However, Harry Richardson noted that today there is considerable evidence that much industry has become 'footloose' and so capable of being sited anywhere. In addition, it is possible that in the future more and more office work will be carried out in the home through the use of computers, either with the worker being allocated a personal computer (PC) and storing the work on discs which will be sent in for processing or, and probably more likely in the long run, transmitting the work to head office over a cable system. Home units may even be connected into an organisation's computer network. However, despite this last forecast, there will still be office buildings and offices attached to factory premises for many years to come. Even if much of the office work of the future is carried out at home, there will still be the need for a central location to collect the information being processed, and to deal with its storage and distribution – perhaps to senior executives and managers who may also be working from their homes. A possible final scenario might be that as sectors of society become richer and more leisure time becomes available, robots could eventually be producing information for other robots to use – and somebody may then ask whether such information is really useful!

These are speculations on the future. Today, in any large city or town, the centre is occupied by buildings housing office workers of one sort or another. These will include: professional peoples' offices, such as those used by solicitors or accountants; the offices of commercial organisations including those of banks, insurance companies and advertising agencies; offices within other organisations, such as the large departmental and chain stores or shops; and offices to keep the records of doctors, dentists and the like. Outside the city and town centres other offices will be found attached to industrial premises and transport undertakings. In the government sector there will be municipal offices for the local government areas as well as offices for central government in some parts of the country. It can be said that probably the thing common to *all* organisations is that, without exception, they require some form of office work to be carried out to enable them to function successfully.

The question that all have to ask is where will it be best to undertake this office work? The answer will depend upon many factors, including: where the organisation's mainstream work is carried out, e.g. does the manufacturing enterprise operate a single factory or does it have a number of these sited at different locations, and in that case how far apart are the locations; if there are a number of locations does the work need to be undertaken near the users or can it be centralised; and what about the costs incurred in actually doing the office work?

The factors to consider when deciding where to site an office

Many organisations already have their offices well established. However, a newly created organisation may be deciding where to site its offices, or consideration may be given to moving an organisation's existing offices to another location. Witness the current campaigns to 'sell' the Peterborough Effect, and Milton Keynes. There may be many reasons for making such a change, including: when organisations merge they may wish to consolidate the new entity's offices on a single site; the organisation may have outgrown its existing office accommodation; or it may be contracting or has to move out of its existing premises for redevelopment reasons. The factors that need to be considered when deciding where to locate the office premises are set out below.

Volume of office work

This is a most important consideration, for it will determine the amount of space required to carry out the organisation's office work. In turn this will influence the location, depending upon where suitable premises are available. For example, the very small enterprise may find that a desk and filing cabinet in a back room will suffice. At the other end of the scale, the very large organisation with factories in many parts of the country may find it difficult to obtain premises of the required size in a prestigious city centre to take all its office staff at an acceptable cost.

The amount of office work an entity requires to be carried out is related to two things: the size of the organisation, remembering that size can be measured in a number of ways, e.g. by the number of employees or the value of the assets employed; and the purpose behind the entity – for example, if the objective of a firm is to manufacture simple products where little quality control or progress chasing is required, there will be less paperwork than where a complex product is made which requires careful checking at each stage of the production process. The attitude of the organisation's management to paperwork also has to be taken into account, since some quite similar businesses generate quite different amounts of paper. This is because the management of one feels that certain aspects of the paperwork can be eliminated whereas the management of the other feels that they cannot.

Number of locations

The number of locations at which the entity operates and where these are will influence the location of that organisation's offices. A firm with all its production facilities in the north of a country is not likely to site its offices in the south. There is the consideration of having the entire office in a capital or large city, or perhaps only a small prestigious office there. This is really providing a 'reception' point for people who wish to do business with the organisation in an area which they regularly visit, especially in the case of overseas clients. Local government offices need to be within the area of government concerned.

When an organisation's units are spread over a wide area there is likely to be more difficulty in deciding where to site its offices, assuming that there is a need for some central location. With the manufacturing organisation, both production and marketing considerations need to be brought into the analysis as well as any factors concerning efficient administration and cost.

Availability of labour

Although office workers need certain skills, the economies of scale associated with the necessary training are not too great, and all towns with a reasonably sized population should be able to provide most of the required labour. In the past, industries operating within the United Kingdom became grouped in certain locations; for example, one of the reasons for firms in the cotton industry going to Lancashire, and woollens to Yorkshire, was because they could draw upon the skilled labour force associated with the industry that had developed in these areas. This is not as important in the case of office work. What is more important is the general availability of labour. Until the late 1970s there was virtually full employment in London, and so office workers could command a higher salary than, say, those offering their services at Great Yarmouth where there was a certain amount of unemployment, and where the cost of living was also much lower. The problem with choosing a location where there is a favourable labour supply is that conditions can change; although an office site may be chosen because the labour supply of the area was favourable at a particular time, a few years later – perhaps because of industrial growth in the area – it may become increasingly difficult to meet the organisation's labour requirements. Forecasts of this nature are by definition complex and subject to rapid change. Nevertheless, an error of judgement in location will have long-term effects.

Social infrastructure

It is sometimes possible to attract labour to an area where there is a good social infrastructure, or for those areas which are fortunate enough to be well endowed in this respect to retain their population. If the social infrastructure is lacking in an area, people, especially the younger ones who are more socially mobile, are likely to migrate to the big cities. Parents bringing up families want good housing, schools, hospitals and other facilities for their children. Transport and entertainment facilities, such as sports grounds, parks and clubs, will also be requirements, as will good shopping areas. Sometimes, when changing an office location, an entity may have to provide housing for some of the key people that it wishes to move with it into the new area, and give an allowance to staff to cover the cost of their having to relocate their families. When an office is located in a decaying area, it may not only be difficult to attract new blood into the area; there is also likely to be great difficulty in keeping the existing staff.

Economic infrastructure

Enterprises in the private sector will be interested in the economic infra-structure of an area. They will want good roads, and perhaps rail, sea or air transportation between the home base and their suppliers and markets. This may be to enable people from these two groups to visit them. Thus if the organisation carries out a lot of overseas business it may be beneficial for it to have some form of premises in the country of operation's capital city, such as London in the United Kingdom. Communication links are also important, although today the telephone, telex and facsimile transmissions are usually available in all parts of a country.

Space for expansion
Some organisations will prudently make provision for future expansion, and so must ask whether the site to be selected will be able to cope with this when it comes along. However, with changes in technology the processing of much office work requires less space. For example, rather than pay for more space to house traditional filing cabinets to store documents, the organisation may decide to record the documents on microfiche.

Cost
Probably the major consideration for most organisations when making office location decisions is cost – both the cost of the site and that of maintenance. There may be State incentives for commercial or industrial organisations locating their offices in certain parts of the country. In the United Kingdom the government has designated development areas where there are high levels of unemployment, and incentives, such as favourable rents and rates, are given to firms setting up business there. Such help, from either central or local government, may also be in the form of cheap accommodation, subsidies for staff, or tax incentives, including those concerning capital allowances.

In the United Kingdom the government itself has moved a number of its major offices outside London in recent years, in order to reduce costs, take pressure off the city, and help provide employment in areas where jobs are scarce. Thus the Vehicle Licensing Department and the Royal Mint have been resited in Wales, and the Stationery Office at Norwich.

Influences on location
Debenham Tewson and Chinnocks[12] collected data on the important influences on companies' choice of property and found that over 50 per cent of them gave location as the most important influence. The factors they looked for in location are shown in Fig. 1.3.

Criteria: Access to	Mentioned by (%)
Motorway network	52
Specialist/skilled staff	49
Markets	30
Good residential environment	28
International airport	25
Domestic airport	14
University/polytechnic	12
Cultural/recreational facilities	9
Railway network	7
None of the above	5
Support staff	–
Suppliers	–

Fig. 1.3 Influences on location (UK)

Locating the office in a major city

There are a number of disadvantages to the location of an office in a major city, especially if it is the country's capital. The opportunity cost of owning a site in a city centre is high, as seen by the rents demanded for buildings in such locations, which tend to be much higher than those charged in provincial locations. The same normally applies as far as rates are concerned.[13] Other occupancy costs such as utilities in the form of heat, light and water tend to be more or less the same within a country, wherever an office building is sited. However, there are exceptions, as in the case of insurance premiums which may be loaded in a major area of population if the risk of crime is greater. Since housing and travel costs are also usually higher in city locations or the commuting area around them, the cost of employees is also generally higher because staff expect to be paid more to compensate them for longer, more expensive journeys to and from work. As an example many organisations, including government entities, with their premises in London pay their staff what is called a 'London allowance' to compensate for the higher cost of living.

Nevertheless, there are some factors which compensate for the high costs of being sited in a major city. There may be a better supply of well-trained office workers to hand, especially those who have experience in the latest equipment, since city firms tend to be among the first to forge ahead. And a factor not to be underestimated is the prestige of being sited in a city. So all these factors have to be considered, and the decision as to where it will be best to site an organisation's offices can become very complex.

Locating the office in a small town

In the United Kingdom there has been a noticeable shift of population from the big cities into the smaller towns and rural areas, thus affecting the location of the supply of office workers. It appears that this is not just because entities have relocated away from cities into the small towns, but also because firms in the small towns and rural areas are doing relatively well and may find it easier to expand than their large counterparts in the cities. As to why this should be the case, Steve Fothergill and Graham Gudgin say 'The balance of evidence points towards inadequate premises and sites as the failure of city-based firms. Most factories in large cities are hemmed in by existing urban development and have little or no room for physical expansion. Therefore as capital intensity of production rises, machines displace labour from the fixed area of floorspace, and employment falls. In the small towns the same displacement of labour by capital occurs of course, but fewer factories lack room for expansion and greenfield sites are more readily available. Firms in small towns are therefore much better placed to increase their floorspace and production during an upturn, and this growth is more than sufficient to allow a net increase in employment in these places.'[14]

Making the location decision[15]

When an organisation is deciding where to site new offices or any other premises such as a new factory, or where to move its existing offices, there are likely to be a number of options open. In considering these there are many influences to bring into the analysis, some of which are easy to overlook. A problem is that although some of the factors, such as the rent of premises and the cost of labour, already have money values put on them which can be directly compared, other factors do not have money value labels on them. Items with money values on them are said to be in *quantitative* terms – as are those which, although not stated in money values, are expressed in other quantitative ways, i.e. they have number values associated with them. For example, the distance from London by road of the various locations being considered can be measured. Or the time needed for a journey can be ascertained, for although one location may be nearer London in single carriageway road miles, it may take longer to drive this distance than to a site which is further away but linked by motorway. Train journey times and flying times can all be calculated, the latter including the time to get to and from the airport; and the cost of journeys can be compared.

However, what employees are likely to think about the local infrastructure is harder to measure since this will depend upon people's subjective valuations. One person may like an area and so value it highly, whereas another may not. This sort of information, which is referred to as *qualitative* information, must also be brought into the analysis.

The matrix approach

The use of a matrix to collate both the quantitative and qualitative information about the different locations being considered has two main advantages. Firstly, it provides a check-list, which helps to ensure that no factors have been overlooked. Secondly, if a weighted points system is incorporated into the appraisal, an attempt can be made to quantify the qualitative information. Although this may be crude, it does at least try to value the siting influences in a more objective way. Figure 1.4 shows the basis to this approach.

The matrix approach in Fig. 1.4 could be developed. There could be a number of matrices, for example one to show the capital expenditures that would be associated with establishing each site, and another to show their annual operating expenditures. Then there could be separate matrices for items already in money values and those which are not, although the items stated in money values could have points allocated to them, or those quantified using the points system could have their points 'converted' into money values. Thus items such as occupancy costs, because they have a money tag on them, could be shown on a separate matrix. The purchase price of the properties, if to be bought, could be transferred into an annuity to enable a direct comparison with rented properties.

SITE (p=points; w=weighting; t=total)	A			B			C		
	p	w	t	p	w	t	p	w	t
OCCUPANCY COSTS Rent									
Rates (property tax)									
Power (light & heat)									
TRANSPORTATION & COMMUNICATIONS Road									
Rail								—	
Air									
LABOUR Availability									
Type									
Cost									
TOTAL									

Fig. 1.4 Matrix approach to collate information for a siting decision, based on a weighted points system

In using a weighted points system the first step is to decide upon the important influences related to the location decision and to list these in the matrix. Each item can then be provided with a weighting according to its importance. The next step is to decide upon the ranking range to be used; this usually runs from 1 to 10. Then each item listed in the matrix is given points on this scale. For example, from the factors listed in the matrix in Fig. 1.4, if the firm manufactured heavy goods, rail transport may be important and air transport less so; in this case the former might be given a weighting of 8 and the latter a weighting of 1.

The weightings and rankings are then multiplied together to give a total rating for the item. This simple multiplication is repeated for each item. All the ratings can then be added to provide a total for comparison purposes. However, it is important to note that the raw comparisons should *not* be taken as providing the decision. For management will have to look at the overall information provided using this approach; although it gives an indication of the benefits of each site, the final decision must be based on management experience.[16]

Design of the office

Generally speaking, the office buildings that organisations move into are already established premises, although sometimes there is scope to make changes. Occasionally an entity is fortunate enough to be able to move into purpose-built offices. This often means that it has been consulted at the design stage; if so, there are a number of important features relating to the performance of office work which the architects should treat as specifications in the design of the building.

Construction

Some countries have a requirement that building plans be approved and passed by an appropriate planning authority, as in the United Kingdom where the local authority has the task of monitoring such schemes.

The architect will be informed of the space requirements and other special features necessary in the performance of the office work, or where special equipment is needed as in the case of the load-bearing capacity of floors, sound-proofing, special lighting and dust-free environments. Consideration should also be given to any additional space requirements forecast for the future, so that provisions can be made to facilitate expansion with the minimum of disruption. Specific accommodation, e.g. for a boardroom, managers, welfare facilities, a medical room, washing and cloakroom facilities, quiet rooms, etc., must be considered.

Provision of communication services such as the telephone, power plugs (bearing in mind the number and distribution of these points), and perhaps a public address system must all be considered, given that it will be much cheaper to install these at the building stage. Not only can it be costly to introduce new points after the premises have been constructed; it may be doubly so with the disruption necessary to do it when they are occupied. If quantities of documents have to be moved during the processing of the office work, there must be sufficient corridors and gangways to allow adequate clearance for this purpose. The expected life of the accommodation is another factor, as is the quality of the accommodation to be provided, since both will affect the building materials that can be employed. The capital expenditure budget is evidently the major consideration in such an undertaking, and provision must also be made for the allocation of capital expenditure for the furnishings, equipment and machinery necessary to make the building habitable and functional. In all this it is probable that some compromise will have to be reached between the organisation's requirements and the capital available.

Building upwards or outwards

Some basic considerations in the design of the office building, depending upon the size envisaged, determine whether the building is to spread upwards or outwards; the size of the site will be a dominant factor.

The *single-storey building* is generally the cheapest to erect, although modern building technology has reduced the differential between it and buildings built upwards, which have the benefit of being able to be constructed on a smaller site. Single-storey buildings can also normally be erected faster, which in some circumstances can be an important consideration, and parts of them can usually be occupied during the construction process if time is crucial.

The single-storey building also makes better use of natural lighting and could have windows in the roof to promote this feature even further. In addition, they are usually easier to ventilate efficiently. An important consideration in countries which have a temperate climate is the heat loss during the winter season, and this is greater in single-storey buildings than in multi-storey ones with the equivalent space – although modern insulation has reduced this differential. Nevertheless, it should be remembered that in a temperate zone, heating bills can be a substantial part of the occupancy costs of a building. Similarly, in hot or tropical climates the costs of installing and operating air-conditioning systems have to be considered.

In *multi-storey buildings*, to supply services costs less since the pipings used require shorter runs and their installation is less expensive. In addition, services can often be placed advantageously. A good example of this is toilet facilities, where these can go one above another. However, these benefits should be seen in perspective. The very tall building will require the costly installation of lifts, which are also expensive to maintain. On the other hand, it is said that it is easier for staff to circulate through a tall building which has lifts, because they do not have to trudge the long distances that they would in a single-storey building. Yet space for services will reduce the floor space available in the multi-storey building, and if column supports are necessary in its construction, these will reduce the available working space even more. On top of this, flexibility in the potential use of floor space is reduced in the tall building.

In the construction of a tall building, the loads that the higher floors will probably have to bear must be carefully calculated. If these floors are likely to carry a lot of weight they will require strengthening in their construction, which will add to the cost of the building, although this point is of less importance for an office building than it would be for, say, a factory. But any noisy machinery, if not too heavy, can be located at the top of a tall building, which isolates the noise from most of the employees.

The separation of departments by floors has its advantages and dis-advantages. The department sited on one floor of a multi-storey building may seem more of a self-contained unit, which can help the feeling of social belonging and morale of its members – although the other side of this is that the department may appear to be, or feel, isolated from the others. This can have an effect on the supervision of employees. Smaller compact offices in tall buildings can be more efficiently supervised,[17] although there is also the danger that it will be easier to oversupervise the people who work in them. But the single-storey building offers more scope for the supervisor to have more people working under him, especially when supervisors can be positioned on a balcony, say above a large typing pool. There is of course no reason why the single-storey office building should not be divided up into smaller units. The pros and cons of open-plan offices are discussed on page 31.

Location of services
When presenting the specifications for the design of a new building, or moving into an already existing building (or indeed, renovating an existing building

which the organisation may have occupied for some time), careful thought must be given to the location of services. Planning at this stage will be repaid in avoiding the need for expensive rearrangements later on, with the costs incurred and the disruption that any process of rearrangement is likely to cause. The matters that have to be considered include the following:

1. Any heavy equipment is best sited on the ground floor; if it is to be situated several floors up, load-bearing must be taken into consideration.
2. Noisy equipment should be isolated as much as possible from the mainstream of personnel, with consideration given to any necessary sound-proofing.
3. Departments should be arranged so that those with the most outside contact are located as near the entrance or reception area of the building as possible; and any departments which are likely to have close working relationships should be as close to each other as is feasible.
4. If there are to be conference or interview rooms, or private offices, the aim should be to put them in a quiet location.
5. If any departments are likely to increase in size in the near future, they should be located in a position that will enable them to do so with the least possible disruption.
6. Departments where close or detailed work takes place must be situated in the best-lit part of the building and so get as much natural light as possible during working hours. For example, offices where drawings or plans are produced would be located ideally on the top floor of a multi-storey building.
7. Office supplies should be stored at a central location, but discarded equipment that is not to be sold off or scrapped could be put in storage spaces which have little other use.
8. Messenger services should be sited in a central position.
9. Cloakrooms, including areas for wet clothes and toilet facilities, should be sited as near to workers as possible; rather than having a single, central location it may be better to provide localised facilities.

The office environment

It has been stated that in the United Kingdom, 'Five thousand injuries every year cause office workers to be absent for more than three days. Contrary to the message on most safety posters, injuries at work are rarely caused by individual carelessness or by "accident prone" workers. The real causes are poorly designed jobs, pressure of work and bad maintenance of equipment and fittings, so most "accidents" can be *prevented*.'[18] Thus the physical conditions in an office, which contribute to the employees' working environment, are very important for a number of reasons. Good conditions lead to a happy and contented staff and can in themselves help to motivate staff. They can also help to reduce both mental and physical fatigue and stress, which in turn should lead to an improvement in output and its quality since fatigue and stress cause a slowing down of production and encourage errors.[19]

Health and welfare

The general environment of the office can also affect the worker's health. For example, a draughty office will not help workers who are susceptible to colds, and will lead to days off; bad lighting will affect workers' eyesight; and noise and overcrowding may affect their disposition and nerves. Then there are the legal requirements concerning the office environment; while these merely specify the minimum legal standards, today many organisations surpass them.

Sanitary and other arrangements are an important factor in ensuring the good health and morale of staff. Some organisations provide staff with lockers, so that the employees have a place to put their outdoor clothes and other personal belongings that they bring to work. Facilities for coffee and meals might in the large organisation be provided from a trolley, although in the United Kingdom these are tending to be replaced by drink-vending machines. Some large organisations will provide a canteen as a service to their staff, perhaps even subsidising the cost of food sold in it. In smaller offices staff will make the tea themselves and might bring in sandwiches for lunch. This could eventually produce a health hazard if not carefully watched. Authorised breaks for staff can help in maintaining good health and in establishing good morale at the workplace. They also cause less disruption since staff take their breaks at a known time and for an established period. Common-room facilities may be provided for those staff who stay for lunch so that they do not have to sit in the office environment during this period.

A sick room will be found in the larger organisation, although even the small enterprise must have some first aid facility. Staff should not be expected to lift heavy loads, and the provision of equipment to move heavy supplies should be considered.

Cleanliness

Much attention is paid to the décor of an office, yet comparatively little to keeping the office clean and the décor fresh. Yet these influence not only the health but also the morale of employees, for the dirty office may give the worker an impression of a non-caring management, which can easily carry over into attitudes to work production.

When deciding how to keep the office clean there are a number of options available. For the small firm it may be that the office worker is expected to keep his own office clean. However, in the large organisation this is unlikely and the choice would be between employing cleaners or using outside contract cleaners, who may also carry out related functions such as ensuring that clean towels and fresh soap are provided in the washrooms.

There has been a move towards the employment of specialist contract cleaners in recent years, since these offer a number of advantages. The firm using contractors does not have the problem of finding and employing staff for this purpose. Also, the contract cleaner's workers will usually clean through the office during the night, when it is closed. The main disadvantage of using contract cleaners is that although their workers are supervised they may tend to become lax.

Cleaning staff can be difficult to find and it is suggested that since office cleaning has become a specialist function, it is best left to the specialist firm. Nevertheless, many organisations prefer to have their offices cleaned by their own staff; a paramount reason for this may be security. However, if an organisation employs its own cleaners, they must be carefully vetted and supervised, and if they are to carry out their work effectively they must be provided with the necessary equipment and cleaning materials. Modern cleaning equipment is very effective, and makes the process more capital-intensive than labour-intensive.

As well as the regular programme of cleaning there should be provision for spring cleaning, when a major purge on dirt can be performed. The general approach to office cleaning is to have a number of cleaning cycles. The shortest cycle involves the work that needs to be done on a daily basis. Then there can be monthly, quarterly or annual cycles, during which other cleaning jobs can be carried out progressively. Such an approach would be combined with the use of check-lists to make sure that all the work to be done during each cleaning cycle is dealt with on schedule. When an organisation employs its own cleaning staff, it must be remembered that they carry out just as important a function as the office staff. So they need a place for their equipment, praise for their work, and access to the organisation's welfare facilities and staff activities.

Safety

Accidents can largely be prevented in the office environment. Preventive discipline ensures safety. This is where machinery has guards and will not work unless they are in place; thus the worker is 'disciplined' to work safely. There should be regular maintenance of equipment so that, for example, potential electrical faults are spotted before they have time to develop and cause an accident. Bernard Duke counsels care with electric office installations and points out that 'The British Standard for "Electrical systems in office furniture and screens" states that "socket outlets should be positioned so as to avoid the danger arising from the ingress of liquids".' Which, he says, 'is a complicated way of pointing out that the electronic office is also electric and that cups of tea and coffee and power supplies are bad mixers'.[20] Stairs must have handrails; open spaces round wells must be fenced off; checks should be made to ensure that gangways are left clear; and cables, especially telephone cables, must not be allowed to trail around all over the place. Floor coverings need to be checked to see whether they are becoming worn; once holes start to appear in them or there are loose tiles, they can cause accidents. And the floors should not be so highly polished that they cause people to slip.

Fire precautions
Similarly, there are established codes of practice with regard to precautions against fire. There should be sufficient fire alarms and extinguishing equipment, and the sophisticated office may have automatic sprinklers or smoke detectors installed. Where equipment related to fire-fighting is installed, it must be checked regularly. Staff must be informed of fire regulations, with fire practices and drills to ensure that they know what to do in an emergency. Employees must also be made familiar with the emergency exits in relation to their place of work – which should be clearly marked and not blocked – and where assembly points are.

Lighting
It should be self-evident that adequate lighting is essential in office work, but this is frequently overlooked in an attempt to create a stylish, if impractical, environment. If lighting is poor it can cause short-term eye strain and headaches, which lead to a slowing down in the production of office work, as well as to more harmful long-term effects on employees. Of course, lighting can be too harsh as well as too dull; thus careful consideration must be given to the provision of lighting of the appropriate intensity in each office. Generally, light which is diffused is better than that which causes pockets of shadow and glare around the office. The siting of desks can be very important. If possible, they should be near windows so that the worker can take advantage of natural light when it is available. However, if they face the window this can cause glare, so their positioning needs to be checked, bearing in mind that requirements will change with the seasons.

The use of natural lighting saves costs. Nevertheless, it frequently needs to be backed up on cloudy, dull days, and artificial light is necessary when the sun goes down. Lighting in an office can be in the form of individual lights on workers' desks which, although useful for some purposes, has the disadvantage of high cost in relation to the luminosity produced. Desk lights can also cast shadows, and because of these disadvantages they are rarely used today.

The forms of lighting usually found in offices are direct and indirect lighting. Direct lighting is suspended from the ceiling, whereas with indirect lighting the light is reflected, for example onto the ceiling and back into the office. This is said to produce a better balance because the light is diffused. Most lighting in offices is provided by fluorescent tubes and although the units for these have a high capital cost, they are much cheaper to run. Where both natural and artificial light is used, the light from the two sources should, if possible, blend together. Because the intensity of the natural light may vary from day to day, it can be beneficial to have the artificial lighting units banked on different switches so that when the natural light fades the artificial ones can be phased in. It must also be noted that lighting will generate heat which may or may not be beneficial according to the situation.

Décor

Décor can help lighting, especially since light colours reflect light. For example, cream will reflect much more light than pale grey, which tends to absorb light. However, the main criterion in selecting the décor of an office is the psychological effect that it can have on people's attitudes towards work. Bright and cheerful colours improve morale, whereas dark and drab colours have a depressing effect. The psychologist states that colours can have an effect on a person's emotions, but that they do this in different ways. Therefore it is probably best to play safe and have colours which are basically neutral, perhaps highlighted by smaller bright areas.

Another factor to consider when choosing colours is the design and age of the building. Some colour schemes suit old buildings better than new and vice versa. Often pictures, posters and notices are allowed to proliferate in offices. Some of these, especially those put up by the people based in the office, can help to maintain the employee's morale. However, they can also spoil the overall effect of the décor. Thus it may be sensible to limit their use. Notices can be limited automatically by having special notice boards on which to display them. If there is no control, the value of good décor might be negated.

Ventilation

Good ventilation is a question of balance between the flow of fresh air and unwanted draughts. Some staff are fresh-air fiends and like to have the office windows open even in winter or when strong winds are blowing through the office like a gale, whereas other people enjoy a stuffy atmosphere. Stuffy offices tend to make people drowsy, and winds and draughts can be most annoying and distract from work, especially when they blow paper about. This is where balance is so important, since draughts can be limited without entirely stopping the supply of fresh air coming into an office. For example, windows can be screened in a way which will direct the fresh air upwards and into the room; where there are doors which let draughts through it might be possible to introduce double doors. The installation of air-conditioning may also be beneficial.

The office temperature

In temperate climates the office has to be heated for much of the year to provide staff with a comfortable working temperature. But it is important to note that staff can be too hot as well as too cold. The most effective temperature is 18° centigrade. When deciding upon a heating system for an office, a major aim must be to distribute the heat evenly throughout the office rather than having pockets of hot and cold. Some form of central heating, rather than stand-alone heaters, is most effective for achieving this objective. In the summer blinds can help keep the blazing sun out and so reduce the heat and glare. In tropical climates the problem is almost the reverse: air-conditioning is used to keep the office cool, and the principles related to the installation of a central heating system apply.

Noise

Noise in the office can be most distracting. It may be caused by equipment and/or personnel and can be exacerbated by open-plan work areas. For example, if an office is sited near a lift and every time the lift passes the floor bell rings, this is likely to distract those working nearby. Noise is reflected from hard surfaces and absorbed by soft ones, so carpets can be used effectively to deaden noise. If there is external noise this can be dealt with by siting the offices as far away from it as possible; in multi-storey buildings this often means at the top. However, double glazing can also be used to reduce external noise. When noisy machinery such as printing equipment is in use, it may be installed advantageously in a special room which can be situated well away from the mainstream of other office activities.

The general absorption of noise can be achieved by using sound-proofing materials on the walls and ceilings of the office and carpets or a rubberoid on the floor. There can also be local absorption of noise to reduce sound at its source, e.g. by having absorption screens round noisy machinery, and insulators under printers or a sound hood over them to deaden their noise.

Layout of the office[21]

Probably the major consideration related to efficiency in the office is the layout of an organisation's offices. B. H. Walley states that 'An office layout study is the analysis of all the factors involved in the siting of work, office equipment, ancillary services, storage areas, functional relationships and work flows, plus the design of the functional aspects of the buildings which house them.' He continues, 'By any standards this can be a highly complex activity' and says that 'Making a technologically perfect layout will rarely be possible. A series of compromises will normally be needed which will encompass various constraints.'[22] One factor to consider is whether the office should be based on the open-plan layout or if the closed-office configuration should be used.

Careful layout of an office provides a number of benefits, which include the following:

1.   Better utilisation of the available space.
2.   Reduction of time necessary to carry out the work since it can be passed from one stage of processing to the next using a natural flow; the natural flow also increases the effectiveness of staff.
3.   Maintenance of the quality of work because of better supervision.
4.   Lower costs in carrying out the office work.
5.   Better flexibility in the use of the resources allocated to office work.

6.   Boosting of morale, especially because a sensible layout can help to establish close working groups which develop the ability to work well together, creating a team approach and group loyalty.

Collecting information

The first stage when considering the layout of an office is to collect information on: the work that is to be done, and how it is to be done; the processing cycle, especially in relation to the balance between the various stages of work, and how long each stage is likely to take to complete; what storage facilities are required at each stage in the processing; where any bottle-necks are likely to occur; and the disposal of the finished work.

Information is also required about any equipment, machinery and labour necessary for the processing. Remember the ancillary things such as power points, cloakroom facilities, etc. There must also be information on the number of employees needed and on the skills they must possess. A subsequent consideration is the communication that will be required during the work process as the work arrives, passes through its processing cycle and moves on to the user. Thought must be given to the position of doors and of any physical blockages in the office such as awkward corners and pillars, and to the location of telephones. In the processing cycles there may be stages at which inspection or general supervision is necessary for the whole process. If so, provision must be made for this. Last, but by no means least, there must be information on the total space available for the work to be carried out.

Alternatives

The alternative ways of laying out the office should be considered. It may be done using a plan of the office drawn to scale and using templates to represent the various pieces of furniture and equipment to be housed. At its simplest this will be a two-dimensional plan on squared paper, although at its most elaborate a three-dimensional model of the office could be used. The position of doors, windows and services will be shown, as will the power plugs, telephone sockets and lighting. The templates of the furniture and equipment can be moved around until the best location for them is found in relation to the overall layout of the office. A much cruder and more time-consuming method is to work by trial and error. Whatever the method used, the first thing is to establish the main thoroughfares that will run through the office, then adding in the subsidiary gangways and the major areas where the work will be carried out. The related minor aspects of the layout can then be installed. The aim should be to minimise the distance of the work-processing routes through the office, making sure that these run logically from one stage to the next and that workers will be located so as to do the work most easily. There will be distractions in the office, e.g. people passing down the gangways. So anyone carrying out work which requires concentration should be isolated as much as possible.

Creative thinking about an office layout often leads to surprising results and an extremely good layout, so planning time must be allocated for this purpose before management rushes into an office and pushes the furniture and equipment into the nearest empty spaces.

Once the best layout for the office has been decided it should be tested 'on paper' by running through all aspects of all the work to be carried out in that office. This will show whether the work sequences flow naturally, and when a number of jobs are carried out concurrently whether they affect each other adversely. Sometimes the plan can be the empty office with full-scale templates used for the furniture and equipment, or the floor marked where it is suggested that each major item will go.

The open-plan office

Some people favour an office layout using open-plan style whereas others dislike this approach. The open-plan system found much favour in the 1950s.

The *advantages* of the open-plan office are as follows:

1. It makes better use of the available floor space and within this the layout can be changed easily so it is more flexible.
2. The movement of staff through the office and communications between them are much quicker and tend to become more informal.
3. Supervision is made easier, especially if the supervisor can see what everbody is doing.
4. There is a better office environment, especially with regard to lighting and ventilation.

The *disadvantages* of the open-plan office layout include the fact that workers can distract each other as they go about their business, these distractions increasing when somebody from outside visits the office. It also has a less personal atmosphere and does not encourage closely knit working groups. Screens can be used to divide off the various sections in an open-plan office, and the workers in such offices will build barriers between themselves and others using filing cabinets, all of which will defeat the objectives of the open-plan approach to office layout.

Private offices for the managers of the various sections of the organisation will often be found associated with open-plan office systems, although these are frequently built in the form of glass partitions to co-ordinate them with the environment's 'openness'. However, these should be kept to a minimum since they also tend to defeat the objectives of the open-plan system. Adoption of an open-plan system raises the problem of privacy when staff have to interview people. So closed-in interview rooms will still be needed.

Office furniture

'Nowadays, administrators are selecting office furniture more sensibly, with high regard to the true needs and requirements of the user and less inhibition about status distinctions.'[23] There are some general points to be considered when making decisions to acquire office furniture. An obvious one is the cost, remembering that a large capital expenditure can be avoided if the furniture is leased rather than bought; in the latter case the purchase could be made on credit terms so that payment can be spread over a period. The construction and design of the furniture will be examined for its likely durability as well as aesthetic qualities. With both these points, standardisation in the choice of furniture will offer some advantages. It looks better to have what is obviously a set of filing cabinets, or set of chairs for the table in the boardroom. This may also provide an advantage in the future if anything gets damaged, since it may be possible to salvage one piece for another. Flexibility in the use of office furniture is another important point. This is especially so if the work of the office or its layout is likely to change over time, for then the furniture can be used for some purpose other than its original one.

A prime consideration when acquiring furniture is that it must be functional. If possible it will be light so that it can be moved around easily. Then there ought to be sufficient space under it so that the floor area beneath can easily be cleaned. It should also be space-saving, which means avoiding unnecessary niceties in its design. There are ranges of executive or prestige office furniture for the senior executive's office where, as much as anything, the intention is to impress visitors.

Ergonomics

The application of ergonomics, i.e. the adaptation of the work environment to the needs and capabilities of the employee, is being used increasingly not only in the design but also in the choice of office furniture.

Ergonomics is defined by the British Standards Institution as 'The relation between man and his occupation, equipment and environment and, particularly, the application of anatomical, physiological and psychological knowledge to the problems arising therefrom'. The International Labour Office defines it as 'The application of human biological sciences in conjunction with the engineering sciences to achieve the optimum mutual adjustment of man and his work, the benefits being measured in terms of human efficiency and well-being'.

From definitions such as these a more comprehensive one has been provided in *A Handbook of Management*, where ergonomics is defined as:

> The branch of technology concerned with the problem of mutual adjustment between man and his work. Drawing upon the sciences of psychology, anatomy and physiology, ergonomics sets out to optimize the design of equipment, the environment and working procedures in respect of both the well-being of personnel and the effectiveness of the working unit.[24]

R. G. Anderson says that as a result of using ergonomics 'Operations are performed in relative comfort and . . . at a high level of productivity. The design of products, such as office furniture and motor cars, is carefully considered to take account of the most comfortable posture for performing special tasks.'[25] He adds that the science of ergonomics tries to locate any dials and controls on equipment and machinery within easy vision and reach of the operators; thus, for example, the seat designed following ergonomics principles for the use of the word-processing operator will be adjustable to the correct height to enable him to see the screen and manipulate the controls comfortably, while providing adequate back support.[26]

Thus ergonomics takes into consideration man's anatomical features, and the behavioural influences at the place of employment in the design of office furniture, equipment and machinery, and seeks to implement these features most effectively in the office layout. When designing chairs, or seats used to operate equipment, the ergonomist will relate design to posture, the expenditure of energy and factors which affect personnel fatigue. It is obvious that people do not all have the same physical characteristics, so there cannot be bespoke chairs which exactly suit the posture of everyone. Nevertheless, the chair used by the word-processing operator will be adjustable for height and angle. Other factors, such as whether the person is right- or left-handed, and what sort of work is being done, must also be taken into consideration in the selection of equipment. For example, how much movement will the work require and will one or both hands be used to carry it out? Is the working surface sufficiently large and of the best shape to take all the equipment necessary for the successful completion of the work, in a way which makes the employee's task as easy as possible? Does the operator require supervision or can he work on his own? In addition, security associated with the work cannot be overlooked.

In the configuration of such items as chairs, desks and side-tables, the principles behind ergonomics should be used for their selection in relation to the working space available, any space necessary for storing ancillary equipment, and the movement of the user between the pieces of equipment being used.

Take two simple examples of office furniture – a chair and a desk. The chair should have a footrest for comfort and health. It is also a good idea to have chairs which can be adjusted in height to suit the user, and then to label the chair with the name of the person that it has been adjusted to suit. When selecting desks, limit their range, with a desk being selected from this range to suit the purpose of the user. This avoids the need for special-purpose desks unless they are essential. Nevertheless, sometimes special-purpose desks will be useful: they may have special fitments to help in the work, for example a collation attachment, or storage facilities appropriate to the job. A desk with a side-table in the form of an L with a swivel chair is useful for the secretary, who may sometimes need a typing surface and at others a flat surface. Probably the only justification for a special-purpose desk is where much repetitive work is carried out, since it will probably be completed more quickly with systematic body movements when the work is being done. An example of this is where there is not room for the typist to have a side-table to his desk for the typewriter, in which case a drop-action desk might be appropriate. Machines with controls should have these at desk-top height. Otherwise, the operator will have to reach up to use the machine, making it much too high for comfortable use.

Conclusions

This first chapter has provided an introduction to the study of office work and the environment in which it is carried out. It has discussed what office work entails and examined it as a system, where there are inputs of data and information created by the environment which must then be processed either on a regular basis or for special purposes to help management in its decision-making, planning and control of activities. The results are then transmitted back to the environment, or retained in storage for later use.

The chapter considered where office work is carried out in differing sectors of the economy, and contemplated the likely future transition to working from home. Concentrating on the contemporary situation, the location of premises, and construction and layout of offices were examined with particular reference to requirements of personnel. Having defined the framework, it is now possible to move on to a deeper analysis – to look at management, services, procedures and means of control.

Questions and discussion problems

1. The systems concept is particularly useful for the analysis of information systems. Using the systems approach analyse any office system with which you are familiar.

2. Discuss the major factors involved in an office location decision and explain how you would appraise the influence of the qualitative factors involved.

3. Explain how, as manager of an office, you would ensure that layout is the most efficient.

4. The September 1980 issue of *Professional Administration* featured an article entitled 'Relocation Management'. In this it was stated that the relocation of an office has a number of 'phases and decision points'. Critically evaluate what is meant by this.

5. Some factors which are brought into the analysis of office location are automatically quantified, e.g. rent, rates, transportation, staff and other costs. Other factors, frequently referred to as the qualitative ones, although having no money value attached to them must still be brought into the analysis. How can management attempt to quantify the qualitative considerations of office location?

6.   Two office managers, who have never met, have agreed to prepare a
       paper for a seminar on office layout. When they meet to discuss the
       paper, Frank East, who controls an office based on an open-plan
       layout, states 'Open-plan has so many advantages . . .'. John Hayes,
       whose office is in the traditional style, butts in 'And disadvantages
       which my staff do not have to face because they work under the
       traditional style of layout where a number of smaller offices are
       grouped together'. Frank East replies 'Well, you write down the
       advantages of your form of office layout and the disadvantages, as you
       see them, associated with the open-plan style; conversely, I will write
       from my side'.

	Advantages	Disadvantages
Open-plan		
Boxed-in offices		

Fig. 1.5 Open-plan vs. traditional office layout

       (a) Using a four-quadrant matrix in the form of Fig. 1.5, write down
       the things that you would have expected the two office managers to
       have included on their lists.
       (b) In what circumstances do you consider that each system is to be
       preferred?
7.   Firms tend to site their headquarters of administrative services in a
       country's capital city. However, pressures on resources have made
       such a practice become less attractive. Citing a country with which
       you are familiar (state clearly the name of the country used):
       (a) Discuss the pressures on resources likely to be incurred through
       operating from the capital, and
       (b) Analyse *both* the advantages and disadvantages likely to be found
       if the headquarters of administrative services are sited away from the
       capital.
8.   Consider six environmental factors which are likely to be conducive to
       greater efficiency within the office. Explain the influences of these
       factors.
9.   Discuss how a knowledge of ergonomics can help to improve
       efficiency in the office.

2
Office management – principles and practice

Introduction

H. R. Light writes that 'Management has, of course, been practised since the dawn of human history. Men have always collaborated with one another in hunting and building and agriculture and many other activities.' He continues that 'Such collaboration for a common good implies arrangements for a division of labour, which in turn postulates the existence of a leader – someone whose task it is both to make arrangements and to see that the remainder of the group carries them out.'[1] This gets to the heart of management and supervision, which play a crucial role in all forms and at all levels of society and within organisations. This is equally true in the operation of an office. Therefore, the person providing office services needs to know something about the application of the principles and practices of management to this area. The objective of this chapter is to give a brief but broad survey of management and supervision in the office.

The following areas must be considered: management as an art or a science; the objectives of organisation, administration and management; the major principles and practices of management and supervision; and a brief survey of the interrelationships a manager needs to be familiar with to make his own operations most effective.

Many questions will arise from this analysis. If the response to the questions 'Is management a science?' and 'Are managers made?' is yes, then it can be taught, whereas if it is felt that management is an art or managers are born it cannot. However, this approach is too simplistic.

It is frequently intimated, even if not wholly accepted, that management is a science. As will be seen later, one of the foundations of the analysis of management is based on a scientific approach. Today the idea of management as a science has been developed even further with the introduction of scientific methods, such as various quantitative and other techniques used to help planners and controllers. All in all the use of quantitative techniques by management helps to reduce the risks faced by their organisations by enabling them to make decisions based on better information.

An early writer in scientific management, Frederick Taylor (1856–1917), introduced the idea that has developed into the so-called *classical approach* to the subject. However, scientific management techniques are less effective when they ignore implications concerning people's behaviour. And in moving from science to art the question is raised of whether a leader is born rather than 'made'. If the former were the case, it would mean that management must necessarily be something of an 'art'. It is this art aspect that puts the gloss of humanity upon management. Thus the suggestion that management is either an art or a science is rather simplistic since it must of necessity comprise the best of both.

From this we are led to another question: is management a 'discipline' that can be taught?[2] The scientific aspects of management can be taught.[3] Yet the best managers seem to have an ability in their management style and practices which defies an accurate definition of the 'art of leadership'. On the other hand, some of the art aspects of management, especially those related to people's behaviour and motivation, can also be taught.[4] People can be made aware of them, and their ability to conduct interpersonal relationships can be improved. People who only have either the scientific or the art attributes of management can still offer much to their organisations. Nevertheless, the manager who can deal with quantitative decision techniques may still need gut feelings, i.e. the complementary art aspects of management, to help him in his decision-making and carry-through. And today, getting the best from employees and colleagues is one area that is becoming more of an art because of changes in employment policy.

Organisations can be analysed in a number of ways. As noted above, the original development of organisational analysis was the so-called classical approach, based upon what are now considered to be the techniques of scientific management. Later the behavioural implications of management were added to provide flesh on this scientific skeleton, and more recently the organisation has been analysed as a system. These most important methods of analysing organisations should not be seen as mutually exclusive; they work best in joint application. In fact it is difficult, if not impossible, to analyse an organisation using any one of these approaches in isolation.

The distinction between organisation, administration and management

The terms 'organisation',[5] 'administration' and 'management' should now be defined. Are they in fact or practice synonymous, or is there some subtle distinction between the meanings given to each? If so, what elements are common to all and what are the differences between their concepts? There is a tendency for people to use the words interchangeably, if only to add variety to what they are writing or saying, and it is interesting to note that some languages do not distinguish between the concepts that underlie them – for example, in Arabic there is one word to cover the two English terms administration and management.

Basically they are all covered by the broad definition of 'getting things done through other people'. This means guiding people, integrating their efforts, and motivating, supervising and controlling them.

G. E. Milward, in his book *Large Scale Organisations*, provides the following definition for organisation: 'Organisation is a process of dividing work into convenient tasks or duties, of grouping such duties into the form of posts, of delegating authority to each post, and of appointing qualified staff to be responsible that the work is carried out as planned'. Milward thus gives four characteristics to organisation, i.e. dividing the work; grouping it into convenient work units; delegating; and appointing staff to fill the delegated posts.

In his book *Business Administration*, L. Hall says that there are no basic rules which have universal application on how to establish a good organisational structure, but continues that there are a number of general principles that may be followed. These are: flexibility to allow for changing policies and circumstances; the determination of the objectives and the means by which they are achieved, thus laying the ground rules for the purpose of the entity; a clear indication of people's responsibilities, with a rider that when a person is responsible for more than one work group, there needs to be some relationship between them; and discipline, which today is not done through coercion, but achieved using more subtle methods.

The separate statements provided by Milward and Hall show that *organisation* concerns the division of work, which in turn leads to some structured delegation through an entity's 'organisation'. Administration and management can now be defined as techniques superimposed on to an entity's organisation to enable it to function efficiently. *Administration* covers aspects of running 'the organisation' by devising systems which will function smoothly under the supervision of administrators who deal with routine 'administrative' work and advise management. Administration thus ensures that procedures are developed and carried out in a co-ordinated manner. *Management* involves making day-to-day decisions and ensuring that other people carry out the various tasks set for them in the appropriate manner. Therefore management tends to be more concerned with the physical aspects of tasks and administration with information service tasks. This may seem to be a rather subtle distinction, yet it indicates why, at least in one language, no distinction is made between the words administration and management.

The definitions of the three words in R. G. Anderson's *A Dictionary of Management Terms* provide a clearer distinction between them. His definitions are as follows:

> ADMINISTRATION: The activity concerned with the smooth functioning of business activities achieved by means of well-designed administrative systems supported by effective management. The administration of a business

is entrusted to a board of directors (partners or proprietors) which is the governing body. The board may be known collectively as 'the administration' of the business. Office managers are also known as administrators; therefore all managers may be defined as administrative managers responsible for the affairs of the business. They are responsible for planning and controlling all business operations to achieve defined objectives.[6]

MANAGEMENT: 1. The expression 'the management' relates to the personnel of the organisation charged with the responsibility of running the business efficiently within the framework of company policy . . . The term management also refers to the activity of managing resources and the tasks of others in order to achieve defined objectives . . .[7]

ORGANISATION: 1. A term used as an alternative to business, company, or corporate body. 2. It is also used to mean the structure of an entity, e.g. a business, that is, the way in which it is organised. 3. The manner of organising resources to achieve a specific purpose.[8]

Although these three definitions refer to a business organisation, they can be applied equally to any other form of entity, such as those in the public sector, charities or social organisations. The definitions bring out a clear distinction between administrative, management and organisational activities, which should be borne in mind in relation to office work.

Herbert Simon points out under the heading of 'Paper-flow' that 'In certain cases – this is typical of organizations handling financial matters, like insurance companies [and] accounting departments . . . . – the organization's work, or some part of it, centers around the processing of a piece of paper'. He continues that this will affect that type of entity's organisational structure.[9] Thus there will be an organisational structure for office work through which the resources allocated to it will be organised to help achieve its performance objectives; through this there will be the administration of the office work function within the entity to ensure that the office services are efficiently provided; and the office work will be managed to ensure that the tasks required of it are carried out effectively.

Together these affect the organisation of resources, especially people and the integration of their efforts which, in turn, must be supervised and controlled. The management aspects are dealt with in this chapter, and the 'people' aspects in Chapter 4.

The functions of management

At a conference held in 1958 to commemorate the fiftieth anniversary of the establishment of the Harvard Business School, the following definition was provided for the rationale behind businesses: they exist to create and deliver value satisfactions at a profit.[10] Analysing the two fundamental points of *value* and *satisfaction* embodied in this definition, it is probable that until the 1950s British industry tended to be production-orientated. Although manufacturers were creating and delivering products, consumers were asking more and more whether these were of the type and value that they really wanted. It was also asked whether all organisations do, or should, exist to create a profit. In fact, the economists' simple analytical tool of profit maximisation has been increasingly questioned in the real-world situation; most enterprises strive to achieve multiple objectives, although at least one of these will be profit.

In a study on managers and their work, Rosemary Stewart found that a manager's job was a varied one, although it did have some elements of repetition, sometimes with activities recurring on a daily basis but also on monthly and seasonal cycles.[11] A knowledge of what the work of a manager entails will provide an indication of the areas in which they need education and training. Some of the major functions of a manager include: planning; organisation; staffing; direction; control; innovation; representation; and communication.

Planning[12]

The basic function of top management is to set objectives for their organisations. These will be policies or goals and the means of achieving them. Even the lower-level manager, who may not have a hand in setting an organisation's objectives, will still influence the extent to which they can be achieved. Once the manager knows the broad objectives, frequently referred to as the organisation's *strategic objectives*, he has to formulate the *operational objectives* which will enable the achievement of the overall aims. With some level of profitability as a primary objective, management must decide how to use the resources under its control to ensure the achievement of the organisation's strategic goals. The plans will be formulated with appropriate time horizons. They will be affected by environmental influences, such as the general economic or political situation and the organisation's place within its industry. Even if it does not reappraise its objectives it will constantly have to readjust the operational objectives to ensure the achievement of strategic objectives in the face of environmental change. At the same time, senior managers must not lose sight of what they expect from lower-level managers, always considering ways of motivating those beneath them.

B. H. Walley points out that 'Unlike many management techniques, planning needs a specific psychological and philosophical approach by the management team'. He continues that 'They must feel that planning works. They must believe that the plans they make must be achieved. Planning must be a part (and an important part) of their life.'[13]

Organisation

The manager will become involved in the division of work, which is the delegating and co-ordinating of work within his area of responsibility. Outlines of the work effort at the lower levels of the organisation must also be considered since there must be co-ordination of departments and work to avoid unnecessary duplication or overlap. The manager should be aware of the informal as well as the formal organisation of the enterprise, since the one may influence the effectiveness of the other.

Staffing
The manager of a large area will likely be filling staff positions on a regular basis, depending on the number of staff employed and the labour turnover ratio. Therefore, the recruitment of staff is an important skill, and it is essential that the manager become involved in the training and development of his staff.

Direction
An organisation must be pointed in the right direction, towards the right objectives. Therefore, another component of leadership is its ability to direct.

Feedback and control
The manager will receive feedback on the progress of his organisation. This will show whether operations are performed so as to ensure the fulfilment of objectives. If not, control will be necessary. For example, using budgetary control associated with feedback in the form of variance analysis, a system of Management by Exception (MbE) may be developed. (This is when only significant differences to plans are reported.) There will also have to be feedback and control to check the use and security of resources, and many other aspects of the operation of the organisation. Although most forms of control will be formulated in financial terms, it is not necessarily the cost of operations that is being controlled.

Innovation
Managers can become so obsessed with the smooth operation of their area of responsibility that they will not allow any interruption. Such managers are often termed 'organisation men'. They will overlook the fact that innovation may be necessary in the form of new equipment that is being developed, as in the realm of information technology. In the United Kingdom today many feel that industry cannot do well because it has tended to cling to outdated methods. So today's managers must be innovators – they must move forward, otherwise they will be left behind.

Representation[14]
A manager has a public relations function in his work. He is effectively an ambassador in his contacts with people outside the organisation. Frequently the only contact that outsiders have with an organisation is through its management, which must therefore formulate an appropriate representational role.

Communication
Communication plays an important part in the mangager's work, and today

has become an essential function. Poor communication is often blamed for the lack of employee motivation and is one of the reasons given for the United Kingdom's industrial troubles. This is such a crucial subject that the whole of Chapter 5 will be devoted to it.

Managing time

One function of managers and supervisors which is frequently overlooked, is that of being able to manage time. Roger Black points out that when somebody makes the statement 'Sorry I just haven't had time to do it', either they have not given that job priority or more likely the constant demands on the person's time have frustrated their efforts to complete all their tasks. He continues that better use of a person's time can 'lead to increased productivity . . . [and] also to personal satisfaction and peace of mind'.[15] Frequently one hears a manager or a supervisor complain of overwork. If this is genuinely the case then it needs to be discussed and readjustments made. However, people often use the time at their disposal inefficiently, in which case they must be educated to use it more effectively. When a manager does not plan the time he has available well, pressures will build up and lead to frustration, worry, stress and eventually a lack of energy. A good manager will also recognise the symptoms of the inefficient use of time in his subordinates and try to help them learn to manage it more effectively.

There are many things that can be done to improve the situation. The first is to plan for the use of time. Sometimes it will be found that work is done twice. For example, when the post is opened, read through and then laid on one side to be dealt with later, this means that the work of reading through it has to be duplicated at a later date. A person must discipline himself to deal immediately with most of the communications received. When reading a document a person should always highlight the key points to save having to reread it later. All too often unnecessary items are filed, especially when they are known to be kept elsewhere as well. Destroy unimportant items and those that are unlikely to be needed again if they can be retrieved from another source – even if this would take a little longer.

Every interruption interferes with workflow. So consider whether telephone calls need to be taken immediately. It might be acceptable to use a telephone answering machine to monitor calls and reduce the number of interruptions. The 'open door' policy may seem fine – but do all those who pop through it have business that must be dealt with on the spot, or could it have waited a little while? And do many callers come in just to pass the time of the day? Above all, when considering the use of time ask what can reasonably be delegated.

Some major principles of management

Numerous writers on organisation, administration and management have isolated some hundred principles of management. Some of these provide only a minor variation on the theme of a more basic principle, however, and some concepts are not uniformly defined. Nevertheless, major principles can be synthesised from the literature, and some of the most widely quoted and accepted of these will be introduced briefly. Not all of the principles discussed here have universal acceptability as being of prime importance to office management. Much will also depend on an enterprise's organisational structure.

Most of the principles which follow have been covered by writers such as Lyndall Urwick, E. F. L. Brech and Peter Drucker.[16]

Objectives

Any business must have some objectives if it is to have a rational existence. All aspects of an entity's organisational structure should then be aimed towards the achievement of these objectives, which will be based on the primary purpose, or ultimate task, for which it was designed and established. The work of the entity's employees can then be valued on the basis of how it contributes to the achievement of the objectives. Obviously, objectives have to be feasible and may be limited by legal, financial or other constraints that the enterprise may face.

Specialisation

Much has been written on the subject of specialisation. One of the earliest references is attributed to Adam Smith, who wrote about it under the heading of *division of labour*. Frederick Taylor developed the idea. Large and usually complex tasks are broken down into smaller, simpler tasks so that the work can be shared among a number of people. Such a breaking down of major tasks into manageable units can promote a high degree of specialisation, to be developed by the people who carry out an element of the task. If people have to acquire only a small area of skill they can achieve a high degree of efficiency in their work. With the concept of *job enlargement*, the idea of specialisation tends to become reversed, although this concept is often applied only to routine, monotonous work where it can have a beneficial effect.

Responsibility and authority

Responsibility and authority are linked. It could be said that the principle of responsibility follows from authority. Certainly, the two complement and reinforce each other.

The relationship between authority and responsibility is formalised into another principle of management, that of the *correspondence of authority with responsibility*. Some writers even state that there must be co-equality between the responsibility a manager has been delegated and the authority he is given within his organisation. However, there is difficulty in how this equality should come about. Lyndall Urwick moved away from complete equality: the correspondence between the two simply means that the person delegated the responsibility of carrying out a task should at least have the necessary authority to do so. It is also suggested that people with authority should take a responsible attitude to the way in which they exercise it. Basically this principle, and its variants, intimate that neither the authority nor the responsibility delegated to a person should outweigh each other to any great extent. Sometimes this principle is referred to as the *law of parity of authority and responsibility*.

Definition

When people have specialist roles these need to be carefully defined. The principle of definition draws attention to one of the problems in any organisation's structure when tasks and roles are not defined. The classical theory states that tasks should be defined as clearly as possible. Lyndall Urwick goes so far as to say that definitions should be provided in writing; thus the vogue of job descriptions and organisational manuals. Such documents are necessary so that: people know the nature of their work; management can appraise the performance of individuals in defined jobs; and other people can stand in for a particular job.

Co-ordination

Following on from specialisation, once a complex task has been broken down into its component elements, the work must be arranged so that it is carried out in the correct order. This requires the development of co-ordination. Co-ordination is especially necessary where tasks have to be carried out in a sequence, if they are to be completed in the most efficient way.

Continuity

Since a business enterprise, especially a company, theoretically has perpetual life, there must be some continuity in its personnel. This occurs in two ways. Any business will need to change in order to maintain its balance in an unpredictable environment. Continuity of existence affects its ability to do so. The organisation must also plan for personnel continuity to protect its future survival through its manpower planning, especially in management education and training programmes.

A balanced structure

An enterprise's organisational system should not be allowed to become excessively weighted in any one direction, i.e. imbalance should not be allowed to develop. For example, marketing should not outweigh production or vice versa. For if imbalances do occur they are likely to cause top-heaviness in the management of the firm. A big problem is that necessary changes may be painful and difficult to make, and frequently will take time to introduce, so that when they do come about it will often be too late.

Scalar chain: unity of command

This principle states that lines of authority need to be clearly defined and must show how the authority runs downwards within the enterprise. Organisational charts will indicate how authority works through from one person to another within the system.

The management principle of *unity of command* states that any individual within an organisation should only receive instruction from, and be responsible to, a single superior. This means that reporting relationships should go in a vertical direction, referred to as the *scalar chain of command*, e.g. as in Fig. 2.1

Fig. 2.1 The scalar chain of command

Unity of command ensures that all resources within the organisation are pulled in the same direction and that any economies of scale are gained from the use of standardisation and common procedures. Employees also know where they stand as far as authority is concerned since they are responsible only to one person, with no possibility of conflicting orders from different people. Nevertheless, the principle of unity of command may sometimes have to be disregarded, in which case alternative arrangements must be clearly stated. This is especially so at the lower levels of an organisation, where people must know to whom they are to report. An example of this would be the delegation of functional authority throughout an organisation.

The matrix structure

In the matrix approach to organisation, as depicted in Fig. 2.2, an individual may be subject to both line and staff authority. This will damage the principle of unity of command. In the matrix approach, the activities are established and a person made responsible for them. For example, there may be departments for cutting, pressing and forming, spraying and assembling in a manufacturing firm, each with a manager. Then a *project* is established for each of the firm's product groupings, again with a leader – e.g. a project for refrigerators, another for washing machines, and so on. The project leader then negotiates with the various departmental managers for the resources necessary to produce the target number of his product. This is said to enable better co-ordination and progress-chasing. However it puts unity of command into disarray since an operative will likely find both his departmental manager and the project leader giving him orders.

Project / Department	X Refrigerators	Y Washing machines	Z Cookers
A Forming			
B Spraying			
C Assembling			

Fig. 2.2 Matrix management

Span of control[17]

This is the principle which influences the shape of organisational structure. It refers to the number of subordinates that a superior has under his control. There has been much discussion and controversy over the application of this principle with regard to how many people a manager can effectively control. The wider the span of control, the lower will be the number of management levels within an organisation, and vice versa. Difficulties can arise if a span of control is misjudged. If it is too wide, tasks may be carried out inefficiently; when it is too narrow, the organisation's resources may be wasted.

This principle does not state rigid numbers for spans of control since these must be tailored to an organisation's needs.[18] A flexible approach is usually required, with different spans of control at each level of management. Thus span of control should be ascertained within the framework of other management principles, and will be especially influenced by the scalar chain. The numbers arrived at for a particular span of control should enable the firm to achieve its goals in the most cost-effective manner.

The span of control, which is also referred to as the *span of management*[19] or the *span of supervision*,[20] should be one of the crucial factors considered when deciding whether an organisation's structure should be vertical or horizontal, and in which way the structure should grow. A knowledge of the factors which influence span of control is important, especially in ensuring that managerial control is effective. These factors include: the activities involved; the skills of those supervised; the organisational level concerned; and the tasks of the organisation. Although these factors will be discussed separately, it is obvious that they have extremely strong interrelationships.

Activities
The more varied the activities of the people supervised by a manager, the

smaller the numbers that he should be given to supervise. In an area such as research, where a vast spread of knowledge may be covered, the number of researchers that can be supervised effectively will be reduced according to the complexity of the work. When many people are supervised we refer to a *broad* span of control; a *narrow* span of control arises when few people are supervised by a manager.

People's skills

By tradition, people working in areas such as the professions are expected to work independently. In such cases the span of control of those 'managing' them can be quite broad. For example, the person who manages salesmen, research workers or other managers can have a relatively large number of these to oversee. Although this may seem to conflict with the activities aspect of the span of control because the people may be undertaking quite varied activities, it is not necessarily the case. Circumstances will dictate the requirements. For example, a highly motivated and experienced research worker would require very little supervision; thus a large number of such researchers could be efficiently supervised by one research director.

Organisational level

The person supervising workers at the shop-floor level, such as the foreman, could be expected to have more subordinates to control than a person managing at higher levels within the organisation. Spans of control can be broad because the tasks are likely to be less diversified. At higher organisational levels, where work becomes more complex, there will be fewer people reporting to a manager.

Tasks

An organisation's tasks, not to be confused with its activities, enable it to fulfil its strategic objectives. These will greatly influence organisational structure and through it the spans of control at various management levels.

Centralisation and decentralisation

A major debate about organisational structure is whether certain areas of work should be centralised or decentralised, and principles of management have developed around these two opposing concepts. Both centralisation and decentralisation have much to offer the office manager. The centralisation of office services has many advantages, such as providing economies of scale, and centralisation can reinforce some of the other principles of management, especially standardisation and simplification – which involve the all-important consideration of methods to maximise cost savings. Nevertheless, the advantages of centralisation have to be weighed against its disadvantages; here an advantage frequently has a disadvantage as a mirror image. Similarly, decentralisation has advantages and disadvantages; and today, through improvements in technology and the lower capital cost of office equipment (much of which has become smaller), there has been a step back towards the decentralisation of some office services. The following will cover the advantages and disadvantages of centralisation and decentralisation, and consider the types of centralisation that can occur in relation to office work. It will also examine the questions that need to be asked when deciding whether or not to centralise office services.

The advantages of centralisation

There are two mainstreams – those associated with office equipment, machinery and space, and those comprising the people who carry out the work. With the former, centralisation promotes economy in the use of equipment, machinery and space, and reduces the need for duplication. It may make the use of specialist machinery worth while, and will enable better scheduling of machines to deal with peak periods of demand. There can also be economy in the use of office personnel, especially in avoiding the duplication of personnel performing clerical functions in a number of local offices.

Centralised office staff can specialise in various aspects of work to be carried out on a standardised basis, although they can still be taught to deal with a number of different functions, enabling one member of staff to cover for another. More important, centralisation will allow the concentration of staff effort on particular functions at peak-load times. All this requires the careful training, allocation and supervision of the centralised staff which, in turn, will generally be executed more efficiently under conditions of centralisation. This is especially true of control over the quality of work and when deadlines have to be met. In addition, communication and consultation with staff are usually more efficient if groups of people are centralised.

The disadvantages of centralisation

With the centralisation of office services, work from all locations must be sent to and returned from 'central services'. This requires logging procedures, which will add to the overall time taken to complete a task given the increase in paperwork. Thus a bureaucracy of rigid procedures may have to be adopted to ensure uniformity in the work produced and to control its receipt and dispatch. Also, since the work is performed away from the originator, misunderstandings and errors which may cause unacceptable delays are more likely.

The advantages and disadvantages of decentralisation

These are more or less the converse of those associated with centralisation, but involve mainly the benefits of flexibility added to the fact that working in smaller units may motivate staff – although there is the disadvantage of not being able to profit from economies of scale. All in all, centralisation has cost in its favour, but there is likely to be better control over the work if it is carried out locally. Local staff also have more opportunity to use their initiative, and seeing what happens to their work motivates them in terms of quality and speed of production.

Forms of centralisation

Centralisation may be either *physical* or *managerial*. The former means where the office services are located in physical terms, as with a word-processing or typing pool, a records department which maintains files, or a print or copying room, all cases where the users of the service 'pool' their resources. Managerial centralisation keeps the production of services with the local offices, nearer to the users, but they remain under the control of a single office services manager to co-ordinate and supervise.

The centralisation or decentralisation decision

There can be many ways in which the centralisation or decentralisation of office services takes place. For in addition to physical or managerial centralisation, the spectrum may run from complete centralisation through scales of partial centralisation (where only selected office functions are centralised, the rest remaining with local user departments), to complete decentralisation. As an example, copying and printing facilities may be centralised in a print room, while the records of individual departments may be maintained in local departmental offices. Or an office procedural manual may require the standardisation of some functions such as form design, or the co-ordination of certain administrative procedures throughout the entity, to provide benefits of scale.

The decision of whether or not to centralise, and if so to what extent, needs to be made with care.[21] It will be based on the criteria of users' needs, especially as related to flexibility, and of comparing the costs of various possible approaches with the benefits ensuing from the use of either full or partial centralisation. The main objective is to make the organisational structure fit the entity's needs as closely as possible. In subsequent chapters aspects of centralisation and decentralisation will be related to various features of office work.

Formal and informal organisation

The concepts of formal and informal organisational structures within an enterprise, and the interrelationships between them, must also be considered. To enable the efficient achievement of an organisation's objectives, attention must be given to the line, staff and functional relationships as well as to the distinctions between them. So formal organisational structures will be examined together with the problems associated with scalar chain and span of control, and the consequences of centralisation and decentralisation. The growth of the informal organisational structures within an entity will also be discussed, especially with regard to their problems and benefits. It will be seen that although organisations have formal line, staff and functional relationships, they are also likely to develop informal relationships which can be superimposed on the formal ones.

The formal organisational structure: line, staff and functional relationships

When analysing an organisation's structure, a number of characteristics should be identified. One of these is the way in which the organisation's employees are grouped into units. When organisational groupings are set up, provision should be made for growth of the entity and its organisational structure. Thus groupings must be as flexible as possible. Various principles, including those concerning the depth and width of the organisational structure, require careful reflection. Some of the factors and principles which should influence an organisation's structure will be considered below. First, however, it will be useful to attempt a differentiation between the three types of relationships, as far as any such distinction is meaningful.

Line operations are sometimes referred to as *task activities*, and are directly concerned with the attainment of an entity's strategic objectives. They are identified with the enterprise's operational objectives and affect how these are organised. A well-known management writer, Joan Woodward, referred to the task activities as the *ultimate tasks* of the organisation. *Staff activities* exist to back up the line operations of the organisation. Joan Woodward referred to these as the enterprise's *element functions*.

The organisation's task functions are considered critical to the entity. Production, marketing and finance are generally classified as the line activities. Some writers add personnel, purchasing, research and development and, with the advent of central information processing (together with the use of computers and microprocessors), information services. Generally the activities in these latter groupings are termed staff activities, because they frequently play the part of a 'lubricant' which makes the line activities more effective. There are no broad rules to this classification, which will depend upon whether the areas are of a critical or a facilitating nature. Basically, it is the line activities that lead to the ultimate success of the enterprise, so the classification will depend upon the operational objectives required for the fulfilment of the entity's strategic objectives. For example, for the retail store the purchasing of items for resale, which is more or less a substitute for production, is a critical function and so is likely to be classified as a line activity for the retailer. But in a service organisation such as an insurance company, any purchasing is usually a minor aspect of the operations of the enterprise; it is unlikely that the items procured are for resale. Thus purchasing would be sublimated as a service function in this sector of commerce. *Functional relationships* are a variant of staff relationships. They arise when a line department also has responsibility for their function in another area.

Forms of staff and functional authority

Although the authority of managers in the line function is quite easily identified, the authority of specialist staff is frequently more difficult to ascertain – especially in discerning real authority. With staff and functional activities, the matrix approach to organisational structures can be used. Here the line authority operates in a downward direction, while staff authority goes across the matrix. This is shown in Fig. 2.3.

Staff \ Line	PRODUCTION	MARKETING
PERSONNEL		
FINANCE		
OFFICE SERVICES		

Fig. 2.3 The matrix organisational structure, showing staff and functional authority

The matrix indicates that while production and marketing management have line authority, they will also be subject to the influence of personnel and finance through the staff authority of the people responsible for these areas. Finance is sometimes considered a line function, although in this case it will also likely have functional authority in other areas. However, the approach shown in Fig. 2.3 is necessarily simplistic; in practical terms, it does not provide any real indication of the extent of staff authority. This will depend upon what top management expects from its staff areas. It may be that staff managers have either advisory or service staff authority, or even may be given complete control over their functions throughout the entity.

Advisory authority
With this type of authority the staff or functional areas offer advice, make suggestions and perhaps prepare plans for their fields of specialisation. This advice is given to line managers for their consideration; if in agreement, they will take the necessary action. However, there is usually no obligation on the part of the line manager to accept any suggestions made or to follow any advice given. For example, a line manager could ask appropriate advisory staff to investigate a problem with which he feels the specialists may be able to provide help – as when a production manager asks the work study team to look into the way an incentive scheme could be introduced in their area, or where an office manager asks organisation and methods to examine one of their areas of work with the aim of improving it. In these cases a course of action will be recommended by the service people, although the proposals do not have to be followed by the person requesting the advice. Thus specialist staff must

develop the ability to 'sell' rather than 'tell' when making proposals, with advisory staff aiming for 'approval' rather than 'rejection' of their work.

Generally, advisory staff will have to wait to be invited by another department to do their work. Even then they may be asked only to write up in a workable form ideas which the line people have already had, although some consultation and discussion about the problem will be needed before complete proposals can be submitted. This will provide O & M with the opportunity to inject some of their own ideas into the report. Other examples of advisory staff authority would be where the personnel staff conduct studies on the various personnel activities within a line department, such as examining their training or management development requirements, and submitting proposals to implement or improve these. But again, the line manager is under no obligation to accept the suggestions. Thus for the work of advisory people to have some chance of acceptance, or at least to be treated seriously, areas with staff authority must be aware of their limits, developing as close a rapport as possible with the line departments with which they are likely to become involved.

Service staff authority

Service staff authority arises where some of the activities carried out in the line department are done under the umbrella of the appropriate staff department. Here the line manager will be obliged to work through the staff manager concerned and follow his advice. An example would be where purchasing was a staff role and clearly delineated, with the responsibility for this function taken away from line managers. So although line managers still have to identify their purchase requirements, the ordering function will be performed by the purchasing section. This inevitably imposes a restriction on the line manager's authority over part of his department's activities.

Usually this separation of a function will occur only when the advantages outweigh the disadvantages. The advantages could include: the development of specialisation in the staff activity; economies gained through the centralised operation of some functions; and standardisation through the use of uniform procedures. Staff service authority does not necessarily have to lead to the centralisation of the activity by its removal from the line department. The work can remain within the line department, the person dealing with the activity becoming responsible to the appropriate staff manager. When variants of service staff authority are used, confusion as to whom staff are to report must be avoided.

Control staff authority

When the staff function has control authority, this means that it is the agent of a higher authority. This type of authority is often delegated to ensure that high standards of performance are obtained, as would be the case when a quality control department is given control authority. The advantage of this form of authority is that the staff of a service area are more likely to be able to identify the need for control action, especially in marginal cases, than would be the case if the line department had to make its own decisions. Thus control authority can initiate control action promptly, which may also help to keep the line departments up to standard.

Functional staff authority

Where functional staff authority has been delegated, people are given authority for their own area of work throughout the enterprise's formal organisational structure. A specialist in a line department may be assigned functional authority for his specialisation outside his line area. For example, the mangement accountant may, as well as running his own department, be given special authority to look after the management accounting procedures in other departments. Obviously, the extent to which this could occur will depend upon a number of factors, including which areas have been designated as line ones, and whether their operations are also carried out in other departments. The possible relationships of the four types of authority to a production department are illustrated in Fig. 2.4.

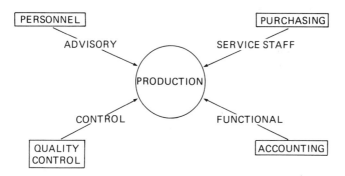

Fig. 2.4 Forms of staff and functional authority

The informal organisation

So far discussion has been centred on formal organisational structures. Although not officially established, an informal organisational structure can often grow up within an entity and exert an important influence on its operation. If management can harness this informal system to the benefit of the concern, it can provide a significant benefit. On the other hand, if left uncontrolled it could act as a brake on activity. Frequently it will be found that the operation of the formal section of a firm's organisation will be tempered by its informal organisation.

The informal organisation can give people status, either throughout the organisation or within one of its smaller informal groupings. The criteria that determine a person's status will depend upon a number of factors. An individual is likely to have both formal and informal status within the organisation. The former will depend upon his position in the hierarchy, and is referred to as his *scalar status*; this comes from the direct authority that he is given to enable him to carry out his work. He may also have a formal *functional status* – the situation where the work is functional, and where the status associated with it will depend upon whether it is considered to be more or less important than that of somebody else. Scalar and functional status may have status symbols attached to them. Examples of such symbols are obvious even to those outside the entity, e.g. those used by military organisations, where the badges of rank indicate a person's scalar status while other badges show such things as the military trade the person is proficient in, thus denoting his functional status. Medals gained in military campaigns provide another status symbol. Thus, in the military environment status has become very formalised and symbols abound.

Even in commercial and industrial enterprises there may be overt, formalised status symbols such as cars, a personal office, carpets and secretaries, all of which provide an indication of a person's scalar status. Functional status may be shown through the different colours and types of overalls or working clothes worn. The uniforms worn by porters and commissionaires, which may even have badges of rank, are a notable example of this.

In addition, individuals are likely to develop status in another dimension within the organisation for which they work. Perhaps this will be achieved through outside activities. For example, the employee who is a well-known local amateur sportsman, or a person who is involved in the local operatic and dramatic society's work, may achieve varying levels of social status according to their importance as perceived by their peer groups.

Social status may even accrue because of quasi-formal status within the organisation, e.g. the union official. It also comes about through character and personality, for example the employee who has become known as 'the life and soul of the party' and is good at telling jokes. Through this people who do not have any formal status within the organisation may have an informal status with which they can exert great influence on their colleagues in the work situation, and therefore on work performance.

One of the problems arising from dual status is role conflict. When a person has more than one role within his organisation, these roles compete and conflict. An example would be where the trade unionist, who is also a conscientious employee, is faced with either following his union's rules to strike, with the feeling that he is letting his employer down, or continuing to work and so going against his union, causing mental and other conflict. If an organisation can minimise any role conflicts that are likely to arise, this will help to ensure that the employee will maximise his work effort, as well as promoting harmony in the workplace.

Various forms of informal organisation may be superimposed on an entity's organisational structure by its employees in a number of ways. It may be through 'formal' groupings within the organisation that people establish relationships and, through similar interests, cause informal systems to grow up. Or it may be outside contacts which provide some employees with additional information about their firm, which is fed into the organisation's various internal communication systems, formal or informal. This occurs because people like to be able to pass on bits of information, since doing this provides them with additional status. For example, in a manufacturing firm the managing director's secretary might have a boy-friend whose father works on the factory floor. There is always the danger that this secretary might say something to her boy-friend about a confidential matter that has arisen in the managing director's office, which he passes on to his father, who in turn feeds it into the internal grape-vine.

Nevertheless, the informal organisational system can sometimes be harnessed to the benefit of an organisation if its managers get to know the structure of the network of informal communication and channel the benefits, some of which are outlined below.

Employee job satisfaction
Job satisfaction generally derives from both the physical and mental environment within the organisation. In the latter case, established routines and a sense of belonging provide employees with satisfaction and security in their work. The informal organisational system can particularly help to promote and underpin this.

Social satisfaction
People at the bottom of an organisation's formal hierarchy have no formal status, but the informal organisation that will grow up, even at that level, will confer respect on them. As an example, informal group leaders may emerge for particular purposes, even those of being the group's horse-racing or motor mechanic experts. The informal organisation thus increases the social satisfaction of employees who serve and support it.

Communication
The informal system of organisation within a firm creates a grape-vine which can help to disseminate information both widely and rapidly throughout the organisation, often more so than the formal channels. So managers must ask whether the informal communication systems can be put to use for the benefit of the enterprise. However, the grape-vine can transmit rumours which have no foundation just as easily and quickly, and it may be difficult to dampen myths or gossip. The informal communication system can also be tapped by management to obtain information about employees' attitudes and can be used as a 'finger on the pulse' to gauge real reactions which may not be forthcoming in a formal context.

Helping internal and external social control

Informal groupings within an organisation can often be channelled by management to help exert additional influence throughout the organisation, even in trying to exert social control. Members of informal groupings who are influenced by management might then use their own influence within their own social groupings to forward management's policies. Alternatively, management might try to use this tactic to influence the formal hierarchy by keeping supervisors in line. In all cases the group's members are being influenced indirectly by management.

Group members

The informal organisation within an enterprise is characterised by an ability to change both rapidly and constantly. However, there are ways of indentifying the various social groupings and their strengths through the use of *sociograms*. The sociometric technique of determining one person's relationships with the others in the group can be used to build up a sociogram. Figure 2.5 provides an example of this.

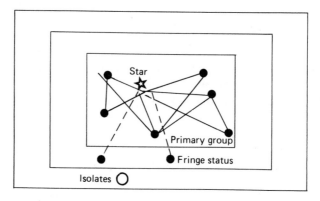

Fig. 2.5 The sociogram

The three types of membership in a social grouping are shown. The *primary* group is the central one, where there will often be a *star*, i.e. the person who has emerged as the informal leader of the group. As well as relating to the star, people in the primary group also relate to most of the other people in the grouping, even if not to all the members of the primary group. Next there are the people who have *fringe status*. They have some relationship with the star but little with the other members of the primary group. Thus they tend to have an unstable relationship with the primary group, perhaps eventually moving into it, or even further away from it as time passes. Finally there are the people without status. These are the so-called *isolates*, who have no connection with any members of the group, not even the star. Although they may be in a group for formal purposes, they tend to exert a negative effect upon the efficiency of its operation. Once isolates have been identified, management must try to fit them in somewhere else within the organisation where they will not be counter-productive.

Organisational units and structure

The people or units within an entity will usually be formed into some kind of departmental structure once the organisation has reached a size which makes this beneficial. The way in which the management units are classified must be approached carefully. Departmental structure may need to be changed as the organisation grows, which may require an increase in the number of tiers of management. Organisational, administrative and management groupings can be made in a number of ways. Some of these are outlined below.

Number
Personnel in the organisation are divided up, providing the simplest method of grouping for management purposes. Effectively this means the division of employees into groups of a size appropriate to the entity, with a manager to supervise each of them. However, this method of grouping employees probably has the greatest disadvantages, particularly if the employees are selected for their group in a random fashion. Among these is the risk that the groupings will not be compatible with the specialised units that exist or grow up within the organisation; nor do the groupings differentiate between the various types of manpower employed.

Function
Division into functions is frequently used when departments are established within an organisation. Such a division may be into the major line or service departments, i.e. production, marketing, personnel, etc., with each department possibly subdivided into smaller units. This division into the areas which are critical to an entity's survival means that their performance can be monitored and controlled more easily.

Product
Grouping by product, or product line, depends upon the size of the organisation and on the product. This method of classification delegates the responsibility for the main product or product areas within an organisation to a single controlling authority. The departments thus established are made responsible for all aspects of that product, from its production through to its marketing. On the other hand, where there is some form of matrix organisation one department might be responsible only for producing certain products, with no control over their marketing. For example, a vehicle manufacturer could have separate divisions for the production of cars and commercial vehicles. The car division could then be subdivided into the

various models of cars produced, but with divisional management retaining control over such things as research and development (R & D) and the marketing of all models. This would have the advantage that while each model could be produced using the most efficient methods, the co-ordination of R & D and design throughout the division would have benefits such as the standardisation of certain basic parts and the co-ordination of marketing effort.

Processes

The division of units by the sort of equipment, production methods or type of work carried out is a special case of functional departmentalisation. It can be implemented when special machine tools or equipment must be used or where the equipment is used serially, i.e. when the product is built up as it moves from one stage of the production, assembly or finishing processes to the next. For example, all the assembly work might be placed in one department, spraying in another, and so on. Or, on the administrative side, all the text creation activities go into one department, and reproduction into another.

Territory

Division by territory, or geography, may occur with production facilities or for marketing purposes. With the former, it may depend on the location of physical resources and factors of production, or there may be external economies of scale to be gained by locating the production processes near markets. As an example, it may be necessary for products with a short shelf life to be near local markets or to have access to good transportation and communication facilities.

Customers

Another possible form of grouping is to divide people into departments which deal with certain types of customers, or with those in various locations, thus providing them with better service. The customers could be divided on a geographical basis, which is one aspect of territorial division, or they could be split into categories such as retail, wholesale and direct customers, or those who buy the different types of products manufactured by a diversified organisation. This will all depend upon the markets catered for and the products concerned. If the firm can differentiate between the classes of product that it supplies to a number of different markets, the use of a judicious differential pricing policy may help to avoid the underemployment of its facilities, although this may, in turn, create the difficulty of keeping the markets separate.

When deciding upon the management groupings for departmental purposes, it might be appropriate to use more than one classification method within an organisation, with different approaches for different levels. The way in which the classifications are formulated will depend upon a number of factors, and there is a great need for flexibility. The classifications should be based upon means which will enable the organisation to achieve its objectives in the most efficient way. Usually the departmentalisation of an organisation will run through *primary, intermediate* and *ultimate* classifications. Figure 2.6 provides an example.

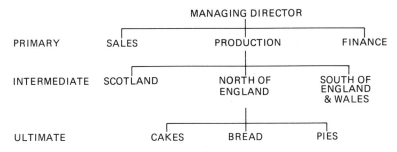

Fig. 2.6 An example of primary, intermediate and ultimate organisational groupings

Different organisations would have primary, intermediate and ultimate groupings appropriate to their circumstances. For example, a consumer durables firm operating in the United Kingdom and manufacturing domestic appliances such as refrigerators and cookers would likely manufacture each product at a central location, whereas it would have a number of regional offices to sell its products, and perhaps district warehouses to distribute them.

Charting the structure

The objective of an organisational chart is to provide a *conceptual representation* of the relationships between and within units in the enterprise. It will demonstrate the main lines of formal authority and responsibility, as well as the communication links which go up, down and sideways. The charting of the management structure of an organisation, or a unit within an organisation such as an office, can be helpful since the chart has many uses. The obvious one is that it helps to provide a *visual representation* of the organisation's structure at that time. Thus it immediately gives an image of the relationships involved and, where the chart supplies the names of the incumbents, it shows 'who is who' at a glance. It also has the advantage that management must consider the relationships of the areas within the chart, for even when compilation of the chart has been delegated, the authority commissioning it will see the result and may contemplate the evidence before agreeing the final draft. Another advantage of an organisational chart is that it indicates *career pathways* within the organisation and shows what promotion possibilities exist for employees.

Producing an organisation chart
When a chart is produced for the first time it is best to start on an outline basis

only, sketching in the major functional and staff areas within the enterprise and then inserting the main components for each of these. Too much detail must be avoided in the early stages. Once the outline has been prepared, the managers of the areas highlighted can be asked to produce an appropriate 'sub-organisational' chart for their own area. These sub-organisational charts can eventually be fitted together like a jigsaw puzzle to make up the whole.

It is usually simpler to prepare an organisational chart or sub-chart starting at the top and working downwards, because once the people at the top of a section have been identified they can be asked to provide a list of those reporting to them. This way charts of each manager's area of responsibility can be built up. Of course senior executives will 'manage' other managers, and a chart of those reporting to each manager at successively lower levels within the organisation can be established.

It is interesting to note a behavioural aspect that can occur. Often, when a number of managers at the same levels in an organisation are asked to produce a chart, they represent their own position on a seemingly higher plane than that of their colleagues who have similar status.

It is also important to note that merely drawing up a fine-looking organisational chart does not necessarily mean that it represents a good management structure, since the managerial posts within it may not have been filled with effective managers. Because organisations operate in a changing environment – and are also affected by growth and internal change – any organisational structure established in the past may have to be altered.

Whether it is preferable to expand an organisation's management structure vertically or horizontally will depend upon a number of factors related to the entity and its environment. Figure 2.7 shows examples of vertical and horizontal organisational structures.

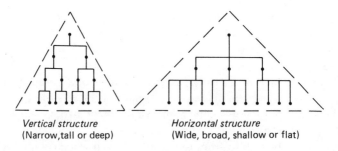

Vertical structure
(Narrow, tall or deep)

Horizontal structure
(Wide, broad, shallow or flat)

Fig. 2.7 Vertical and horizontal organisational structures

Vertical growth and structure

Vertical growth is often referred to as the *scalar* process of growing because growth occurs by adding more and more levels to the organisation's structure, just like adding rungs to a ladder. As this process takes place there is continual delegation of authority and the assignment of responsibility further down to each new stage or tier in the structure. This eventually produces what is referred to as a *tall* organisational structure.

The vertical organisational structure, which may also be referred to as the *deep* or the *narrow* structure, has many levels of management, all requiring co-ordination. The advantage of this form of structure is that it provides better cohesion within a management group; and since the size of each area of management tends to be small, it enables far more contact and better communication between the members of a group. Greater informality is likely to develop under this structure, which may or may not be considered a good thing. Numerous small groupings are also likely to provide better prospects for promotion, as well as more opportunities for people's managerial skills to be fitted into an appropriate part of the system.

The disadvantages of the vertical structure may be identified as follows. A superior manager may not delegate as much of his work, whereas he would be forced to do so if he had a lot of subordinates to control. Because the manager has only a few people to 'manage', he may tend to *overmanage* them by supervising them too closely. This form of organisational structure will also cause a decline in the quality and speed of communication between people at the top and bottom of the system because of the number of management levels the communication process has to work through. Employees at the lower levels of the organisation are bound to feel that they are remote, even alienated from the top, which might affect their morale. And the many junior managers in the system might feel somewhat underextended because their area of responsibility is limited.

Horizontal growth and structure
Horizontal growth is the sideways growth of the organisational structure, with more functions or departmental divisions being added across it. This form of growth may also occur by increasing the span of control at various levels within the organisation, and produces the wide organisational structure shown in Fig. 2.7.

The features of the horizontal organisational structure, which is also referred to as the *wide, broad, shallow* or *flat* structure, are that there are few levels of command within it and that a manager at each of these will have many subordinates to supervise. One advantage is that the short chain of command makes for better communication within the organisation. It also increases the area which the manager can oversee, thus reducing organisation-wide co-ordination and communication problems. And there are greater economies in the use of managerial resources because there are fewer managerial posts.

Nevertheless, there are inevitably disadvantages in this form of structure. Management may become overburdened through having too many people to control and so face great problems in co-ordinating work at the local level. However, the extent of the problem will depend upon the nature of the work concerned. The prospects of promotion in the horizontal structure will be lessened, so employees may become demotivated because they are likely to get stuck in a job which does not extend them; at the same time, they will realise that they have few opportunities for promotion or higher status. The management skills and ability required from one level to another may also increase abruptly so that when a person does get internal promotion he may not be equipped for, or may not be able to cope with, the much greater responsibility and work-load at the next level.

Office manuals

Office manuals are sometimes known as *organisational* or *procedural* manuals. The latter name is the most graphic since it highlights their functions. These are to provide a list of the rules governing staff and the procedures that have been established for tasks to be carried out by the various functions within the organisation.

The office manual should not be confused with an employee's job description, which sets out the work to be done by a particular employee (and which will be discussed in Chapter 4). The manual takes a broad-brush approach, dealing with the tasks and methods of an area rather than the tasks of an individual. It should be emphasised that there may be a number of different manuals within an enterprise to cover different aspects of rules and/or procedures. Examples could be: a manual concerning staff rules; in organisations where safety aspects of the work are important, there could be a safety manual; within a particular office there could be the department's own office manual; and so on.

The advantages and disadvantages of the office manual
There are both supporters and critics of the formalisation of procedures through an office manual. The obvious advantage is that any rules or procedures will be clearly defined and standardised, either for widespread implementation or for the various sections within the organisation. Such manuals are freely available for reference; thus all staff can understand why certain things are to be done in a particular way. Employees will also be able to see the interrelationships between their own and associated areas of work within the organisation, which should help them to cope with the difficulties one department may have in linking its work to that of another.

The office manual is of particular benefit to management since it provides guidelines to refer to in the supervision of work. The manual also makes a good impression on people outside the entity. Then in cases where a dispute has arisen as to who does what, or how a task is to be carried out, the manual can be referred to. Standardisation also means that the various areas within the firm should follow the same procedures for the same sort of work. This should promote co-operation in the use of resources throughout the entity. With the standardisation of tasks it should also be easier to learn how to perform them, especially for new employees, because many of the existing employees will be familiar with the tasks. And standardisation of office tasks provides more flexibility in that office workers can more easily interchange from one area to another when there are peak-load periods in one area that coincide with a slack period in another.

The other side of the picture shows the disadvantages associated with the use of an office manual. The obvious one is bureaucracy, with its rigidity and lack of sympathy. Office manuals are often written along the lines of 'Theirs not to reason why, theirs but to do and die'; thus staff may feel they must blindly follow the rules laid down, even when they realise that they are inappropriate to a particular situation. Or staff may be made to follow outdated procedures precisely because they are in the rule book! This problem becomes particularly acute when the office manual becomes out of date, which is increasingly the case these days with rapidly changing technology. There is also the danger that the procedures in an office manual may be ambiguous or vague. This emphasises the importance of ensuring that the manual is drawn up accurately, with little room for error or misinterpretation – although it will be impossible to state every task precisely, and to keep the manual completely up to date at all times.

Nevertheless, the application of instructions from a manual may highlight the fact that there is a better way to carry out the task, and enlightened management, after evaluation of the alternatives, will amend the existing manual to enable employees to do so.

The office supervisor

The supervisor could be defined as 'The foreman of the office'. Owen Hiner writes, 'Foreman is a well-established title in the manufacturing and construction industries, but supervisor is more commonly used in offices and service establishments and seems to be gaining in popularity in all trades because of the superior job characteristics and status it implies to many people.'[22] Supervisors do not formulate an organisation's strategic or operational objectives. The former are established by the entity's directors and senior executives and the latter by middle management. The supervisor's job is to *implement* the operational policies for his area of responsibility and to *supervise* the workers directly responsible to him.

The qualities of supervisors

Since the supervisor leads and to a large degree motivates his section, he needs to have the same basic qualities – although perhaps not all of them, nor to the same depth – as the manager. The leadership skills required for the position of supervisor are set out in the following pages.

Technical ability

The supervisor must have the technical ability to carry out the work done by his subordinates, and he must know how to operate the equipment used in his area. (This is not so necessary for the manager, and is less important as he moves up in the organisation, although it can still prove to be a bonus when a manager is familiar with the work of the people he has to manage.) There are three reasons for this. Firstly, the supervisor can show by example that he knows as much as those under him and so win their respect. Secondly, he should be able to advise his staff on how to overcome any of their operational problems, making a knowledge and understanding of their work necessary. Finally, he may have to do some of the work of his section, perhaps in the normal routine of things, but especially if some staff are absent through holidays or sickness. Or there may be work to be done urgently, making it necessary for him to become involved if the deadline is to be met.

Ability to lead

Employees cannot and should not be driven. Thus the supervisor must be able to lead those he is responsible for. When leadership was discussed earlier, it was suggested that the very top leaders probably have an inborn ability to lead, although people can be trained in the skills involved. This is especially so with communication and the approach taken to subordinates.

Communication

It is very important for a supervisor to be skilled in communication, especially where he needs to give instructions to the members of his group. This must be done clearly to ensure that they understand what is expected of them, and subordinates *must* be encouraged to ask questions when they do not understand. This highlights why the supervisor must be approachable and sympathetic.

The supervisor's communications will go in three directions: downwards, in the form of orders and instructions; upwards, as feedback to higher management, perhaps in the form of reports; and sideways, as when leaving instructions for the next shift, communicating with supervisors at the same level to co-ordinate the work of a number of groups, obtaining advice, or offering the services of his area to others.

Maintaining discipline

There are a number of considerations in the maintenance of discipline, such as having the strength of character not to be obstinate and unprepared to change or bend when this has become necessary. In maintaining discipline, the demands made on subordinates must be seen to be reasonable. Here example is an important ingredient in the maintenance of discipline. Thus if there is a 'no smoking' rule the supervisor must not break it, for if he does he cannot expect to reprimand others for doing the same without causing resentment.

Example is also important in the maintenance of the quality of his own work where he carries out some of his area's work himself. Sometimes courage is needed to maintain discipline. The supervisor must be prepared to back his judgement and always carry out what he said he would do in the case of a disciplinary matter.

Decision-making ability
The supervisor must be able to make decisions. He should be taught to do this methodically, which is possible because usually he will be involved only in lower-level decisions. His major decision will be on how the work is to be allocated, which calls for careful planning to produce the right scheme. In decision-making the supervisor must have a reasonable time horizon and be able to look ahead to the likely effect of his decisions. He should always be on the look-out for new processing methods, and know where their introduction will affect the work in his area. The supervisor requires good judgement; for example, he must be careful not to push his staff past their breaking-point. This may lead to extra production in the short run, but may cause them to leave and so have a detrimental effect in the long run. Above all, he must be able to make his decisions on time; a decision made late may be of no benefit whatsoever.

Justice
The supervisor must be, and must be seen to be, impartial in dealing with his subordinates. Otherwise, he will be unable to inspire confidence, win respect or gain co-operation from his group as a whole, and this will undermine the projects undertaken.

Administrative ability
Generally, a supervisor will be involved with some paperwork, such as completing forms, writing reports (including staff appraisals), and so on. He thus needs to have some administrative ability.

Consistency
The supervisor must be consistent in the way in which he deals with his subordinates. This applies to how matters are dealt with over time, and to his dealings with different employees. An able supervisor will represent a constant within an organisation – a focus of stability and a source of some security.

The work of the supervisor

The supervisory role entails a number of functions. Some of these are set out below.

Control
Probably the most obvious function of supervision is that of controlling the

work and the people. The supervisor must control his work-force in the speed and quality of their output. He must also control the other resources at his disposal, such as materials, ensuring their cost-effective use.

Interpretation and implementation of management's plans
Top management will formulate plans and policies for the entity, and these will be broken up into smaller operating plans and targets for each supervisor's area. The supervisor therefore has to interpret the plans for his area and plan how operations will be carried out. There will be detailed plans for the methods to be used, who will do what and how, using which materials and equipment. Then he has to activate his plan. Finally, he must control the process to ensure that all is going as planned.

Motivating
The supervisor must be able to get the best out of his work-force, and his manager should help him there. Although the supervisor can do many things himself to motivate his subordinates, as by setting a good example, there are still a number of goals that can be achieved only with the support of higher authority. However, the supervisor can make suggestions to his manager, and the personnel manager may be brought in as well.

The law of the situation[23]
This is a principle of management suggested by Mary Parker Follett (1868–1933). She stated that the supervisor should inform his subordinates of the facts of the situation and that this requires good communication. In addition, where possible, the supervisor should allow his subordinates to make their own decisions about how they carry out their work. This would help the supervisor in the exercise of authority since, to some extent, the subordinates would be permitted a degree of self-determination in their work, thus increasing motivation and satisfaction.

Discipline

The maintenance of discipline has already been mentioned as one of the necessary characteristics of good supervision. The law of the situation stressed the importance of communication and this, together with setting an example, can lead to high staff morale and make employees more willing to obey rules. For example, if a person is ordered to do a job in a special way without being told why that method has been prescribed, he may use his own initiative to do it in what he thinks is a better way. He may cut corners, which could lead to a loss in quality and to his being disciplined. If the reason for the instruction had been carefully explained to him, there would have been no trouble. Without prior explanation a reprimand may cause justifiable grievance. Discipline can sometimes be preserved by using rewards, as in a bonus given for maintaining the quality of work or for increased productivity. In the last resort a superior must have the right to enforce his reasonable requests and to discipline those who deviate from them – with the sack as the ultimate deterrent.

Discipline can be classified into two types, constructive and negative.

Constructive discipline, which is sometimes referred to as *positive discipline*, is the establishment of rules in a way which makes them automatically obeyed and so ensures co-operation. An example would be where there were two types of film which could have the same use in microfilming. However, one is very expensive and designated for a special camera used to copy architectural drawings, while the other, which is much cheaper, is used in a camera to mass-copy text. Both films are supplied in cartridges. The equipment can be designed so that although the films and their housing are similar, each camera will take only the appropriate film. This could be done by 'notching' both cartridges differently so that they will only fit into the housing of the appropriate camera.

Negative discipline is the use of threats or force to instil acceptable behaviour. Today this does not tend to work as well as it might have done in the past, for the use of 'the big stick' and threats of unemployment are no longer feasible. Even when it was thought to be a deterrent it did not necessarily work, since employees were always trying to find ways round the rules; thus the threat of discipline had a negative effect.

Disciplinary action

Unfortunately there will always be cases which require disciplinary action. Sometimes this will arise because of deliberate disobedience, or because there was deviation from instructions. The personnel department has an important role in educating supervisors to deal with disciplinary matters. It must ensure that the supervisor knows the steps to take according to the organisation's 'rule book', and the limits to his authority.

There are several types of disobedience; however, the severity of the offence will sometimes depend upon the frequency of its occurrence. For example, if an employee is late once or twice over a long period, this is not a great disciplinary matter. However, if somebody is regularly late, and continues to be late even after having received a verbal warning, at some point the offence would be classified as a serious one. On the other hand, the first time somebody left the guard off a dangerous machine, it would immediately be classified as a serious offence.

Serious offences

Serious offences are those which could lead to instant dismissal, depending upon the circumstances. These would include: not obeying a lawful order; immoral behaviour; causing deliberate damage to the organisation's property; causing damage through incompetence; being involved in an act likely to cause bodily harm or injury to other workers; and misappropriation of materials through pilfering.

Minor offences

These are offences which tend to become more serious through repetition and would include: absence without a reason, continual lateness; time-wasting through malingering; being away from the work area without permission; and disobeying regulations such as no smoking or safety rules. Even seemingly minor offences would move up into the serious category if they led to injury.

The punishments used

The punishment should fit the crime. The possible forms of punishment, in order of increasing severity, are: the *verbal reprimand*, where the person is warned of his misdemeanour but no record is made; the *recorded reprimand*, where the employee is also told that it will be recorded; and *suspension* of the person who committed the offence, which may be for a predetermined period or while waiting for the outcome of a case which may lead to the employee's dismissal; there is likely to be an appeal mechanism built into this procedure.

Dismissal can prove to be a long and tedious business because of the Employment Protection (Consolidation) Act 1978.[24] And dismissal especially instant dismissal, can also lead to problems with the union and other workers. Where the employee has some seniority there can be demotion, where he may be moved to a lower grade on the payment scale or rung on the managerial ladder. Dismissal generally comes about only after suspension, and will be the last resort after all other disciplinary devices have failed. It must be carried out by a higher authority, and must follow clearly defined rules. This should all be under the advice of the personnel manager, and any legal requirements, such as written warnings in the United Kingdom, must be followed rigorously. The employee should be given the opportunity to state his side of the case and be allowed to have representation – whether union official or a friend – to speak on his behalf when being heard. This is to avoid the indiscriminate dismissal of employees through malice and is part of the justice concept in personnel policy.

Conclusions

When proposing the toast to the Institute of Chartered Secretaries and Administrators at their Annual Dinner in 1983, His Royal Highness Prince Michael of Kent said 'Specialists in administration are increasingly in demand . . . This . . . brings about the need for people who are skilled in the knowledge of corporate structure and administration'.[25] Many people have written or spoken about the importance of good management to a country's economic performance.[26] Thus the need for – and the opportunities available to – good managers, especially in the area of administration and the office, are there. However, such people need to know about organisation, administration and management. And to be successful in office administration and management, it is important to have a knowledge of the principles and practices of management and how these affect the structure and operation of the enterprise, especially its information-related services. Some major principles of management can be discerned, many of which have particular application to the provision of office services. An example is the question of whether or not to centralise office work. Many factors are involved, such as the state of technology and the behaviour of employees. Early in the twentieth century, when offices were based on labour-intensive processing methods and there was not much machinery available, services tended to be decentralised. After the 1950s, when office equipment improved through major technological advances, machinery tended to have a high capital cost and to be bulky. The large photocopying machines, and especially the mainframe computer, were prime examples. There was a tendency towards the centralised use of such processing equipment.

Today, however, developments in office technology have moved forward rapidly and equipment has become smaller and less expensive. So there has been a drift back towards the decentralisation of office work. There is even talk of the office employee of the twenty-first century working in his own home since the use of terminal equipment will bring the processing technology direct to him.

When organising office work, charting the system can also offer practical benefits. The formal organisational chart is useful in ascertaining the lines of authority and responsibility, as well as the channels of communication within the enterprise. With the latter, the development and workings of the informal system must not be overlooked. Both formal and informal organisational structures come in all shapes and sizes. While there is no 'right' way to establish the formal structure, there are basic principles which should be followed, especially those concerning the scalar chain and the span of control. Thus there remains a strong element of choice which will be influenced by the circumstances. Getting it right can have an important effect on the efficiency of the office system, and through this on the success of the organisation as a whole.

Generally, it is either impossible to stop the informal system from being established or, once it has become established, to destroy it. In fact it would probably be counter-productive to try to do so because the informal system would quickly re-form itself in one way or another. Therefore the most sensible course of action for management is to try to identify it and, if possible, to tune into the informal system and thus harness it to the benefit of the organisation. At the very least, management should tap the current in order to ensure that any potential harmful effect can be mitigated.

Questions and discussion problems

1. Organisational charts and manuals have a number of important functions.

(a) Explain the functions of both types of document.

(b) Draw a chart showing an organisation's or department's structure, preferably for an office-based system, with which you are familiar.

2. The following terms are frequently used associated with the office:
(a) formalisation;
(b) specialisation;
(c) centralisation;
(d) standardisation.

Explain what you understand by *each* of these terms, and discuss the benefits they can offer in the running of an office.

3. 'The company started seriously to investigate the feasibility of centralising administration.' From *Administrator*, May 1982.

The company concerned had, at that time, office units established in various geographical locations within the United Kingdom.

(a) Discuss the factors involved when making a decision to centralise administration from diverse locations to a single site within a named country of your choice.

(b) Assuming that a decision has been made to centralise administration, describe the stages that the process will go through from the time of the decision until the completion of the task.

4. What are the advantages and disadvantages associated with the centralisation of office services? In your answer use examples from the centralisation or decentralisation of reproduction services.

5. Draw up an organisational chart for an office with which you are familiar.

6. Are the words organisation, administration and management synonymous, or do you think there is a difference in the concepts which underlie them? Give reasons for the stance that you take.

7. The following questions are often asked in relation to management:
(a) Is management an art or science?
(b) Are managers born or made?
(c) Can management be taught?

Briefly provide answers to *each* of these questions.

8. State, and explain, *five* of the major principles of management.

9. Carefully explain:
(a) the scalar chain, and
(b) the span of control.

In your answer state how these two principles of management should be taken into consideration when developing the organisational structure for an entity.

10. (a) Distinguish between formal and informal organisation.

(b) Explain how the informal organisation can influence the operation of an entity and indicate the possible problems and benefits that may arise if an informal organisational structure grows up.

11. (a) Distinguish between management and supervision.
    (b) What are the functions of a supervisor?

12. Two identical offices have supervisors who hold quite different attitudes towards the respective budgets for which they are responsible. One supervisor feels that there should never be underspending on a budget, and that his job is always to utilise fully the budget for his office. The other supervisor cuts expenditure to the bone, sometimes even to the detriment of office efficiency. He feels that the greater the favourable expenditure variance, the more successful the supervison has been. Explain your views on the approaches taken by the two supervisors.

3
Office services and methods

Introduction

This chapter will look at the services and methods used in offices, related to text origination, copying and storage. The emphasis is on the use of office equipment and machinery within the framework of a systematic analysis of work requirements. The selection of the most appropriate way of carrying out these functions will be based on the type of output required and the most efficient methods of obtaining it, all seen in relation to the cost of processing.

The origination of copy

Copies of information can be produced in many forms, some of them more durable than others. For example, Moses chiselled the Ten Commandments into stone, and the Egyptians used papyrus scrolls for their hieroglyphic writing. In the Middle Ages in Europe, when few people (even among the nobility) were literate, the profession of clerk or scribe was important and influential. As writing spread, instruments such as chalk, charcoal or the quill pen, and more recently pens with metal nibs, came into use. Fountain and ball-point pens are a relatively recent development. Instruments with a keyboard or keypad, such as the typewriter and the stenotype, were invented in the nineteenth century but still provided a record of the information on paper. Today the information may be recorded and stored electronically using a computer or word processor. Nevertheless, the principles behind recording information electronically are the same; it is only the method of storing information that is radically different, especially since people do not have direct access to it. It must be called up on a visual display unit (VDU) and a 'hard copy' printed out before it can be accessed in the traditional sense.

As will be seen in Chapter 5, effective communication is of the essence, and while it may be neither appropriate nor necessary to use a word processor for all forms of written communication (and indeed there is still much to be said for a clearly handwritten memo), the objective is *clarity*.

More and more people carrying out office work are having to become familiar with the operation of the keyboard. The person who can touch-type using the QWERTY keyboard has an advantage, as do those who can record figure work using the keypad without looking at it. In fact most computer keyboards have three banks of keys: the standard QWERTY keyboard; a keypad for the quick entry of numbers; and a set of function keys, all of which are applied when computer technology is harnessed for word processing. There are two major groups of people who input data: those trained in keyboard skills, with the job of inputting data, and casual users; and today many managers have computers on their desks to provide them with an electronic work station. With the former a certain dexterity is important. With the latter, few are trained to touch the correct keys without looking at them as the touch-typist can, although as managers become more reliant upon personal computers in the future this will obviously be beneficial.

As with playing a piano, some people have a natural ability with keyboard skills. Thus selection of keyboard operators using speed tests can be worth while, with rigorous training for those who have to acquire the skills.

The typewriter

The *Encyclopaedia Britannica* states that the typewriter is 'a writing machine, enabling the operator to produce writing resembling printer's type at a speed far greater than that possible with the pen'.[1] The history of the typewriter goes back some 250 years, when on 7 January 1714 an Englishman, Henry Mill, was granted a patent by Queen Anne for 'an Artificial Machine or Method for the impressing, or Transcribing of Letters Singly or Progressively one after another, as in Writing, whereby all Writing whatever may be Engrossed in Paper or Parchment so Neat and Exact as not to be distinguished from Print'.[2] However, no drawings of the proposed machine appear to have survived. Although there were several attempts to produce writing machines after that date, the first practical version did not come along until Christopher Shole's design in 1867. Although his machine was much slower than today's manual typewriters, it produced copy far quicker than could be done in handwriting. This machine was not marketed until 1874, when it was produced by a firm of American gunsmiths, E. Remington and Sons, and sold under the Remington name. Over the years the typewriter has become more sophisticated, with Thomas Edison producing the first electrically operated machine in 1872 (although an electrically operated machine suitable for office use was not produced until 1920). There was the development of shift keys in 1878, a great step forward, and many other refinements such as automatic carriage return in subsequent years.

The early typing machines were originally operated using the 'two-finger' method, and it was not until the last decade of the nineteenth century that touch-typing took off – although in those early days there were few proficient typists. It was probably the typewriter that led to the employment of women in the office in great numbers, for they had the dexterity to use the new device well, and it was introduced at a time when employment in domestic service was declining. The shortage of trained typists promoted the establishment of typing schools, which in many ways were the forerunners of today's commercial colleges in both the public and private sector. The First World War caused a shortage of male clerks, which speeded up the process.

The first really workable portable machine came on the market in 1909, and the electrically operated portable was marketed in 1956. Other developments since then include replacing the keys – the original device to enable the typewriter to produce text – with a single element, either in the form of a golf ball, as developed by IBM, or now with a daisy wheel. These both have the advantage that different balls or wheels can be manufactured using different type styles. These are interchangeable on the appropriate machines, giving a machine versatility because different faces and sizes of type can be used in the creation of a single document.

The typewriter has many advantages. It produces clear, even text. It can tabulate work easily, i.e. line up columns of information. And, using carbon paper, it can usually provide more copies of a document than can be made even by the firm handwriter. The most recent development in the typewriter world has been the electronic machine, which is a move in the direction of word processing. Electronic typewriters may have limited storage facilities, and some can be linked up to equipment such as the VDU, external storage, or printers.

The word processor

The word processor is a collection of four pieces of equipment: the keyboard; the processor; the visual display unit (VDU); and the printer – all of which may be in modular form and linked together, or integrated as a dedicated word processor. The first and last pieces of equipment are based on typewriter technology. The word processor is a development of computer technology; the VDU is necessary if the person keying in the text or anybody else wishes to see what has been entered and stored without getting hard copy at that stage, or perhaps wants to make corrections to, or edit the text. Kevin and Kate Townsend write: 'Word processing represents the power of the computer brought out of the mystique of the data processing profession and into the commercial environment of the office.' They continue: 'It is for anyone and everyone to use.'[3]

There are two categories of computers which can carry out word processing: the machine *dedicated* to word processing, i.e. built solely for word processing and so 'dedicated' to this task; and the machine, perhaps a personal computer (PC), which can be used for word processing if the appropriate software package is loaded. The major expected advantages of the dedicated word processor are that it costs less and has been tailored to produce text as efficiently and effectively as possible. The disadvantage of such a machine is that it is generally limited to the word-processing function, although some machines also have limited facilities to carry out simple calculations.

The software for today's PCs has become more sophisticated for word processing. For example, programs such as Microsoft's WORD are prepared so that people without computing skills find it relatively easy to use; it is thus said to be *user friendly*. It shows the text on the VDU in exactly the same form as it will appear on the hard copy, thus 'what-you-see-is-what-you-get'.[4] Software such as WORD has been developed to use various combinations of the function and other keys to enable it to carry out different aspects of editing simply, quickly and automatically – e.g. underlining, double-spacing, indenting paragraphs, and inserting running headlines, page numbers and footnotes. It also allows the writer to 'cut-and-paste' text, i.e. move text from one part of a document to another, or to merge documents through the use of a *window* facility. Windows mean that the VDU screen can be split so that different documents, or parts of a document, can be seen on the screen at the same time. In addition, it has a facility to search for the spelling of words or check through a text and highlight those that it feels have been incorrectly spelt.

Other software developments, such as that of LOTUS 1 2 3, provide integrated facilities, the 1 providing the filing system, the 2 a speadsheet and the 3 a graphics module, all linked together. The extension of this into SYMPHONY, which is more or less LOTUS 1 2 3 4, has a fourth module added to provide word-processing facilities, thus enabling the incorporation of information from any of the other three modules into a document.

The concept behind the word processor is that the user keys in text which is stored electronically. Any corrections or changes are also made electronically. Thus when the originator of a document requires changes to any proof that he has checked, there is no need to use correcting tapes or fluids to make them.[5] With the word processor additions or deletions to the text cause the original or remaining electronic characters to be pushed outwards or closed up automatically and more or less instantly. Another feature of word processing is that, unlike typing, a carriage does not have to be moved up and returned at the end of a row to begin a new line, for the better word-processing systems automatically 'wrap' the lines round and along in the right places (as with WORD's wordwrap). To read through text keyed into the machine there is a facility to scroll through the document.

When the text produced has been printed out, the 'copy' in the machine can be stored within it electronically. When all the capacity has been used there may be external storage on a floppy disc which can be conveniently kept elsewhere. The storage capacity of machines can be colossal; for example, a double-sided double-density floppy disc, which is made of flexible plastic 5¼ in. in diameter, can store 330,000 characters – the equivalent of 220 single-spaced pages of A4 text. IBM discs of quadruple density hold 1.2 million characters, or up to 800 pages of text. Hard discs can hold 2–25 million characters or from 1,300 to 16,000 pages of information, depending upon the type being used.

It is also possible to use the machine to incorporate standard paragraphs into letters or to produce form letters. Once the basic information has been keyed in the machine can be instructed to 'chainprint', i.e. print more than one copy of this information, and then to merge it with the names and addresses of a number of recipients from a separate mailing list.

Shorthand and audio typing

Even with the advent of word processors, Andrew Doswell points out that 'The initial preparation of the material' has to be considered 'prior to keyboard input'. He continues, 'The dominant method is manuscript preparation by longhand, although in specific organisations and specific jobs other methods of initial preparation, audio or shorthand dictation, may be more significant.'[6] Shorthand and audio typing are used as convenient and efficient ways for an author of text to communicate it to the typist, avoiding full-length longhand drafts or time-consuming dictation.

Shorthand is a compressed form of writing which allows twice as much information to be sent and recorded in a given period. The first English shorthand system was published in 1588, when Dr Timothy Bright invented a code for writing which he dedicated to Queen Elizabeth 1.[7] In 1837 Isaac Pitman published a shorthand system which, with the advent of Roland Hill's Penny Post, gained national and international recognition. In this century other effective shorthand systems have been developed using either symbols or letters of the alphabet to record sounds. Pitman and Gregg are the most widely used of the symbol shorthand systems, while Speedwriting has since 1924 come to dominate the alphabet-based systems in the United States and the United Kingdom.

Symbol-based systems allow the experienced shorthand writer to achieve speeds of 140 to 160 words per minute, the world record being 300 words per minute for five minutes. The principal disadvantage of a symbol-based shorthand system is that it takes considerable time to learn and not everyone has the linguistic skill to master the code.

Alphabet-based systems allow a shorthand writing speed of 100 to 120 words per minute, with exceptional writers achieving 140 to 160 words per minute. The principal advantage of alphabet-based systems are ease of learning and a marked reduction in training time. In 1969 Pitman produced a simplified form of their shorthand, Pitman 2000. This is easier to learn although the speeds attained are somewhat slower than those achieved using Pitman classic. The advantage of any form of shorthand is that the documents or letters a manager wants prepared can be dictated at his normal talking speed and later keyed into a typewriter or word processor to produce text. It also helps the planning of work and its more even distribution over the working day.

Audio typing merely requires that the originator of the text record on tape what he wants produced as typescript without the need to have the person who will eventually transcribe it present. It is then played back, usually on a transcribing machine with a foot control to enable the audio typist to listen to a manageable passage of dictation, stop the tape and key in the text. John Derrick and Phillip Oppenheim write:

> Dictation equipment is not commonly thought of as the most exciting type of business equipment when it comes to technological advance, but it has nonetheless not managed to escape the onslaught of the microchip. The all-electronic pocket memo is not far off, and over in Japan, designers are busy inventing dictation machines that will automatically turn your speech into typed copy without the need of a human secretary to have to transcribe it. That, however, is still some way off in the future.[8]

Nevertheless, today's technology has enabled the miniaturisation of tape cassettes, allowing executives to carry pocket-sized dictating machines or 'pocket memos', and if away from the office to mail in tapes for transcription.

Printers

Word processors can be linked to printers, which currently fall into two major categories, the matrix printer and the daisy wheel printer. However, there are also jet printers, and the introduction of the laser printer is coming up fast; given that it is in a much higher cost bracket, its introduction has thus far been limited.

The *matrix printer* produces the text in the form of small dots which are imprinted by thin rods on the paper. Original versions of this printer produced a crude quality of output; the dots were spaced far apart in a character, and it was obvious that this type of printer had been used. However, the dot matrix printer has two advantages. The first is that it is much faster than the daisy wheel printer: it can produce more than 300 characters per second. The second advantage is that it is more versatile and can, using the right form of word-processing software, produce characters of different style, for example mixing Gothic and italic, and different-sized characters in the same text. The daisy wheel printer can do this only if the machine is instructed to stop and so enable the operator to change wheels, thus slowing the printing process. The dot matrix printer can also print graphics. Over the past few years the quality of the work which dot matrix printers can produce has improved dramatically. Today there are dual-speed dot matrix printers on the market which can produce letter-quality work at 80 characters per second and, where quality is not so important, drafts at 200 characters per second.

The quality of the work produced by the *daisy wheel printer* is superb but it is much slower than the dot matrix printer, operating at about 40 characters per second. This type of printer is also less versatile, especially as it cannot be used to produce graphics. The *laser printer* can produce characters of a very high quality from multifonts. It has all capabilities including the printing of graphics. The process used by the laser printer is based on that used by some photocopiers, but whereas the photocopier places the image on the paper using reflected light, this sort of printer does it using a laser. A sheet of paper is fed into the machine and a complete page printed out at a time. Laser printers can produce up to eight pages per minute. In terms of characters per second, their output can be as high as 350. *Jet printers* come with disposable ink-feeds which are effectively the print head. The printer is based on a thermal process which heats up the ink to vaporise it before jetting the characters on to the paper. These machines can produce up to 150 characters per second.

Copying information

In the Middle Ages if a copy of a piece of written information was required the scribe, or a number of scribes according to how many copies of the document were required, would sit down and make the requisite number by hand. Fortunately, there has been much progress since those days, through the carbon copy to the use of duplicators, photocopy machines and printing equipment. Copying is a method of providing information to a number of people at the same time in an orderly and efficient manner.

This section will introduce the copying facilities available to organisations and discuss the points to be considered when deciding on the method of copying to be used for a particular assignment.

Duplicating

Documents are often reproduced using some form of duplicating process. Although this way of obtaining copies may seem somewhat crude today, it is surprising how frequently it is still used. Duplicating has the benefit of requiring equipment with a relatively low capital cost and of being economical when a reasonable number copies, say ten to 200, are required. The quality of duplication does not compare with that of copies produced using a photo-copier, and the production process can be somewhat messy. Nevertheless, it provides copies which are quite suitable for disseminating information around an organisation. One major disadvantage of the duplicator is that unless there is an electronic stencil-cutting machine available, it cannot make copies from already prepared text, the text having to be prepared again on a stencil. There are two basic types of duplicator, the spirit and the stencil duplicator.

The spirit duplicator

These machines, which can be operated by hand or electrically powered, are very simple to use. A master sheet of special coated shiny paper and a sheet of hectographic carbon paper are required. These are placed with their coated surfaces together. The matter to be copied is then written using a hard-pointed instrument such as a special stylus or ball-point pen, or typed to transfer hectographic carbon on to the master sheet in the form of a mirror image. One of the advantages of spirit duplication is that different-coloured carbon sheets can be used to produce a form of coloured artwork which can be printed in a single run. This provides a very useful facility when line or shaded drawings, and charts or graphs have to be produced in quantity.

The master is then mounted on the spirit duplicator's rotary drum, and the machine damps it with a special spirit. Special paper is loaded into the machine's paper tray or feed, and the machine is then switched on or its handle turned. The master and a sheet of the special duplicating paper are passed through rollers which make an impression of the image, the right way round, on the paper as it is fed through the machine. A major disadvantage of this process is that the number of copies produced is limited to the amount of carbon transferred to the master; and although the pressure applied by the rollers can be slightly increased every now and then as the run proceeds so that more copies can be produced, there is a limit of about 100 good copies from each master.

The stencil duplicator
These machines can also be either manually or electrically operated. With the stencil duplicator a thin wax-coated or nylonised stencil, which is attached to a backing sheet, is used to produce the master. The surface of the wax is broken to let ink seep through and produce the copies. This may be done using a special stylus and board to obtain the correct pressure without tearing the stencil. When a typewriter is used to prepare the stencil the ribbon is moved out of the way, usually by setting the typewriter ribbon control to a stencil setting, which drops the ribbon and so enables the keys to make their imprint straight on to the stencil.

To save having to 'cut' new stencils when the text is already available, an electronic stencil-cutting machine may be used to produce a stencil from copy. This is done by mounting a blank stencil on the machine's special drum and feeding the text into it. The copy is read and the machine makes the appropriate impressions electronically. Using the electronic stencil-cutting machine, photographs can be reproduced in halftones, as can shading. However, the use of these machines can constitute a health hazard.

The stencil duplicator can be of the *flat* or *cylinder* type. The flat version is rather basic, with the stencil mounted on a thin silk screen, paper laid under it and a rubber roller, which is inked by hand, rolled with a slight pressure over the stencil to produce a copy. It is a rather slow and laborious process. The cylinder version, especially when electrically operated, is much more efficient. The prepared stencil is mounted on a drum, through which ink is forced from a reservoir; the special duplicating paper, which absorbs the ink, is fed into the machine. When the drum is rotated, a slight pressure is automatically applied to it and the paper feed under it to produce the imprint. Since the ink used is slow to dry, it is important that special semi-absorbent duplicating paper is used to make the copies. The cylinder machines have a counter which can be pre-set so that the machine produces the required number of copies. The latest versions of cylinder duplicators have interchangeable drums to allow the copies to be produced in different colours. If copy of more than one colour is to be produced, a different stencil has to be cut for each colour and a drum change made with the paper fed through for each colour. Another advantage of the stencil duplicator is that stencils can be stored for re-use.

Photocopying

The use of photocopying machines has increased rapidly since the 1960s, and tremendous strides have been made in the development of the equipment used (the generic term commonly used for photocopy equipment is Xerox). Julie Harnett writes, 'With every new development in the copier market one suspects that technology has reached its limit. One is always proved wrong a few weeks later.'[9] There are many photocopy machines on the market and they use a number of different principles to make the copies. According to Julie Harnett, 'You could be in for a surprise if you look at the new copiers on the market'.[10] For today's machines offer numerous facilities, such as being able to: backprint, i.e. produce text on both sides of the paper; collate the print run, i.e. sort out separate pages in the order required, usually numerical; produce reduced or enlarged copies of the original text, some even having automatic zoom capabilities; and produce work in full colour. Today, with the increased efficiency of photocopy machines, the marginal cost of producing a copy is often less than that of producing a copy using a stencil duplicator, with the added advantage that it looks much more professional. The equipment is also easier and cleaner to operate.

Common technology used by photocopy machines includes the dye-line, transfer, reflex, heat transfer and electrophotographic methods. Basically the differences between these methods are as follows: The dye-line method produces copies in a way similar to that used by photographers to obtain prints of their photographs, but uses a positive master instead of a negative. An important point about dye-line technology for copying, and one of its major disadvantages, is that documents to be copied must be translucent (i.e. let light through), so opaque material cannot be copied. The technology is based on light passing through the original document and creating an image on the sheet of special paper on which the copy is to be made. This sheet is then 'developed' in a liquid, the surplus of which is squeezed out through rollers. This method of copying is not used by the latest machines.

Transfer copying uses both positive and negative paper. A 'negative' is made of the text to be copied using the negative paper, which is then placed next to the positive paper. The two sheets are passed through rollers in a liquid to develop. The sheets are then separated to obtain the copy of the document. This method of copying can be used for opaque documents, but is rather slow and messy and has again been overtaken by improved technology.

The reflex method of copying has the advantage that the positive and negative can be developed separately and so can be used to produce more than one copy. The heat transfer or thermo method makes the copies through the transfer of the image by heat onto special chemically treated paper.

Most copying machines manufactured today use electrophotographic technology. The process is based on using light and static electricity to make the copy. This technology offers many advantages, the major one being that it produces dry copies, and equipment using this method can produce copies very quickly.

In discussing decisions about the acquisition of copying equipment, Julie Harnett says that 'The choice of copying machine and the method by which it is obtained depend not only on available finances but on copy volumes'. She continues that machines can be acquired through purchase or a leasing agreement, and that perhaps the most dificult factor of all to bring into the analysis is that of service costs.[11]

Offset lithographic equipment

These are the machines found in the modern print room when large numbers of copies of a document are required cheaply and quickly. They can be used to print drawings, handwriting, illustrations in halftone and copy produced by typewriters and word processors.

The quality of the master litho plate used will depend upon the length of the run required, and may be paper-, plastic- or metal foil-based. To prepare a master the image is formed on the top surface of the plate in one of three ways: directly, by writing or typing on to the master (in this method a graphite typewriter ribbon, which contains grease, must be used); electrostatically, in which the image is fused to the plate by an electrostatic process using carbon powder, which also contains grease; or photographically, using special photographic equipment to print the image on to a sensitive master. Some machines using this last process have reduction and/or enlargement facilities.

The lithographic process is based on a rotary mechanism and the concept that oil and water do not mix. When wetted, the part of the surface of the master which contains the image on a grease base repels water, whereas the rest of the master will absorb the water. Thus when water and ink are spread over the master the wetted area attracts the water and the image attracts the ink, which is then offset to create the reverse of the image on another surface. This is in turn transmitted in reverse, which puts it the correct way round on the copy paper. The process provides an exact copy of the master image.

Comparing the three basic technologies

Spirit duplicators are very flexible, but unless a careful handling drill is established they will be messy to use. These machines are suitable where not many copies are required. A disadvantage of the copies produced is that they tend to be unstable to light. The spirit duplicator is simple to work and produces cheap copies, which can incorporate colour in a single run on their special glossy paper.

The *stencil duplicator* is simple to operate and cheap to run, and the copies it produces on semi-absorbent paper do not fade. However, a number of runs are required to produce colour work. The *dry photocopy* machines can produce a large number of good copies economically, and this is the machine usually found in today's office.

The *offset litho* can be the most expensive method, both in capital cost and running expenses, since a fully trained operator has to be employed to work the machine. The copies are superior to those produced by any of the other methods and do not fade. These machines will accept the widest range of paper, from flimsy to quite thick.

The choice of machine will depend upon a number of factors, including the purpose for which it is required, the likely throughput, and whether the organisation has a central print room. Often an entity will have a number of each of these machines. Some large organisations will centralise most of their reproduction facilities in a print room, although many departments will still have a small photocopier at local sites for convenience, when the odd copy is required quickly. A print room has all the advantages and disadvantages usually associated with centralisation. The decision will tend to be based on the organisation's office locations, the throughput of copying and printing and its management's attitude towards centralisation.

Reprography (or replication)

The Council of the Institute of Reprographic Technology agrees with the following definition:

> Reprography is the technology of producing and reproducing two-dimensional visual communication media in business and administrative operations.

A reprographic manager's work is likely to cover a much wider area than merely the copying of text and in-plant printing. Sometimes it will include the preparation of text using word processors, preparing artwork and making plates, any finishing required, and even the dispatch of the work internally or externally. The reproduction responsibilities may also include those of producing records on film and the preparation of photographic and visual aids.

Frederick Cox notes that 'Reprography covers every technique used to handle and reproduce alphanumeric information in business, government and other offices'. And because today more information is being conveyed in ways which are neither two-dimensional nor visual, he feels that the following is a better definition:

> Reprography is the management of communication technology in business and administration.[12]

Information storage: records management

An effective and efficient way to store information is required as soon as an entity starts to accumulate it. This involves filing but can be looked upon, and is generally referred to, as records management. Records have a life cycle which runs from their creation through retention, maintenance and preservation (with retrieval as necessary in this section of their life cycle), to their transfer to long-term storage or their ultimate disposal. Records can be stored today through manual or automatic methods, the latter being electronic storage via the computer. John Graeme notes 'It has been said that a filing cabinet is a "device for losing things systematically".[13] Whether this is true or not depends on the filing system used.' Obviously, it is essential that any records can be located speedily when wanted.

The principles of records management

There are a number of principles to be followed when devising a filing system. There should be accessibility of records so that they can be produced quickly when required. The system should be simple enough to be understood and easily operated; otherwise there may be confusion over which record is required, with delays in retrieval. It should be possible to adapt the system in the event that circumstances change. This flexibility should include 'elasticity' so that the system can expand and take increasing numbers of records. Economy in the cost of installing the system (its capital cost) and in its running costs, mainly the labour costs of operating it, must be considered. Compactness can be an important consideration in ensuring that the system fits into the space available. Safety against such things as fire[14] and the deterioration of the records from dirt, dust and loss, and the security of confidential records, must be looked at.[15] The overall suitability of the system for its purpose within the conditions in which the entity operates is another consideration. The indexing of the system should be appropriate for the purpose and provide sufficient cross-referencing for documents that cover a number of areas. There must be controls to keep track of any documents removed and to trace them if necessary. The system should be accurate, i.e. kept up to date, with the filing not falling behind.

An organisation thus has to tailor its filing system to its needs and ensure that the system is flexible enough to cope with changes, especially those related to the expansion of the system and the current requirements of management.

The classification and indexing of records

To facilitate retrieval, records must be clearly classified into major areas and subgroupings, and must be indexed and cross-referenced.[16] The classification and subsequent storage of records can be arranged in five ways. Each of these has its use depending upon the type of documents to be stored, the reason for storing them, and the method of storage. (Records can be stored electronically on a random basis, for retrieval can be automatic if the correct address, i.e. the file name, is known.)

A manual filing system must have an efficient storage arrangement which allows for the division of the records and the expansion of both the system and the records in any part of it. Any of the following approaches, or a combination of them, can be used.

Alphabetical

The alphabetical or alpha approach is based on the *name* of the record. The divisions and subdivisions of this system can be arrived at on a scientific basis, e.g. by asking what the most common names in a country begin with. In the United Kingdom these start with the letters S, B, M and H, whereas the least common names begin with X, Q and U. Then there are generally three times as many Bs as As, 20 times as many Hs as Ts, ten times as many Ts as Us, and so on. The divisions in the system can then be ascertained statistically. Once the *primary* divisions have been decided upon they can be subdivided into *secondary* classifications. Expansion of these divisions and subdivisions should be allowed for to minimise any further subdividing at a later date. The alphabetic classification of records has a number of advantages and disadvantages. The advantages are: direct reference is given to the record so no index is required; it seems the 'natural' way to file; it is easy to understand; and a check can be made quickly to see if there is any misfiled material. The disadvantages of this method include: where common names like Smith arise there will be a congestion of records; and if the system grows too large it will take time to retrieve any record required.

The alpha approach can be modified to cover subjects instead of names. This may make it possible to file a document under a number of different headings. However, the use of some form of coding, such as colour coding, can help overcome many of these difficulties. The alpha method can also be based on a phonetic system such as the US soundex code, or on UK vowel filling where the first letter of the file word is followed by the first vowel.

Subject

This is a variation of the alphabetical method, with documents put under the primary classification of a subject heading, such as insurance or property. Within each primary classification there will be secondary classifications; for example, the primary classification of insurance could be subdivided into fire and vehicle.

The difficulties here are that there may be a problem in the formulation of sufficient suitable classifications, a lot of cross-referencing is usually required, and sometimes a complex index is necessary. Often when this classification method is used a large miscellaneous file builds up with many different items in it, whereas in a good system a file will hold only related items. This seems to be through a reluctance to open up a separate file for each subject in the miscellaneous file. Nevertheless, this classification method can be easily and conveniently expanded. It also provides a useful approach where the subjects are clearly identified, and where people are familiar with them this makes retrieval easier.

Geographical

Using a geographical approach, the files are arranged by location such as county, district, town, and so on for their primary classification. Then alpha subdivisions may be used for the secondary division. The geographical method is sometimes referred to as *location* arrangement. It is easy to understand because the concept behind it is simple and users are likely to have or soon acquire some familiarity with the geography involved. This approach also has its advantages and disadvantages. The advantages are: it enables a number of people to use the files at the same time without getting in each other's way; it is simple to understand; and retrieval is convenient if the location is known. The disadvantages are: users need to have some knowledge of the geography involved, especially if there are a number of similar place names; the location for a piece of information must be known; and the method needs to be supported by an index.

Numerical

The numerical method of classifying records is convenient, especially when the documents are already numbered. This method can operate in several ways. There can be a numbering system which allows for unlimited expansion, based on a classification such as the *decimal numeric* system used by many libraries in the United Kingdom; or *terminal digits* can be used. When this is done by reading the numbers from right to left, it helps to eliminate errors since people are not used to reading in this way and so are more careful when doing it. The numerical approach can also be used to disperse the filing activity, and it enables the easy removal of dead material.

The advantages of the numerical approach are: it can easily be expanded; it provides some secrecy; it enables the effective identification of items, which means both a greater speed of operation and greater accuracy; and the file number can also provide the reference number. The disadvantages are: the costs of preparing an index and the time taken to refer to it; and if the figures of the reference numbers are transposed, the item will be put in the wrong file – which, unfortunately, is all too easy to do.

Chronological

Here the documents are filed according to some time sequence, usually that of the date, or possibly the time of origination. The files may be divided into days, weeks, months, quarters or years, depending on how much material is being saved. This system is usually used in conjunction with one of the other methods of classification. Thus it will be common to file material alphabetically, using chronological order within the file.

Reversing the traditional UK method of presenting the date, i.e. changing 31 12 86 (31 December 1986) to 86 12 31, provides a convenient automatic sequential date numbering system which has many useful applications.

Indexing

There is a distinction between classification and indexing in filing. Frequently there will be a choice of suitable classifications that a piece of material could go under. For example, when classifying a customer who is both a wholesaler and a retailer, either classification could be used. If put under the former, it is inevitable that sooner or later somebody will be looking under the latter. The solution to such problems is indexing. An index can be defined as a *finding tool*.

There are several ways of providing an index to a filing system. The one to use is that which relates well to the classification method. A good indexing system needs to be flexible, so that it can be changed quickly and easily if necessary. The index should also provide for *cross-referencing*. The basic classifications used to store the documents can be the key words in the index, and the major subclassifications can also be used as reference points. The index should list a file word under any other possible classification, in the same way that the index for a book would do. It should then be possible to locate a record through whatever sensible heading is consulted. This sort of index is often referred to as a *relative* index. It is also important that an index be kept up to date, i.e. it must be current, especially when new words are introduced into the sytem.

In making a decision about the form of a file index, a number of questions must be asked. For example, what is to be indexed? Can the items be located easily through their normal classifications, thus making the use of an index redundant? Are there other indexes available for other systems which might be adapted for the files under consideration, and if there are quite different systems should there be some relationship between the indexes for each of these? Would the index be better in the form of a list or a card system? How will things such as abbreviations and synonyms be dealt with in the index?

The headings in the index should provide the obvious place to look, and where there are several indicators they all need to be introduced, although the more cross references there are the more complicated the system will become.

Installing a filing system

When a new filing system is being considered, there are a number of points that must be considered from the outset in its design. These include: the expenditure to be allocated, including both the capital and revenue costs; whether there are any space constraints, remembering that the provision of space has a cost associated with it; the time period over which the records are to be retained, e.g. whether it will be on a permanent basis, and if not what will be the arrangements for the disposal of dead files and records; if the records are in regular use, whether those that require constant retrieval will be easily accessible; what calibre of staff there will be to operate the system; and whether hard copies are to be made from the records. The classification and location method used in the system will partly depend on the answers to these questions.

Principles of good filing
There are a number of important principles to follow for the operation of a good filing system. Efficient containers and dividers should be used to hold and separate the various classifications of files. The containers, whether they be files, concertina envelopes, boxes or whatever, must be able to hold their probable contents. A clear division every five files is a helpful device in locating files. The use of colour coding on name tabs gives instant recognition to the classification of a file using a particular colour. The file material should always go behind the guide. The latest material to be stored should go into the front of the file.

The order of file classification should follow that of items which are likely to be recalled first. For example, when names are used the surname should go first followed by initials, or if countries are the primary classification these should be followed by cities and towns. All filing classifications based on words should be alphabetical through the word or sequence of letters; compound words, such as co-op, should be treated as one word. Abbreviations in file names should be avoided. The use of synonyms should also be avoided.

Material should be broken down into smaller groups for storage. Thus material in an alphabetical grouping may be divided into files which cover from A to F; G to L; M to R; and S to Z. The same applies to material filed numerically, geographically or by an other method.

The tickler file
This is the name given to a file that 'tickles' the memory about any unfinished work or matters that require further attention in the future. It may contain items that have fallen behind schedule or need to be followed up. To be of any value, the file should be gone through on a regular basis.

The physical maintenance of records

There are many different types of equipment available for the storage of documents and records. However, the objective of this section is to discuss the principles behind the storage of records rather than the equipment that has been designed for this purpose.

Although retaining the text of documents on paper is not the only method of preserving information, it is still an important one and is commonly used. In the small enterprise or the department of a large entity it may be the only method used. And even the largest organisation generally keeps some records in paper form. When paper records are retained there will inevitably come a time when some cramming and overflow occur unless something is done about it. Sometimes the cramming and overflow come about because careful thought was not given to a records maintenance system in the first place, in terms of its divisions, the amount of material that would be generated under each of these divisions, and how it could eventually be thinned out. When this happens, if there is spare space elsewhere in the system it may be possible to reconsider how the material is divided and arrange the records in a better way. However, this may provide only a short-term solution, and a complete reorganisation of the filing system may be necessary and more efficient in the long run. When the overflow situation arises the person responsible for the system, together with those who use it, must decide whether to withdraw and destroy the older documents or store them somewhere else as archival material. In the latter case the records maintenance system will have the current records to hand for day-to-day use; the archival files, which are not likely to be required for immediate use, are very often stored somewhere else where the space has less value. It is important to note that some archival records must by law be kept for a prescribed period.

It is not easy to use overloaded files since it becomes harder to push even more material into them, which can damage existing records in the process. As a result, the records currently being received may be left in a pile to be dealt with on another day – which is one of the behavioural aspects of filing.[17] Thus it is important to thin the old records, and if necessary cut out some of the divisions which have become obsolete before things go too far.

There must then be a clear policy as to: when a record will be declared dead and is to be disposed of, or put under suspended animation in the archival storage; when thinning and withdrawal will take place; how dead records will be destroyed, with special care for any confidential documents; and who is to be responsible for all this. Policy here will usually establish predetermined intervals when the records are reviewed, ideally during slack periods. Often archival files are merely document containers which house a number of files and give them some protection. These containers will generally be numbered and their contents recorded in a book; a record sheet detailing archival files, or files that have been destroyed, will be placed in the appropriate current file. This record sheet will state the location of any withdrawn files in the archives and provide a description of any files disposed of, the date when this was done and by whom.

Access to files

The final and perhaps major consideration is access to the records. It must be decided whether there will be *open* access, which means that anybody can use the records. Where this is the policy there is always the danger that users will not return the records, or when they do that they will put them in the wrong place, or not even attempt to put them away but just dump them. Thus where there is open access there must be well-defined rules governing the operation of the system. Then there can be *selective* access, where only a few people are authorised to use the system. Or the records may be maintained in a *closed* access system, with only the staff employed in the area authorised to extract records for users. This last form of access is the best in terms of control of the issue, use and return of the records. However, it has the disadvantage of being more bureaucratic and thus more costly to run. Open access has its costs too, although these tend to be hidden since they are borne by the user; there may also be high costs associated with searching for lost or misplaced records.

Records management systems and equipment

At its simplest, records may be kept in cardboard or some other type of cheaply produced boxes, which can be placed on the floor and stacked one upon another. For better accessibility, racks can be provided on which to stack the boxes. Today sets of such boxes especially manufactured for the purpose can be obtained relatively cheaply, some of which even have strong frames, stacking lips, and a primitive form of draw.

Lateral files

This is a relatively recent development in the provision of space for files of paper documents. The files are placed in a lateral configuration through being suspended horizontally, i.e. side by side. Normally the suspension rails will be installed in purpose-built steel locker-type cabinets, although there are executive versions of these made in wood to blend in with office furniture.

This method of storing files has a number of advantages. The major ones are as follows: existing cupboards can be used by fitting them with suspension rails; the special-purpose manufactured lateral filing cabinets take up less space since there are no drawers to pull out and the weight of their contents can be distributed over a narrower area; they are relatively thin and can thus be positioned round the walls; when installed in rooms above ground-floor level they are less likely to cause weight problems (as opposed to drawer-type filing cabinets which, when full, can cause floor-loading problems through the way in which their weight is distributed); the lateral files can be extended up to the ceiling, with the less-used records at the highest levels, whereas it is difficult to access drawers higher than four in vertical cabinets; the side-by-side approach shows at a glance how thick the contents of a file have become; since files are suspended horizontally it is easier to notice when a document in the process of being filed 'misses' its folder, whereas in the traditional filing cabinets it could fall unnoticed to the bottom of a drawer.

Drawer files

The drawer type of filing cabinet is the one typically seen in most offices. The cabinets usually house two or four quite deep drawers, although some have three. There are a number of disadvantages to these cabinets, such as: they protrude and so take up a lot of floor space, especially when opened; because of their total depth when drawers are open, four drawers are the limit of their practical height, although their flat tops do have the advantage of providing additional storage space; they are heavy, which may pose weight problems if a lot of units are used in an upper office; strength is required to open drawers full of files to their complete extent; and if a full top drawer is opened when the bottom ones are relatively empty, they can be unstable and dangerous (although most cabinets of this type now have a mechanism permitting the use of one drawer at a time to prevent overbalancing).

Indexing equipment

The simplest 'equipment' suitable for an index to filing systems, or for any indexing purpose, is a ring binder which holds sheets of paper for each major classification within the index – e.g. one page for each letter of the alphabet.

Cards can also be used for this purpose. The cards may be in a tray with insert cards to identify and separate the various classifications and sub-classifications within the index. These guides may be offset, staggered or of different colours to make the divisions clear at a glance. Offsetting has the advantage of providing a visual check as to whether any division is missing. A disadvantage of cards filed in boxes or trays is that they can easily be lost. This problem can be overcome by having security devices such as rods to go through holes punched in the bottom of the cards. Cards may also be fixed to a carousel so that many can be stored in a very small area, providing quick and convenient access.

Cards to be used for indexing must be designed carefully for the information and sequence of information being collected. The principles of form design, dealt with in Chapter 5, also apply here. Another form of indexing uses a special frame into which the information to be indexed can be slipped. These frames have the advantages of flexibility and that photocopies can easily be made of the current index for distribution to users.

When cards are used their edges may be cut or punched in different places and ways to represent the major features of the item being recorded. For example, holes may be punched to indicate various geographical locations, making it easy to sort the cards into batches for each location. This is referred to as a *features index*, although today it has been overtaken by applying the same principle to records stored in the computer. The computerisation of records makes their electronic retrieval under the features required much easier and faster.

Microfilmed records

A major problem with document storage is the sheer physical space taken up by manual records. Two major developments have taken place to overcome this problem: firstly, the general use of microfilm to miniaturise and retain records; and more recently, the wider use of computer storage, especially with storage on discs away from the computer. This function is being used increasingly as developments in computer technology have made the machines cheaper and smaller. It is not within the scope of a book such as this to deal with the latter in depth; however, the former will be covered in this section.

The use of microfilming as a technique in records management has gained popularity in recent years through two main reasons. Firstly, improvements in the equipment used to make the copy and to view it or provide hard copy have made the process much easier, quicker and cheaper. Secondly, the increasing cost of the space required to store original documents and the cost of staff to maintain and access these has made management think hard about how it will carry out this function. Management has often been able to justify large capital outlay on equipment when this is balanced against the costs of the entity's physical expansion to accommodate storage.

When a document is microfilmed the information on it is miniaturised. This means that it can take up less than 1 per cent of the space of the original document. But there are other *advantages*, which include: records of a uniform size can be produced; filing of the document can become a by-product of the filming process; once documents have been filmed, duplicate copies of a batch of records can be made cheaply and quickly for use at other locations – for example, catalogues of the spare parts produced by a manufacturer for distribution to service agents, or of books held by a central library for use at branch libraries, usually in the form of microfiche. The major *disadvantage* of all forms of microfilmed records is the problem of updating, unless a system that mounts lengths of the filmed records on to frames is used, enabling strips to be exchanged for more up-to-date ones. Thus microfilm is best for records which are not subject to rapid change.

There are firms which specialise in microfilming documents, returning the finished work in the form of a non-combustible film record of the information copied together with an index.

There are several ways in which records may be stored on microfilm, the microfiche being the most widely used. The same concept underlies them all; it is only the format which differs.

Roll and reel

In this method the documents are copied on 16 mm or 35 mm film in sequence along the roll. The use of 35 mm film, although taking more space, has the advantage of greater clarity – which is very useful when, say, architectural drawings are copied. Because documents are recorded in sequential order, they must be grouped before filming and put in some reasonable order. It is not possible to access documents filed this way on a random basis, so where this method is used it is better for files of documents to be in a particular order which is not likely to change, such as date order. This effectively makes the reel of film containing such records a file in itself. For example, many newspaper companies maintain records of the issues of their daily, weekly and other publications in this way. When a batch of like items has been stored on a particular reel, it will be helpful in their retrieval.

To read the film, i.e. the record, a *microfilm reader* is needed. If a hard copy of the document is wanted a print reader has to be used to produce it; some of these will provide a copy at the size of the original, or at a reduced size if required.

Cassette, cartridge and magazine

The approach of housing the film in a cassette, cartridge or magazine is merely an extension of using a roll of film; it is put into a 'casing' of some sort, which makes it easy to load in the microfilm reader and helps in running it through the machine. It also affords the film a degree of protection from dust, dirt and wear. The disadvantage of this approach is that it is bulkier. Yet it can easily be sent through the post and provides a strong, automatic packaging. Some organisations use these to replace their catalogues sending information on their products or spares to their depots or customers this way.

Microfiche

The microfiche is a sheet of film which contains multiple rows of *micro images*. A microfiche 6 in. by 4 in. (c. 152 mm × 102 mm) could have varying packing capacities, the reduction used depending upon the quality of the material to be filmed. With clear text, 60 A4 pages would become 60 'views' by 'packing' them on to a fiche using the jacket method, i.e. 12 channels or rows across the fiche which were five deep. With a step and repeat camera this density can be much higher, equaling that obtained in micromation (see page 93). Thus many records can be stored in a small space. To view a microfiche a special *microfiche reader* is required.

The microfiche is usually filed in a transparent sleeve in a double-sided wallet, the size depending upon how many records are to be housed. The wallet will indicate which fiches are kept in it and each fiche will clearly state which images of documents are stored on it across its top, these usually being marked during the photographic process.

The UK Registrar of Companies maintains records of information which companies must deposit as a legal requirement, such as financial statements, and these are filed in microfiche form. This is an example of a vehicle to store records which are historical and so not subject to change, although they will be added to after each accounting period when new financial statements are produced. The Registrar of Companies can produce duplicate microfiches of each company's records, and if an organisation wishes to make a company search it can be supplied with one of these for a nominal charge.

Frames and jackets

To provide a more flexible version of the sequential storage of records using microfilm, frames and jackets to house strips of microfilm have been developed. The microfilm jacket will take a channel, i.e. a strip of microfilm which is usually 16 mm gauge, and using special equipment mounts it on to the jacket card developed for this purpose. The flexibility arises when the information on a strip changes, since it can be extracted and replaced with another one containing the new information. However, the density of storage of the records is limited with this approach.

Tab or aperture cards

Tab or aperture cards to house the microfilm have been developed to help in the retrieval of information. With these a single strip of microfilm is mounted on a punch card, which is indexed with information on the contents of the microfilm record. Rapid retrieval of information can be achieved by sorting out the cards housing the information mechanically. This method is often used to store drawings and plans where regular access to them is required. Once a card has been retrieved the film on it can be read using the appropriate microfilm reader.

Micromation

The process referred to as micromation or *computer output on microfilm* (COM) is a relatively recent development in records management. It has combined the use of the computer with microfilm images. One of the problems with computers is that they can produce vast amounts of output which can be stored electronically within the computer or using some form of external storage such as disc or tape; this is done more or less instantly. However, when readable text is required, the printer can be very slow. For although the VDU provides more or less instant access, it does not give a permanent record. So technology has developed a device to transfer this instant output from the VDU on to microfilm. The process is automatic, and provides a copy of the information which can be viewed using a microfilm reader or by having a hard copy produced. Thus text initially stored electronically in the computer, which might take many hours to print out according to its volume, can be filmed in minutes. In this process the images can be merged on to preprinted forms. Another advantage of using COM is the saving of space, in two ways. Firstly, once the information has been moved out of the computer (and at electronic rather than printer speeds), the computer storage can be cleared and so be released for other uses. Secondly, since the information has been stored electronically, it is in perfect form for copying and does not present the problems sometimes encountered when reducing unclear documents. COM can be produced on the fiche using landscape or portrait style, the mix being specified by the user. Fiches come in British Standard sizes. Using the 24× reduction and storing the information in portrait form, there will be seven rows and 14 coloumns, giving 98 views; the 48× reduction can produce 270 views over 15 rows and 18 columns. The last view on the fiche is generally used for indexing. Computer print-outs can also be reduced.

The acquisition of office machinery and equipment

A major decision about the processing of office work is whether it should be done manually, mechanically, electronically or in some combination of these, and if some form of machinery is to be used, which sort? The question is one of *balance* – balancing the *costs* associated with doing the work in one way against the *benefits*. Where change is being contemplated, the old method should not be discarded without thought, since it might still be the best way to go about things. It should be noted that both the *quantitative* costs and benefits (i.e. those given in terms of numbers) and the *qualitative* costs and benefits (those not directly stated in numbers) must be brought into the analysis. It will be difficult to measure on the latter, however. For example, one cannot easily quantify the comfort of office chairs of different designs, or put a number on the quality of drinks produced by the tea lady and those which come from a drinks dispenser – although individuals will have clear ideas as to which they prefer and be able to rank their preferences. Nevertheless, an attempt must be made to quantify such factors when making a decision involving qualitative information.

New machinery may be acquired for one of three reasons, namely: to replace existing machinery; to be introduced as a small part of an existing operation to improve it; or to change a processing methodology completely. The first reason will sometimes, but not always, involve replacing like with like, and if so quotations should be sought from potential suppliers. The second may be associated with an organisation and methods (O & M) study, a technique dealt with in Chapter 6. The last may also concern O & M or a complete systems analysis.

The following points should be considered in the acquisition of new office equipment and machinery: whether different equipment can improve the performance of existing work; what feasible alternative processing methods are available; the comparative costs of the possibilities under consideration, including both capital and running costs; for capital costs the length of time over which the capital expenditure can be depreciated; whether the running costs include any likely maintenance or labour costs, including any training necessary for operatives; what are the benefits of each alternative, e.g. ease of operation of equipment, and speed and quality of its output. From the balance of the costs and benefits of the feasible alternatives a decision can be made. A capital and operating budget can then be established to enable implementation of the decision.

Labour- vs. capital-intensive processing

There are two extremes on the spectrum of possible ways of processing office work: more or less completely manual, i.e. labour-intensive; or highly mechanised, i.e. capital-intensive. There are a number of advantages and disadvantages at both ends of this spectrum. In moving from the former to the latter, the best mix, and the position at which the organisation ends up on the spectrum, will depend upon several criteria.

The advantages of mechanisation
The major advantage of most forms of mechanisation is that a reduction in staff costs can be expected to follow, all other things remaining equal. For the use of mechanisation in the processing of office work invariably leads to it being done quicker using fewer staff. This speed and economy in the use of staff results partly from a greater division of labour through the development of specialisation. Once up-to-date equipment is installed staff must be trained to use it proficiently; and, perhaps surprisingly, the use of such equipment will often lead to greater job satisfaction since it may reduce the monotony of the work. However, it is also suggested that if staff have to specialise in a job they will have to carry out the work on a repetitive basis, producing the opposite effect. Machinery will reduce the fatigue associated with much office work. For example, the manual depression of typewriter keys requires about 500 per cent more energy than that necessary to activate the keys on an electric typewriter.

In terms of *general costs*, machinery not only reduces labour costs but also reduces other costs associated with employing people, such as the provision of welfare facilities. If fewer people are required, the introduction of machinery (depending upon its size) may save on occupancy costs since less space will be needed for those undertaking the processing. The work itself may be improved qualitatively, and the quality will be more standardised. For example, carbon copies of documents are not as clear as those produced using a good photo-copier; and nobody except the operator knows about the mistakes corrected when the word processor is used, whereas if typing errors are corrected with a correcting fluid they can still show up as unsightly blotches.

The use of mechanisation can provide more information to management. For example, an additional copy of data needed for another manager can easily be produced using a photocopier, whereas without such a machine he may have had to do without. It can also provide the information in a way that makes it easier to assimilate, as with a computer using integrated spreadsheet and word-processing software. Accuracy can be improved; again using the word processor as an example, when text previously keyed in requires minor corrections, the author can be sure that any unchanged text will be printed out exactly as before, with no need to check through it again.

The disadvantages of mechanisation
The most noticeable disadvantage of mechanisation is usually the high initial costs of acquiring office machinery and equipment. A related problem is that equipment is often quickly overtaken by new technology, so may become obsolete soon after it has been installed. Where this is likely to be the case, high depreciation charges will be necessary to write off the equipment over a relatively short period.

When new equipment – especially if based on a new, more complex technology – is introduced, there may be high installation costs, including those associated with staff acceptance or rejection and any necessary staff training. Sometimes the new equipment affects the working environment, perhaps by generating heat and noise. If so there may be additional costs in its installation, e.g. sound-proofing, and since it is likely to be electrically operated additional power plugs will be needed.

Sometimes there will be high costs in the operation of equipment that introduces a new technology. This may require the use of special stationery, or there may be staff training or retraining costs. Once complex equipment is introduced, the maintenance costs can be high.

Mechanisation can also render the systems used to process work less flexible and so bring rigidity into the office. These systems depend upon the operator, and often can carry out only a limited range of processing functions, not dealing with the isolated one-off situation. Machines will be specialised in performing a single function, whereas a worker, after suitable training, can undertake a variety of work. Nevertheless some equipment, such as the personal computer, can be loaded with a range of different software which can be integrated, thus making it more versatile.

Purchasing second-hand machinery and equipment

People often have an inbuilt resistance to purchasing items which have belonged to somebody else. Although most British people are quite prepared to acquire second-hand buildings and vehicles, it seems to be less acceptable to buy such things as furniture and clothes second-hand. The same seems to apply to office furniture and equipment. With the latter this could be justified, since much second-hand equipment is available because its initial purchaser has changed it for a later model, or found that it was past its prime. However, the second-hand item may also be avoided through psychological factors rather than rational justifications. The only advantage of buying second-hand is that the price is usually much lower than the capital required for a new version of the same item. However, there are a number of disadvantages in acquiring equipment that was used previously by another organisation. It may be less efficient both in its speed of operation and the quality of its output. It may require repair and costly maintenance. The design may be old-fashioned and if it is a very early design using older technology, it will likely be more difficult to use and certainly to integrate into modern systems. If the equipment becomes out of date or obsolete quickly, its resale value may drop more in percentage terms than that of the new.

Nevertheless, with some office equipment, especially office furniture, second-hand bargains can indeed be found. Such items as second-hand desks and filing cabinets can frequently be picked up for bargain prices. And reconditioned office machinery, such as golf ball typewriters or photocopying machines, can be obtained for prices which are markedly lower than those charged for new machines. Often the price of second-hand equipment will be so low that any difference between the price paid for it and the eventual scrap price will not be great.

Thus the purchase of second-hand goods should not be summarily dismissed, especially when they are guaranteed by the supplier for a short period and maintenance contracts can be taken out on them. It is obviously important that they be obtained from an established and reputable dealer.

Financing the acquisition of office machinery and equipment[18]

The use of office machinery and equipment may be legally obtained in two ways, through leasing or purchase. With the former, the lease may be either short- or long-term. Purchase of the asset may be outright or using extended credit terms, or may be through a hire-purchase (HP) agreement.

Leasing

By leasing equipment an organisation can acquire its use without having to finance the cost of an outright purchase. The equipment is purchased by some entity, generally a finance house or a bank, referred to as the *lessor*, which then hands over the use of the assets to somebody else, the *lessee*, who pays a rental for this priviledge. For the lessee, the main advantage of leasing is that he does not have to find the finance necessary to acquire the use of the asset by purchase. The advantage to the lessor is that he obtains a return on the money he invests in the asset through renting it out. The accountant calls the short-term lease an operating lease, and the long-term one a finance lease.

Operating leases, also called operational or risk leases, cover leasing such assets as office furniture, equipment and machinery over the short term. Perhaps this is to fill a gap while the lessee's own equipment is being repaired; while waiting for new equipment to arrive; or for a particular purpose, e.g. where special machinery is needed to do a job on a short-term basis. An advantage of the operating lease is that it can be entered into to acquire the short-term use of machinery that is subject to technological change, or where it is known that the manufacturer is about to introduce a new model. With assets obtained on short-term leases, the lessor invariably carries out any maintenance and repairs necessary, having costed the possibility of these in his rental charge. Insurance is normally included in the package as well.

Finance leases, which are also called full payout or capital leases, involve the leasing of an asset over a long period. During the period of the lease, although ownership *de facto* remains with the lessor, the contract effectively provides the lessee with possession over the asset since he will gain any economic benefits from its use over a relatively long period. This is because he commits himself to a long-term obligation to pay the rental and so bears the risk of having to continue to pay the rental on an asset which has been overtaken by technological developments. With the finance lease the lessee is also invariably responsible for the insurance, maintenance and any repairs necessary. Often the lessor is a finance house which effectively provides the finance necessary to enable the lessee to acquire the assets he has chosen. Part of the lessor's gain, in the United Kingdom, will be any tax benefits from the purchase of a capital asset, and he really does not want to know about any problems that arise during the asset's use. The lessee can charge his rental as a tax-deductible expense. To the accountant, since the lessee has the long-term right to the use of the asset, he has in effect a right to its ownership. Thus the accountant says that the finance lease provides a form of finance, albeit 'off balance sheet finance', so it should be included as one of the lessee's assets in his financial statements, with a corresponding charge also shown for the amount due under the leasing agreement.[19]

Purchase

An organisation must have sufficient free capital to be able to purchase office furniture, equipment and machinery, or at least access to the finance. The purchase of an asset, whether using some form of credit, HP facilities or cash, gives immediate ownership – and the problem of dealing with possible breakdowns. There are benefits to both sides when financing the acquisition of the asset on credit terms through a finance house. The seller immediately receives his asking price for the equipment from the finance house, and the buyer gets immediate ownership.[20]

Lease or buy

The decision of whether to acquire the use of office machinery and equipment, or even furniture, through either purchase or leasing depends upon an evaluation of the costs and benefits of the alternatives, and also on the availability of finance if purchasing would be the most favourable option. The major questions when making this evaluation are:[21] is there finance available for purchase; for how long is the equipment required; and how quickly is the equipment likely to become obsolete, especially in terms of being overtaken by new developments? Generally, if the answer to the first question is yes, and the equipment is required for a long period and not likely to date too quickly, it will be beneficial to buy. However, whether the finance is available or not, if the answers to the other questions are either that the equipment is not required for very long or that it is likely to be superseded by technological changes very soon, then it will be better to lease.

Repairs and maintenance of office machinery

Office machinery is susceptible to breakdown, whether it is new or reconditioned. If machinery has just been purchased there is likely to be a manufacturer's guarantee, and even when reconditioned equipment is bought it will probably be given a short guarantee by the supplier. These guarantees are usually for one year for the former and three months for the latter. It is often possible to add to the period covered by the guarantee by taking out an extended maintenance contract, although these tend to become more expensive as the equipment gets older.

Management must decide how to deal with the following categories of repairs and maintenance: routine maintenance and service; breakdowns which can be dealt with by the organisation's employees themselves; breakdowns which require an outside engineer to deal with them; and preventive maintenance. When equipment is out of order or a computer is 'down', staff productivity is reduced; so it is in an organisation's own interest to ensure that it is kept in good working order at all times.

Routine maintenance and service

Machines have to be kept clean if they are to work at their maximum efficiency. Therefore operators should be trained to carry out the routine servicing of equipment. The general cleaning and any oiling necessary to maintain the machinery may be part of the job of its operator, as may dealing with minor servicing such as replacing the printer's print ribbons, or keeping the photocopier fed with the necessary ink or toner.

Breakdowns of a minor nature, e.g. when the paper jams in the photocopier, may be dealt with locally by the operator, and staff should be trained to carry out minor repairs on equipment. If an organisation has a large quantity of office machinery, it may be beneficial to employ its own engineers for maintenance and repair work.

Outside maintenance

In this case the machinery is maintained and repaired by an outside agency, e.g. engineers from the manufacturers or suppliers of the equipment who have been especially trained for this function.

Preventive maintenance

Machinery and equipment should be serviced at regular intervals, whether there is anything wrong with it or not; this is referred to as preventive maintenance. It may be carried out by either the user's own staff or outside engineers. Preventive maintenance is done so that the equipment will be kept in better condition and be less susceptible to breakdown. One major additional advantage is that the servicing can frequently be done at the user's convenience rather than when the machine breaks down, perhaps at an inconvenient time such as a peak-load period when it can be disruptive and costly – and not always possible to find a technician. The service intervals can be planned on a time or usage basis. The time basis involves carrying out the service at some predetermined interval such as monthly, quarterly or annually. Use involves service intervals based on a unit of usage; for example, a photocopier could be serviced each time a certain number of copies had been produced. There may be a number of preventive maintenance cycles providing different levels of service. Thus after a short time period or low usage figure, a basic service can be undertaken; at longer intervals an increasingly longer check can be run, even to the extent of automatically replacing major components of the equipment at prescribed intervals.

Using inside or outside engineers

When deciding whether to employ in-house maintenance engineers or use those provided by an external agency, management must consider two major factors: the comparative costs of the two approaches, and the convenience – in terms of greater experience or speed of service. When comparing the cost of these approaches, management must take into account the following factors: the amount of equipment to be maintained; the range of this equipment; how vital the equipment is; and whether experience has shown that the machinery is prone to breakdown. The greater the amount of equipment involved, the more likely it is to be beneficial on all counts to employ staff to look after it. Convenience may also figure strongly here, especially with the costs of delays in having breakdowns rectified. For example, one printer feeding a number of word-processing units can rarely afford to be out of action.

A facility offered by many service firms is a maintenance contract. This is an agreement between the owner of the equipment and the outside agency that the latter will be responsible for keeping the items under the contract in working order in exchange for a prescribed sum paid on an annual, quarterly or monthly basis. The agreement may be a full one, where every cost associated with the repair is covered, i.e. all labour and material costs. Often there is a guarantee to carry out any necessary repairs within 24 hours during the working week. If the repair cannot be carried out on the user's premises within that time or the equipment has to be taken back to the workshop for repair, an equivalent piece will be left on loan until the owner's own machine can be returned in full working order. The contractor often carries out preventive maintenance at regular intervals, which is clearly both to his and the user's benefit.

The limited maintenance contract does not cover the cost of everything necessary for a machine to be put back in good working order. Limited maintenance contracts can operate at various levels. For example, there may be a call-out charge, exclusions for the supply of certain parts, or no loan of replacement equipment when the owner's is out of action. Obviously, it can be costly to take out a full maintenance contract, but with a limited contract there is the twin risk of the even higher cost of a spate of large repair bills and zero production.

Centralisation and decentralisation of office services

Chapter 2 discussed the benefits of both the centralisation and decentralisation of office services and the disadvantages of these two approaches in the processing of office work. That discussion was couched in general terms. In this section these considerations will be related to specific aspects of office work. The centralisation of office work and services tends to provide economies of scale, and especially to reinforce standardisation and simplification. However, centralisation can frequently lead to: increased bureaucracy; the loss of flexibility in carrying out the work; a loss of control over the speed at which the work is done; and a reduction in the quality of the work compared with what would be obtained under local facilities. The following subsections will consider some of the pros and cons of centralisation and decentralisation as related to a number of office services.

Communications

An entity's communications network is an obvious candidate for centralisation, especially the telephone system and mail room. With the former, most organisations install a centralised telephone switchboard. Many also have a centralised post room for the distribution of both internal and external mail, and telex and facsimile transmissions. Centralisation of these facilities can lead to many economies – although even here it may be necessary to provide for that odd event with which centralisation cannot cope.

Text origination

Text is originated by 'keying' the characters which produce the information, either using a typewriter, or increasingly today through the use of a word processor. Thus it does not mean being the author of the text to be originated, but rather the transcribing of this text from drafts or tapes. The usual advantages of centralisation here are the concentration and use of expensive equipment in a single centre, and the more effective use of and supervision over the staff operating it. This is a sensible approach for routine volume work, e.g. the origination of the text for reports or of the minutes of meetings, where immediate production is not of the essence.

The decision of whether or not to centralise text production services is not a simple one since there is no fail-safe guide. Nevertheless, the principles related to both approaches can be applied. In the production of routine text a pool can frequently provide the best service, although problems associated with motivation should be considered here since some people do not work as effectively when 'pooled'.

The advantages of central text creation

There are several advantages in a central text creation pool. There will likely be reduced costs in the supervision of staff and better control over the work. Also, because it pools the resources for this function, it is more likely that specialist equipment can be acquired with different but appropriate types of machines available for the range of work. For example, equipment to produce form letters for bulk mailing can be of a kind especially developed for this purpose.

Economies can often be achieved when accessories for equipment can be linked. One example of this is a golf ball typewriter; one sited alone in an office could not justify a complete range of golf balls, but if a number were placed in a pool a wide range of these could be provided, including those used infrequently. Again, if a word processor is the only one at a local station it will require its own printer, whereas a number of word processors at a centralised location can share fewer printers and there can be a range of these for different purposes. Furthermore, the pool may justify having its own photocopier to make copies of work for several users, which may not be the case when the text is produced at a number of locations.

Another advantage of the pool is that it can provide a better means of covering for sickness and holidays without having to call in temporaries from expensive agencies. The supervisor of the pool can also route the work through a system of priorities according to the order in which it is to be done.

Centralised text production staff

The centralisation of staff who key in the text also has its advantages. It may permit a system of job grading; if there are different categories of work, some staff will be able to specialise in the more complex work and so reach a higher grade. It is also easier to devise a limited system for career progression within the pool, and the larger it is, the better the chances for advancement.

Nevertheless, it should be remembered that despite the organisational benefits derived from specialisation, when a person has to carry out the same routine work on a day-to-day basis frustration and demotivation can result. Thus job enlargement or job rotation may be necessary to keep such staff satisfied.

The disadvantages of centralised text production

There are a number of disadvantages in the production of text on a centralised basis, including the time and effort expended in getting the original copy to the centralised services for processing. This can be aggravated by the number of drafts required, especially since the originator of the draft is not to hand and therefore in no position to give immediate feedback on what may be a minor problem. Control over the arrival and dispatch of work will mean some form of paper record.

The senior executive and the centralisation of text production

The major opposition to the complete centralisation of text production services comes from those working at the higher levels of management. They may provide persuasive arguments as to why they should retain a personal secretary who, as well as producing text for them, will likely have to perform a range of other functions. The senior manager who is about to lose his secretary through centralisation is bound to say that this will cause him problems, especially in the production of correspondence which needs to be done quickly and confidentially. He may also claim to lose the advantages of the initiative of the competent secretary who formulates suitable replies to enquiries or other correspondence. Nevertheless, arrangements can be made for the executive to telephone such correspondence to central services using a number on which his requirements will be recorded and then keyed in to produce text, with some system of priority. The executive can also record the information required for longer documents such as reports and send the tape along for processing. However, when executives' secretaries get consolidated into a central unit the managers lose their services for individually tailored tasks such as maintaining diaries, making appointments and travel arrangements, and keeping local files – unless arrangements are made to deal with such matters on some other basis.

A strong case can be made for the senior manager needing a personal secretary. Many senior executives are highly paid and demands made on them are great; a secretary can help to ensure that their time is used more effectively. The rapport that can be established between manager and secretary should promote the best possible use of time and resources, freeing the manager from routine administration and minor organisational problems so that he can concentrate on major objectives.

Calculation services

Calculation services can be carried out centrally, although today these tend to be a function of the computer. Where the odd calculation arises it can be done by individuals using a small calculator. However, if bulk computations are required, centralisation will bring the advantage of being able to use the most suitable equipment for the task in tandem with the specialist training of personnel to operate it. But again, there are the costs and delays of increased handling to get the work to the centralised location. Further delays can arise because one result may be needed before deciding what to do about the next calculation in a chain of statistical work. Therefore, with today's improved calculating equipment it is invariably better for this function to be carried out locally. Centralisation also poses the problem that a pool of machine operators can easily become careless when keying in work, and expensive double-keying may be necessary to ensure that there are no errors.

Copying and printing

Grouping together all the entity's duplicating, photocopying and printing facilities brings many advantages. In the very large organisation there may even be separate facilities for photocopying and printing. The obvious advantages are not so much derived from the specialisation of staff in relation to photocopying equipment – although this advantage does apply to printing machinery – because the equipment is normally easy to operate, but rather from economies of scale through the use of specialist machinery, such as photocopiers that can enlarge and reduce, backprint, and perhaps the installation of colour printing equipment. Nevertheless, centralised staff can be trained to use the equipment more efficiently and deal with any minor breakdowns such as paper jams, and to provide any routine servicing required.

The centralisation of copying and printing becomes more important when the following two conditions apply: the type of equipment used is expensive to purchase and yet necessary to produce the quality required, for example where offset lithographic machinery is used extensively; and where the volume of work is heavy. Here an advantage of centralisation can come into the analysis, with the central purchasing and stock control of supplies such as paper – although it is not necessary to have the purchasing of stationery central in order to obtain the advantages of centralised copying, or indeed vice versa, since the centralisation of either of these functions can stand alone.

Once the centralisation of copying and printing has been accepted, the various types of peripheral machinery, e.g. collators, guillotines, punching and binding equipment, can be obtained; and the use of specially designed and printed stationery may become feasible. Since a large printing department lends itself to the use of factory mass production techniques, the print room may even be able to produce headed stationery, forms, catalogues and so on more cheaply internally than by acquiring these from external sources, which undoubtedly helps in the running costs of the unit.[22] There should, however, be a definite policy on how users will be charged for the work. And, as a form of control, it would be useful to obtain quotations from external agencies or bureaux for the same work so that a regular check can be kept on internal production costs.

Nevertheless, there are disadvantages to the centralisation of this service, including the bureaucracy established to control the input and output of work, and delays in getting the work done. This is because it has to be sent to and returned from the printing department, which will have to establish a graded priority system to build in the necessary flexibility to deal with peak workloads.

A way of helping to overcome the delay problem in situations where users require single or only few copies of some items quickly is to provide small, localised photocopying machines. These will also avoid the high unit costs of sending a document to central services for a single copy. However, it is important to ensure that any large amounts of copying are carefully planned and sent to central services; otherwise 'crises' will occur and the local unit will be used for long runs of copies needed urgently, at a high cost. This raises the point that smaller units of photocopying equipment – although fairly cheap to purchase – are generally economical only for short runs; expensive equipment which provides copies for a low unit cost must be centralised, and to get the full benefit of the investment must be utilised at maximum levels.

Filing

The advantages and disadvantages of centralisation also apply to records management. A major disadvantage is that the retrieval of records from a centralised location will inevitably involve some delay. The introduction of computerised records systems overcomes this problem when the computer, usually a mainframe with great storage capacity, is linked to a network of local terminals to provide the instant retrieval of information.

The main advantages of the centralisation of records management are the possible economies in the use of staff and equipment at a central location. Staff can be trained to look after certain sections of the records, and will develop a specialist knowledge of them. But the greatest advantage of centralised records is that an overview can be taken in planning the system, with the entity's total records requirements being considered in order to produce a central record bank. Here the classification of records will be standardised and a comprehensive indexing system can be prepared and distributed to users. There may also be an economy in the use of stationery, since when records are kept locally duplicate copies are sometimes needed. Even where this is not the case, when some documents are distributed to many locations there will be the temptation to keep them, causing a costly duplication of record retention throughout the entity.

On the other hand, if local users frequently require documents from a centralised system, especially if urgently, frustration can arise through delays in obtaining them; or it will be costly to send someone over to the central records bank to get the file quickly. One solution where there is no computerisation of files as yet is to have local 'mini' records systems installed to house the major, frequently used and urgently required records in local offices – although clearly this somewhat defeats the purposes behind the centralisation of an organisation's records.

The establishment of records on microfilm, as with a microfiche system, makes it possible to realise economies of scale. Such a system has the advantage that copies of each fiche can be made quickly and cheaply and sent to any local offices requiring them – where only a little space will be needed to maintain the records, but where a microfiche reader must be available.

Purchasing

There are many advantages in centralising the procurement of office equipment and supplies.

The advantages of centralised purchasing

The major advantages are as follows: there can be a consistent buying policy; goodwill can be developed with suppliers, especially if fewer suppliers are used, and as a result it should be possible to negotiate better prices for bulk purchases; specialist procurement officers can be employed; fewer suppliers and bigger orders lead to economies of scale in the processing of orders, especially since centralised and uniform purchase records can be maintained; through standardisation in the equipment and stationery used there can be better stock control; and there should be better financial control over the use of stationery throughout the organisation.

The disadvantages of centralised purchasing

The disadvantages of centralised purchasing must also be considered. These include: the responsibility for ordering and holding stock of stationery is taken away from the user, which may cause delays and loss of flexibility in purchasing; liaison between users and purchaser must be good to ensure that the user gets what he wants; the user may be able to draw only from a standardised range of supplies; and the paperwork involved in ordering, controlling, and dispatch to users will increase.

Solutions

There are two solutions that can help to overcome the problems of centralised purchasing. The first is that although most purchases will be made centrally, there will also be a budget for small local purchases. The second is the establishment of an authorised suppliers list and negotiation of contract prices centrally for the organisation's stationery requirements, with local users purchasing direct from the list at the special prices. Accounts are usually settled centrally in this system.

Conclusions

The area of office services and methods is wide. The acquisition of machinery and equipment and how it will be used must be considered. Whether to lease or to buy the office equipment and machinery must also be considered in relation to the organisation's needs and financial resources, with servicing and maintenance borne in mind. Then decisions must be made about the most efficient way of using it, with careful consideration of whether the users' needs should be met on a localised basis or an attempt made to gain economies of scale through centralisation of some services. For a particular organisation, some services might benefit from centralisation whereas others would be best left at the local level. There is not one single right answer: what may be right for one entity may not be the best approach in another; what is right within one part of a large organisation may not be good in another part of it; and what is the best way at one time may not be so at a later date. Therefore, the system used must undergo regular review if the entity is to adopt the best approach at any particular time in the provision of its office services.

Questions and discussion problems

1.   The ways in which an original document can be produced have undergone rapid development since the mid-1970s. The latest of these is the advance from the electronic typewriter, with its refine-

ments for correction and storage, to the word processor. When an organisation changes from a typewriter-based system for text production to a word-processor-based system, a number of clearly identifiable stages can be discerned. What are these stages? In your answer explain their significance for the introduction of a word-processing system.

2. You have just moved to a different firm as their central services manager. On your first day you learn that the typing pool is shortly to receive its first word processor. However, you find that apart from the order having been placed, no other action has been taken. How would you plan for the arrival of this word processor?

3. 'In the installation of a word processor, compromises frequently have to be made.' Discuss this statement.

4. 'The word processor has become a status symbol rather than a means of improving productivity.' Do you agree with this statement? Explain why you take the view that you do.

5. When word processors are installed in an office they are likely to lead to both pre- and post-installation stress among those employed in the office. Discuss why you think this is so and suggest ways of minimising the stress.

6. What factors need to brought into the analysis when one is deciding upon the optimum method for document reproduction? Describe two methods of document reproduction.

7. 'Not only are the copier manufacturers developing products to cope with the computer age, but they are not forgetting, as so many new technology industries are, the normal day-to-day business operations.' From 'Catching on to the copying market' by Julie Harnett, *Administrator*, April 1984.
    Discuss the latest developments in copiers and relate these to changes which have taken place in the office in recent years.

8. Critically analyse the factors which should be taken into account when considering copying and/or printing in respect of:
    (a) initially installing equipment;
    (b) making copies of a particular document.

9. The storage and retrieval of information within an organisation has become more complex because of the vast increase in the volume of information to be processed. This all requires storage facilities and lengthening retrieval times. Describe ways in which this problem can be minimised and analyse the advantages and disadvantages of one method of dealing with information storage and retrieval.

10. (a) It is suggested that indexing is the most vital factor in ensuring efficient and effective retrieval from a filing or document storage system. Explain why you agree or disagree with this.

(b) Discuss the major factors in index classification, stating the advantages and disadvantages of each in relation to its appropriate use.

11. In document storage confidentiality and security may not be the same thing. Differentiate between the two and discuss how they can be maintained in document storage.

12. (a) Distinguish between classification and indexing in filing.
   (b) Describe (i) *four* methods of classification, and (ii) *four* methods of indexing, stating the advantages of each of the methods you describe.

13. The ABC Trade Association provides a number of services to its members. One of these is to answer queries on home and overseas markets. Because the Association's premises are situated in an old building in the capital city, the staff of the technical services department are spread over seven rooms. Three of these house information about the UK market, one each for the South, Midlands and the North. The other four rooms are used to store information on overseas markets: the Americas, Europe, the Far East, and the Middle East and Africa. Staff have been allocated to particular rooms and tend to operate independently using quite different filing systems developed in the past.
   The facilities and equipment used to store material, and the retrieval system, are rather outdated. The Association's membership has grown in recent years, and each member is making far greater demands on technical services than in the past. Increasingly, the nature of the query requires information from more than one room. Because of the high costs incurred in the city, the Association has decided to move to a site in the provinces. Thus the opportunity for the long-needed reorganisation of its technical services department arises. However, because of the nature of the information to be stored, it does *not* lend itself to computer storage.
   Required
   Assuming that you may start from scratch, suggest the factors you would consider and the approach you would take to reorganise the Association's technical services, carefully stating the advantages and any disadvantages likely to be associated with your solution.

14. 'Companies which rent a large amount of equipment will have weighed the advantages of rental against outright purchase.' From 'To buy or not to buy', *Administrator*, October 1984.
   Explain the advantages of renting *vis-à-vis* the purchase of office equipment and consider the disadvantages of both approaches to equipment acquisition.

15. During the 1970s there was an increase in the number of organisations offering leasing plans for office furniture and equipment.

Taking a cost/benefit approach, analyse this leasing option from the viewpoint of an organisation requiring the use of office furniture and equipment on a long-term basis.

16. Although many firms lease office premises, only a relatively small number lease office equipment. Why do you think this is so, and what benefits might an entity miss out on by not leasing where this is likely to be appropriate?

17. Two sales people working for firms that manufacture and distribute similar office furniture meet at a conference. Brian Wood's organisation sells furniture, whereas Alan Cook's firm leases out the furniture that it produces. As they talk about their jobs, Brian Wood says 'It's much easier for me to make a sale because I can talk about the benefits of buying and these far outweigh those of leasing'. Alan Cook smiles and says 'Don't believe it. I point out all the disadvantages of buying and emphasise the many benefits to be gained from leasing'.

   (a) List the advantages and disadvantages of buying and leasing office furniture that you think the two salesmen would bring out as they continued their conversation.

   (b) If the sales people had distributed office machinery and equipment, what additional points could be made?

18. (a) What information should be sought when making a decision to purchase a business machine?

   (b) Critically discuss the advantages and disadvantages of the use of a selection committee to decide which business machines an organisation should procure.

19. Two companies, Baldwin Ltd and Patons and Co., decided to merge. One of the companies operates a system of centralised office services, while the other allows individual departments to provide for their own services. When they heard of the merger proposals the two companies' office services controllers decided to take early retirement. Management decided that it would take this opportunity to consolidate the merged organisation's office services under a single controller. However, it had an open mind as to which of the two approaches to use. At the interviews for the job of services controller, one candidate, Elsie Ellis, advocated the centralisation of the overall structure of the office services. However another, Nan Govan, pressed that they should be supplied within user departments.

   (a) List the advantages likely to have been stated by both applicants in support of their views.

   (b) What major factors should be taken into consideration before management decides which approach to adopt for the newly merged organisation?

20.   Write a special report on the possible introduction of a centralised purchasing system for office supplies, to replace the current system where they are bought by departments on an individual basis. Make appropriate assumptions for the contents of your report, and pay particular attention to its layout.

4
People in the office

Introduction

Laurie Mullins writes, 'The effectiveness of any work organisation is dependent upon the efficient use of resources and in particular human resources. The human element plays a major part in the overall success of an organisation. Proper attention to the personnel function will help improve the efficiency of the labour force and the level of organisational performance'.[1] Until the 1950s employers tended to be authoritarian in their attitude to their employees. Management, particularly in the nineteenth century, was based upon direction by coercion, playing on the fear of unemployment. There was what is termed the paternalistic approach – where an employer took an interest in the social and economic welfare of employees – thus providing some respite in an otherwise exploitive environment. Even so, there was the constant anxiety of losing a job if you did not work hard and give the employer complete loyalty. This no longer applies, although some would say that with today's high levels of unemployment in the United Kingdom the fear of losing a job and not finding another does provide a lever to keep people on their toes in the workplace. It is not so much the fear of being sacked as it is the contemporary evil of firms having to close down because they cannot survive in a competitive market. Or, just as bad for some, firms may have to slim down through redundancies, perhaps with the most expendable employees shed first. The United Kingdom's social security system, although not enabling a person to maintain living standards at employment level, does to some extent cushion the most adverse effects of unemployment. Unions also have greater strength than they had 50 years ago, which gives them more muscle to look after their members.

Employment in the service industries grows in mature economies, and office work is a service which now takes an increasing proportion of those in employment. With the developments in office technology, opportunities for employment in the office are affected in two ways: reducing the numbers required; but generally improving the skills of those left to do the work. For example, staff in a large typing pool may be cut by up to one-half if the pool installs word processors to replace electric typewriters. At the same time, the reduction in people required to use the new equipment is usually tempered by the fact that greater automation produces more paper or higher-quality information. Because of this staffing levels within the organisation are maintained: although fewer people are used to process work, more may be required to analyse what has been produced.

Recent developments have also had an effect on the motivation of people in the office. The changes in the management environment that have taken place since the beginning of this century have meant that managers must look for other ways to motivate the workforce, thus propelling them into the realm of human relations. Management has realised that this is the way to get more from staff, and that good personnel policies will provide better trained and more contented workers – with the effect of reducing the unit costs of employing staff. This has also come about because entities have developed a greater social conscience. The aim here is to encourage greater staff loyalty. Showing more interest in staff work will, in turn, help the quality of production. All these elements provide a bonus to the employee in the form of greater job satisfaction and quality of life.

In Chapter 2 the organisational charts of the entity showed personnel as a staff function. With the importance of people to an organisation it could be said that this function has become more akin to a line one, as has the information function in many organisations today. This makes it extremely important for the manager and the supervisor in the office to increase their understanding of and contribution to their organisation's personnel policy.

One aspect of the personnel policy is for the entity to develop harmony of objectives. An entity's personnel policy can go a long way towards ensuring this harmony and preventing conflicts. Major problems can arise when two different areas of management have two different objectives and cannot reconcile them. The idea of harmony in objectives has been formalised by the concept of the unity of management objectives.

Chapter 2 also discussed the influence of the informal organisation on an entity's organisational structure and through this its performance, which links up with the harmony of objectives. It is important that the organisation's interests do not conflict too much with those of the employees, and a sound personnel policy should go a long way towards promoting both aspects. The employee must see that the objectives pursued by his organisation are for the common good, and that he will share in the rewards of achieving them.

The personnel function

Personnel services cover a wide area which goes much further than aiming to ensure that employees obtain some satisfaction from their work and so are motivated to be loyal to their employer or entity. There is also an interest or involvement in all stages of the 'life cycle' of the employee, from the time that a member of staff is recruited to the time that he leaves the organisation, and including training, advancement and remuneration, as well as welfare and motivational considerations. Throughout, the cost of employing a member of staff has to be weighed against the benefits obtained from that person's output. The personnel function is also involved in office work in its own right through the maintenance of personnel records and statistics.

Personnel work can be classified in two ways, routine and advisory. *Routine* personnel work involves recruitment, selection, engagement, training, promotion, or any changes of direction in employment within the organisation, plus dismissal, resignation and retirement of staff. A number of routine functions will be involved here, including the maintenance of personnel records, the communication of personnel policies to managers, supervisors and employees, and possibly the payment of wages and salaries. The *advisory* aspect of the personnel function involves the co-ordination of personnel policies throughout the organisation and advising management on personnel matters. With the latter, personnel must be in touch with line and functional managers, for example when decisions are made about the personnel records that are to be maintained, or what personnel statistics will be made available and the uses to which they will be put. In the first case a manager may require non-standard aspects of information on his staff to be recorded; or when statistics on labour turnover indicate that the ratio for a department or area shows a departure from the norm, he will want to investigate the reasons.

An extension of this consultation may involve the industrial relations aspect of personnel, where personnel may be brought into negotiations with individual employees or unions. On a lower plane, perhaps a manager feels that one of his staff should be paid more and will discuss this with personnel; at the highest level it may mean negotiating wages on a plant-wide basis with a union when the wage structures and levels of all the firm's work-force are under scrutiny. However, this may be felt to be so important in a large organisation that industrial relations becomes the responsibility of a special department.

Several aspects of the personnel function are described below.

Pecuniary rewards

Most people work because they get paid, and it can be said for many that they do this only because they need money to live. The financial rewards and the effort that has to be put into work will influence an employee's attitude towards his employer – how co-operative he is, his level of morale, and so on. Remuneration for various jobs should be set at levels which eliminate constant discussion and bickering among employees who feel that they are underpaid in relation to each other, especially where it seems that they are carrying out very similar work, either elsewhere within the organisation or in relation to people working for other entities.[2] This means that remuneration must be, and must be seen to be, calculated fairly and appropriately.

One important function of personnel is to monitor what employees in other organisations are being paid, especially when carrying out the same type of work. Personnel needs to consider such things as whether it would be advantageous to the entity to use some form of time rate or a bonus or productivity agreement to pay employees, and advise management accordingly.[3] It is also important that the entity's employees are paid a wage which provides them with a reasonable standard of living, so that domestic worries are not brought to work. Nevertheless, it seems normal for people to believe they are overworked and underpaid!

Fringe benefits

As well as the pecuniary remuneration that an employee derives from his labour, he may receive some fringe benefits, referred to as perks; these provide a form of indirect payment. For office workers, fringe benefits may include the following: holiday entitlement; sick pay; subscription to medical or life insurance; sometimes a rent allowance; possibly a car, a car allowance, or other transport to take employees to and from their workplace; a pension fund which may be contributory, i.e. the employee has to make some contribution from his earnings, or non-contributory, where the employer pays the full subscription to the fund; profit-sharing or share option schemes; luncheon vouchers; and discounts on the firm's products or services. Not all organisations offer all these fringe benefits; it depends upon management policy towards them. And it must be remembered that the provision of such benefits adds to the entity's costs. Which (if any) of these fringe benefits an employee is entitled to may depend upon three factors. These are: the work performed; status in the organisation; and/or seniority. For example, an office manager responsible for the work of a number of offices sited at different locations may be entitled to a car allowance. The sales person may receive a company car, the value of which may depend on his status. The employee with long service may get the benefit of longer holidays as a sort of loyalty bonus.

Fringe benefits became more important in the United Kingdom in relation to remuneration packages in recent years because many of them were not taxed (and many still are not), whereas the receipt of additional salary would be subject to taxation. However, government has brought in legislation to tax some of these perks, e.g. the use of a company car.

Welfare facilities

Sometimes welfare facilities are bracketed with the fringe benefits an organisation provides to its employees. Nevertheless, it is helpful to discuss them separately since they approximate to what the economist would describe as a public good as far as employees are concerned. This means they can be consumed by all, although there may be some restrictions on some of these facilities to certain categories of employees. Some will be able to take advantage of them more than others; for example, older staff may not be able to use any squash court facilities provided, while the younger ones may not want to play bowls. And some will make great use of the facilities, while others who do not will not perceive them as a perk.

Entities' welfare facilities would include social or sports amenities, with some organisations having their own clubs or hiring premises for these purposes. There may also be medical facilities, a canteen, and so on.

Security

One of the highest priorities for most employees is security of employment. This includes such matters as channels to protest against unfair dismissal, and whether a trading or manufacturing firm has a secure enough base to enable it to survive into the future. In the past one of the advantages so-called staff employees[4] had over those who, for example, worked on the factory floor was that their employment tended to be more secure. However, various government policies relating to unfair dismissal have gone some way towards mitigating the less secure position of wage-earning employees, and this imbalance has all but disappeared. The security aspect of personnel policy becomes more important to employees as they grow older, especially when their work requires physical effort. Employees want to be assured that they will not be dumped on to the scrap heap but retained by the organisation and possibly moved to lighter work. Sometimes pensions are included under the heading of security, although in this book they have been discussed under fringe benefits.

Advancement

Employees, particularly younger office workers who may start out on a relatively low salary, want to know about their opportunities for advancement. The carrot of promotion prospects can be one of the greatest factors in the motivation of employees. It at least helps to ensure that the ambitious are always on their toes and carrying out their work effectively and efficiently, in the expectation that their efforts will be recognised and promotion to a higher-grade job will eventually come along. Thus there must be a personnel policy concerning the internal promotion of employees, and it must be communicated to staff. Such a policy will frequently be linked with the education and training of employees. As examples, a typist may automatically be given a rise if he passes one of the Royal Society of Arts typing examinations; or it may be policy that a person has to attend, and be successful in, a course on supervisory management before he will even be considered for promotion to a position which will entail the supervision of other staff.

Thus if it is known that whenever possible the organisation's policy is to fill any senior vacancies in its offices by internal promotion, this will provide a great motivational influence. At the same time, staff should not be given the impression that promotion is a right, but rather that there is a policy of internal promotion, with examples of how this has happened in the past.

Status

Chapter 2 discussed the influence that status can have on a person's attitude towards the workplace. As in other areas of employment, in the office status can be gained in a number of ways. Status may be formal, i.e. where the person is the office manager, or informal, where the person has some special outside position and the influence of this spills over into the way in which he is treated in the office by his colleagues. Even at the lowest level in the office, 'status' can be generated if people are made to feel their work is important. Thus management should be concerned and appreciate what employees do, not treating them as if they were just another piece of furniture. The higher up a person is, the easier it is to ascertain his formal status. Sometimes this can even be seen by the way in which the office manager's office is equipped and furnished, or whether he rates a secretary. Then there are those who have the status of a company car, and usually the bigger it is the higher the user's status.

Environment

The working environment requires special attention. Such things as the congeniality and comfort of the surroundings and safety factors at the work-place have to be considered. The employees' environment can have a tremendous effect on their attitudes and motivation towards their work. Everyone likes to work in nice surroundings, but this does not necessarily mean that they expect a modern office building; it means rather that the premises they work in – and these may be old buildings – are made as nice as possible in relation to their age and design. It will often be found that people like to give their office a homely feel by having plants and pictures in them.

The safety aspect of the workplace is also very important, although offices tend to be much safer than factories, where there is usually moving machinery. Nevertheless, there can be dangers in the use of office machinery and in an office where things are left around for people to trip over. There are legal safety requirements governed by a number of Acts in the United Kingdom, including the Offices, Shops and Railway Premises Act 1963 and the Health and Safety at Work Act 1974. Many office functions are carried out on the factory floor, and for people working in the factory there is the Factories Act 1961. Today, with more and more machinery in the office and with greater mechanisation of office work, especially where there is electrically operated machinery, safety has become an important factor.

The personnel policy in relation to safety in the office should not just ensure that the minimum legal requirements are being met – but, where necessary, that these are exceeded so that the office environment is a safe one. Unfortunately, accidents cannot always be prevented. It is important to keep records of these, analysing them at regular intervals – and, if accidents repeat themselves with the same type of equipment or keep occurring in the same place on a regular basis, to find out why and prevent their recurrence. In

Chapter 1 the importance of ergonomics in the office was explained. The good design and layout of office equipment can often help ensure safety in its use.

Education and training

The education of employees in what new office equipment will do, training them in the skills of using it, and educating management in organisational and administrative procedures as well as training them in supervisory and management skills, is important. As already mentioned, education and training can be linked to the remuneration a person receives and/or to promotion prospects and career pathways. Equally important, management must recognise that money spent on education and training can give a range of benefits. The obvious one is that the more efficient a worker is, the lower will be his unit costs of production. This will occur not only because he will be able to carry out tasks quicker, but also because work should be of a higher quality and there will be less wastage of materials and other resources in the process. For example, the typist who makes lots of mistakes will have to keep stopping to correct them, and sometimes may even have to retype text, with additional costs of time and materials.

Problem solving

Often the personnel department is asked by the line manager to advise him on how to solve a staff problem. The problem-solving interview can be used to help, although it has a much wider application in problem-solving situations. In this case somebody from the personnel area meets the person with the problem. 'The conversation between them may have been initiated by either the interviewer or the respondent on the grounds that the latter needs help in defining his problem and deciding how best it can be solved. This means that the interviewer must help the respondent to accomplish two tasks; first to clarify the facts so that he can see precisely what his problem is, and secondly to clarify his attitudes towards the problem situation so that he is enabled to take these into account when he comes to make his decision about how to solve it.'[5]

Justice

Workers must be treated fairly; it is important that they and their colleagues are *seen* to be treated equitably. Personnel policies have an important role to play in this aspect of employment, and in the last resort there should always be the right of the worker to discuss the problem with the organisation's personnel officer, or the person who carries out this function. After that if the employee still feels he was treated unfairly or still has a grievance, there should be an appeals system available. This will ensure that employees know they have protection from unfair treatment or even dismissal[6] and certainly have recourse to justice if it is felt that a superior is victimising them.

The heading of justice can also cover the principle of equal opportunities for all employees, who should know that there will be no unfair discrimination in the organisation based on age, class, race, religion or sex.[7]

Industrial relations

In some very large organisations the industrial relations aspect of personnel policy is rated so highly as to be given a separate department. This may have full autonomy or be under the ultimate control of the personnel department. Industrial relations covers mainly the relationships between the organisation's management and the work-force, which is usually represented by a trade union, and in particular this concerns the conditions of employment of the workers and their remuneration. It should be noted that poor or even non-existent communication has frequently been held responsible for management–union conflict.

Aspects of personnel

Every organisation has to pay some attention to the personnel function. Thus for the self-employed the owner–driver will have to consider his personnel policies, even if he does not think of them as such, once he starts to employ people. As an organisation increases in size it will have to decide whether it will formalise the personnel function and establish a personnel department, or whether the managers of the various line and staff areas will be made responsible for their own personnel arrangements. Once an organisation does employ a large number of people there is a good case for having a trained personnel officer. The decision about whether to do this, and if so when, will depend upon a number of factors including: the size the organisation has reached; the numbers in its labour force; the depth it wishes to take its personnel policy to; current or potential labour problems; the labour turnover ratio; the level of training carried out; and so on.

The advantages of a personnel department

There are many advantages to the establishment of a specialised personnel department. Some of these follow.

A personnel department enables the co-ordination of a consistent personnel policy throughout the organisation. Without a personnel function there is always the danger that in the large firm managers will have different attitudes towards personnel requirements. A personnel department will iron out any major differences in the ways in which employees are treated in different areas of the organisation.

A by-product of co-ordination is the standardisation of personnel matters throughout the organisation. As well as having administrative advantages, this also makes it clear to employees that they are all being treated in the same way and have equal opportunities, enjoy equal facilities, and have the same justice meted out to them. There will be continuity in the organisation's personnel work, both over time and in dealing with any personnel problems. Records will be established to promote continuity, and one member of the department can be allocated to deal with each problem and follow it through to the resolution, rather than the person with the problem being directed from one authority to another.

Specialisation provides an obvious benefit in personnel work in that the tasks to be carried out can be divided and done by people who are specifically trained in them. They will also gain experience and expertise in dealing with the problems in their specialist area. Following on from standardisation and specialisation, economies of scale can be achieved, especially since duplication of work is avoided and areas such as recruitment and training can be dealt with on a centralised basis. The personnel department can organise training centrally, often bringing together the same training needs of a number of different areas, and ensuring that it is carried out on a systematic and economical basis. With a personnel department welfare considerations can be looked at for the organisation as a whole, with the added benefits of economies of scale likely to accrue.

The organisation of the personnel function

Assuming that an organisation has a personnel department, an important consideration is its position within the organisation and its range of authority. To an extent this will depend upon the size of the entity, the personnel function itself and management attitudes. The personnel department may either provide this function or service throughout the entity, or simply have the role of advising the various line and staff areas as to how they should carry out the organisation's personnel policies – although even in the latter case, personnel records will usually still be maintained centrally. When the personnel department is given functional authority throughout a large organisation, especially when the entity operates from a number of premises at different geographical locations, assistant personnel officers will likely be located at each major site. But even if this is not the case, personnel staff will have to be 'organised' in an effective scheme. Figure 4.1 illustrates the sort of organisational chart that could be found in a large personnel department.

The accommodation of the personnel department and its location also require careful consideration. Especially in large entities, many employees are likely to visit personnel, and indeed so may many potential employees and employers, for whom this will be their first contact with the organisation. Interviews will mean that the personnel office should be removed from noise as far as is feasible, but should also be accessible to visitors from whatever source. Thus the siting of the personnel offices near the main reception or office area of the organisation would be convenient. It is also important that the personnel offices are clearly signposted. In addition, they must be reasonably well decorated and furnished, especially since potential employees will likely get their first impression of the entity here.

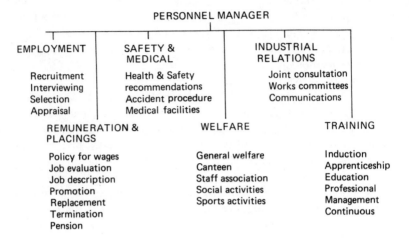

Fig. 4.1 Possible organisational chart for personnel department

The personnel manager

From the above it is clear that the selection of a personnel manager is all-important. The qualities and characteristics required for this role are numerous and varied, although the importance and extent of these will also depend on the size of the entity and on whether it is sufficiently large to employ specialists to support the personnel manager and assume the burden of some of the specialised personnel functions. The personnel manager needs to be both an industrial psychologist and a good administrator. He must be able to handle people, which includes his dealings with management on personnel matters as well as with lower-level employees. Good communication at all levels is of prime importance, as is showing impartiality in decision-making. On the administrative side, he is likely to be responsible for the operation of his own department, which may be a large one, and equally must be able to supervise the administration of the organisation's personnel records.

The success of the personnel manager will depend upon a number of criteria, even when the right person has been selected for the job. Top management must recognise the importance of the function and be prepared to give it full support, ensuring that the status and authority necessary to the role are fostered and understood throughout the organisation. However, the co-operation of middle management is also important if the department is to succeed, and this co-operation must work both ways; otherwise, the effectiveness of the personnel policy will be reduced. Then there must be support for the work of personnel from the organisation's employees in general – and this will come about only when there is confidence that personnel is genuinely concerned about their welfare.

The development of personnel policy

The principal function of the personnel manager is to carry out the organisation's personnel objectives and policies. Nevertheless, he should provide management with advice and recommendations when it is formulating these objectives and policies.

When a personnel manager joins a new organisation he will encounter a number of potential difficulties. Some organisations have no personnel policy. When this is the case the personnel manager will not know either what his role is supposed to be or what aspects of personnel work he is to carry out. Thus he will probably try to formulate his own personnel 'rules' as he goes along which, if generally accepted, eventually provide the basis of the organisation's personnel policy. Clearly, this is unsatisfactory and if he is faced with such a situation, his duty should be to encourage management to develop a personnel policy. Another possible problem is that he may find little co-operation or even active hostility from the organisation's senior or middle management, or indeed its employees, especially if it appears to any of these groups that he is playing safe and seems to be a yes-man. This may be even worse if the personnel manager is put into the situation where although he does not approve of some aspect of management's personnel policy, he still has to carry it out. The personnel manager may have a lack of knowledge of the various functional areas of the firm; for example, although he will have been trained in personnel matters, he should also know something about the problems of the other major operations within the firm, whether they be production or marketing. For in a matter concerning employees it may be that the problem cannot be solved using traditional personnel methods. Thus, the more knowledge he can assimilate about the operations of the organisation as a whole, the greater the opportunity of dealing with problems promptly as they arise.

Personnel records

The major routine job in the personnel function is the maintenance of personnel records. Apart from the use of these to provide biographical information on the individual employee and his employment, they have an important use in the provision of general statistical information. For example, they can highlight departments with high absentee percentages, labour turnover ratios and accident statistics, which it may be beneficial to look into. The growing use of the computer to compile and maintain personnel records is a great help. There may also be a legal obligation for an organisation to supply government departments with information on the number of people that they employ. Personnel records can provide the basis for these statistical returns and should enable them to be collated and presented more easily and quickly – and more cost-effectively. One entity's personnel statistics can be compared with those of another, similar organisation with the objective of seeing whether they differ, and if so whether this is favourable or unfavourable and why. Thus there are two basic sets of personnel records that can be utilised: information on individuals, and group statistics.

The individual's personnel record card

The personnel record, which is sometimes referred to as the employee's history or data, can be created and maintained in a number of ways. It can be on paper in the form of a card or sheet, or within a computer, although if it is computer-based the provisions of the Data Protection Act 1984 have to be taken into consideration. Any information retained as an employee's personal data needs to be relevant to the purpose; otherwise the size of the record will become unwieldy. To be of any practical value, the record should present an accurate work history of the individual and should be a reflection of positive *and* negative attributes, conduct, etc. There is a case for the maintenance of a separate record containing any adverse information on a confidential basis. Even when all the information on an employee could be classified as being good, the confidentiality of the record must still be taken into consideration. For if such records are seen to be lying around it may give the impression that all the information held by the personnel department is treated in the same way.

The purpose of employee history cards

It is important to ask what purpose an employee's record card is to serve, especially since this can help in the design of the record's format. For example, when the records are maintained on paper it might be economical to have different sheets or cards for different categories of employees, each designed to fulfil the particular record needs of the group concerned. There are a number of reasons for maintaining personnel records containing the history or other information on individual employees. Already mentioned above was the need to prepare group statistics, which will be culled from each employee's individual record. The organisation will also want to have certain basic information available about its employees, such as their addresses in case of accidents or illness at work. This will normally be collected under the headings which follow, although those used and the information gathered should be tailored to the organisation's needs.

1.   *Dates*, such as when the employee started with the organisation, dates of changes in his position, salary, location of employment and status, and when he eventually completes his employment, would all normally be recorded.

2.   *Basic personal information* is required – obviously, name and address and if appropriate, telephone number. It is also usual to include the date of birth under this heading and perhaps marital status and information of the employee's family, e.g. the name of the next of kin and the number of dependants. Sometimes information on any special interests or commitments will be detailed here.

3. Information on the employee's *education and training* will also be collected. This will include his academic achievements, any trade or professional qualifications, courses of training or study that he has, or is, undertaking and any training given within the firm itself, including on-the-job training.

4. The employee's *work experience* may have a separate heading, although it could be included under the heading of education and training. Work experience will be divided into that in previous employment and that within the organisation.

5. *Absences* through sickness or accidents will be listed, although it is not usual to include details of official holidays in the records. Information about timekeeping will be shown if the employee is habitually late or, alternatively, is prepared to work overtime or on shifts.

6. Finally, information about any *reprimands* given to the employee will also be recorded although, as mentioned above, this may be done separately.

A typical layout for a personnel record card is shown in Fig. 4.2 and Fig. 4.3. Even when the records are maintained using a computer, a structure similar to these will be used, the main difference being that the records are maintained electronically.

Once a system is set up the records must be protected from deterioration, especially if in a factory floor location, and from possible damage or loss. Duplicate sets might be maintained either for multiple users or as a back-up in the event of loss. Finally, access to personnel records must be restricted to authorised users.

Compilation and storage of personnel information for individuals

As stated earlier, the personnel records of an individual may be maintained in a number of ways, such as on paper or cards which can be kept in a record envelope so that other documents relating to the employees can be put with them, or using some form of computer storage. In the storage of personnel records all the principles of records management should be followed and their safety and retrieval considered. Whether the records will be maintained at some central office or at the various locations where the people are employed must be decided, together with the control aspects of keeping personnel records centrally. If not kept centrally, it must be decided whether there will be branch personnel offices at the decentralised sites.

Group statistics

When group statistics are prepared from individual personnel records they must not be considered in isolation. As with all statistics they should be looked at in comparison with other personnel information. These comparisons can be made in three ways: on an *intertemporal* basis, i.e. looking at information from

CORRECT TO:	PERSONNEL RECORD	REFERENCE:

SURNAME .... FORENAME(S) .... ADDRESS .... CHANGES (1) .... (2) .... TELEPHONE	PAYROLL NO. NATIONAL INSURANCE NO. SUPERANNUATION NO. DATE OF BIRTH NATIONALITY SINGLE/MARRIED CHILDREN/DEPENDENTS NEXT OF KIN ADDRESS................................... ....

EDUCATION and TRAINING

SCHOOL/COLLEGE/COURSE	FROM	TO	DETAILS and AWARDS

PREVIOUS EMPLOYMENT

NAME OF EMPLOYERS	FROM	TO	POSITION and REMUNERATION	REASON FOR LEAVING

OTHER INFORMATION

EMPLOYMENT	COMMENCED	TERMINATED

Fig. 4.2 Layout for a personnel record card (front)

POSITIONS HELD			
DATE	DEPARTMENT	JOB	COMMENTS

ANNUAL HOLIDAY			OTHER ABSENCES		
YEAR	COMMENCES	DAYS	FROM	TO	REASON

REASON FOR TERMINATION

NOTES: REMUNERATION : Details of wages, bonuses, termination pay,etc., are recorded separately by the wages department

ANNUAL REPORTS: Filed in an envelope system.

Fig. 4.3 Layout for a personnel record card (back)

the same source for different time periods; through *interfirm* comparison, i.e. with other organisations' personnel statistics; or through *interdepartmental*, interdivisional or interbranch comparisons, where the statistics from different parts of the organisation are compared. (These are often abbreviated as: intertemporal comparison (ITC); interfirm comparison (IFC); and inter-departmental comparison (IDC).) And it is important to stress the need to compare like with like. Thus with interfirm comparison only entities in the same sector of the economy, and organisations in the same industry and with similar organisational structure, size, etc., should be compared. If there are great differences between the personnel statistics being compared, these should lead to the question of why the differences might have occurred. Although group statistics will be useful to the personnel department itself, they will probably be of more immediate use to management to help in its man-power planning. They might also be helpful when used in conjunction with other statistics in order to make an appraisal of the general progress of the organisations – e.g. in combination with production information to obtain a ratio of output per production worker, or with sales to show the sales made on average by each sales person.

The sort of personnel statistics that can be useful include those which show the numbers for the following: applications for employment, especially when divided into the media that attracted the applications; attendance or absences; time lost through lateness; days lost through, say, sickness or accidents; average earnings of various groups of employees; overtime paid; use of the canteen; days of training undertaken, and success in examinations where appropriate; support given by employees to the various welfare and social activities provided by the organisation; labour turnover ratios; and many, many more.

Examples of the use of group personnel statistics

Three examples of the use of this information – absentee percentages, labour turnover and accident ratios – will be given.

Absentee percentages

These can provide useful information in some industries, such as mining or the docks, where employees are frequently absent, especially on Mondays. The statistics may show that there are trends in the absences, although it is obviously important to segregate absences through sickness[8] or holidays.

Labour turnover

This is an important ratio, especially when related to an organisation's recruitment and training costs – which can be surprisingly high. If the statis-tics indicate that one organisation has a much higher labour turnover ratio than what appears to be the norm for a trade or industry, or where this ratio is high for one part of the organisation in relation to that calculated for other areas, questions should be asked and remedies sought. For example, the turnover of word-processing operators might be found to be high. This may be because there are few promotion opportunities for them so they become frustrated and move elsewhere. The labour turnover of a certain section of the work-force may be high because they are paid much less than the going rate for the same job elsewhere. A department with a high labour turnover may be highlighted, with investigation showing that the way in which the manager treats his workers has an 'expelling' effect. At least the identification of problems such as these will give management the opportunity to put things right.

Accident ratios
These can also provide useful information, especially in showing the trends of accidents that take place in a department. If the record is poor something must be done about it – and this may require the 'education' of employees to use the equipment in the department properly.

Evaluating work

There is a distinction between *the evaluation of a job* and *placing a value on a job*. The latter has no connection with the employees who carry out the work or their efficiency in doing so. Another technique, *merit rating*, indicates how efficiently an employee carries out his work; this will be dealt with in a later section of the chapter.

It is also important to note that *job grading* is used in relation to placing a value on administrative work, usually carried out by salaried staff, whereas *job evaluation* does the same thing for factory work. Nevertheless, the terms tend to be used synonymously and both are about the values of various jobs or work.

The advantages of evaluating work
Evaluating work offers a number of advantages. It groups jobs of the same order of importance and responsibility together. The same salary levels can be attached to jobs that are given the same classification, and this can minimise dissatisfaction between people who carry out similar work. Another use of the technique is that standard costs can be built up for jobs, and budgets prepared from the information gleaned during the job evaluation exercise. The information obtained can be used to help in the recruitment of staff to carry out the work, as well as to develop any training requirements necessary. Then, because at recruitment people will have been matched to the jobs and in subsequent training will have been given more confidence in their ability to carry out the work, it will help efficiency. And since the grading provides employees with information about their job and higher, related ones, they know what it will entail if they move up to the next rung on the ladder. There is also the advantage that during the job grading procedure information will

have been collected that will help in the drawing up of organisational charts and the writing of procedural manuals to help employees in their work.

The limitations of evaluating work

Although the evaluation of work can have many benefits it also has its limitations and difficulties. Firstly, it may give the impression of providing a perfectly scientific way of matching jobs of equal value. Yet this is frequently impractical, since in the process of the evaluation of quite different work some subjectivity must enter into decisions about the relative values of different jobs and the placing of some of them in the same categories. Thus instead of causing harmony it can sometimes be the very cause of dissatisfaction between people who get paid the same for jobs which have been rated the same, e.g. when one of the parties feels that his work is much more difficult and has a greater importance to the organisation than that of the other. This shows the importance of consulting with staff when evaluating work and of trying to get their agreement to the gradings proposed through careful explanations as to why quite different jobs may have been put into the same category.

Job evaluation is often used to establish rates of pay for various jobs. However, sometimes rates of pay have to take into account the supply of labour for a category of work, whereas the evaluation does not do this. This may cause problems. Then job evaluation does not make allowances for the different abilities of employees, for example in speed and quality of output. Nor does it take into account the experience of an employee. Merit rating may be used to overcome some of these problems.

Finally, the work content of some jobs is continually changing, yet job evaluation rarely takes place on an ongoing basis. Thus if an employee finds a way of improving his performance he is likely to feel aggrieved if his job is not re-evaluated promptly.

The steps in evaluating work

Evaluating work needs to be done in a systematic way. The steps involved are to establish the job description, evaluate the work using job evaluation, and then rate it.

The job description

The job description involves an analysis of the work being performed, listing the duties and responsibilities. The job specification also states the qualities required of people doing this work. There is no standard way to describe jobs, the methods varying between entities and even within the same organisation for different classes of work. Nevertheless, within an organisation it is sensible to use a few standard formats, with the number of these limited and their headings tailored to suit the different kinds of work. Very often several seemingly different jobs can be grouped together into broad categories with forms used as the basis for collecting the description of a job in a category.

Each job should be given a precise title. For example, describing the job as clerical work would be too broad, whereas the use of copy clerk, filing clerk and so on might be suitable. The name of the job may be abbreviated using a reference code, or a reference number may be assigned to each job description. The essential parts of the work involved in the job will be clearly stated, with a note as to why the function is necessary and what is achieved by doing it. When and where the work is to be done and how it is to be carried out will also be specified.

The requirements of holders of the job (education, skills, and any special mental or physical attributes) will be stated. Information on the environmental conditions in which the work is to be carried out (e.g. if it is associated with physical discomfort or is monotonous) will be given. How responsible the work is with regard to such things as accuracy, reliability, own initiative or supervision will be indicated.

Methods of gaining information to describe work include observation of or consultation with the people currently carrying out the work and their supervisors and/or managers. Whatever method is adopted, there should be agreement between those employed to do the work and the personnel carrying out the job evaluation on the final job description. Sometimes a draft job description will be 'exposed' to the employees doing the work, who will be given the chance to appeal before it is finalised. An example of a job description form is provided in Fig. 4.4.

Job evaluation

Jobs may be evaluated in a number of ways. A popular method is to use a *weighted points* system. When using this, first decide upon a number of key components for the job. These may be common to a number of different jobs in the area, or to similar work carried out in different areas. These key components provide the standard when comparing work. The problem is to rank an existing or new job being evaluated into a perhaps already established ranking scheme, which is difficult to do because different jobs will have different mixes of components. The objective here is to quantify the qualitative aspects of the jobs for payment purposes. The ranking of the units of work may be done using a points system, perhaps on a scale from 1 to 10. This approach may be further refined by giving weightings to the more important features identified in the work. Once all the points are weighted, the final 'scores' for different jobs can be compared. Appropriate bandings for salary purposes can then be decided upon and jobs placed in these according to their scores.

Another way of evaluating office work is to use the *factor comparison* method. This has a major disadvantage, however; it can be complex and can lead to misapprehension and confusion. With this method work is normally broken down into six elements, although there can be more or, conversely, some of the elements could be grouped together. These six elements are: education, skill, mental effort, physical effort, responsibility and environment. Some key jobs

```
┌─────────────────────────────────────────────────────────┐
│                 JOB DESCRIPTION FORM                      │
├──────────────────┬──────────────────┬────────────────────┤
│ DEPARTMENT       │ JOB TITLE        │ REFERENCE          │
│                  │                  │                    │
├──────────────────┴──────────────────┼────────────────────┤
│ ESSENTIALS                           │                    │
│                                      │                    │
├──────────────────────────────────────┼────────────────────┤
│ ANALYSIS                             │                    │
│                                      │                    │
├──────────────────────────────────────┼────────────────────┤
│ ENVIRONMENT                          │                    │
│                                      │                    │
│                                      │                    │
│                                      │                    │
├──────────────────────────────────────┼────────────────────┤
│ REQUIREMENTS                         │                    │
│ SKILL/EDUCATION                      │                    │
│     Basic education                  │                    │
│     Training                         │                    │
│     Initiative                       │                    │
│     Dexterity                        │                    │
│                                      │                    │
│ MENTAL/PHYSICAL EFFORT               │                    │
│     Concentration                    │                    │
│     Strength                         │                    │
│                                      │                    │
│ RESPONSIBILITY                       │                    │
│ For  Equipment                       │                    │
│      Costs                           │                    │
│      Quality                         │                    │
│      Time                            │                    │
├──────────────────────────────────────┴────────────────────┤
│ NOTES                                                      │
├────────────────────────────────────────────────────────────┤
│ DATE                     ASSESSOR                          │
│                                                            │
└────────────────────────────────────────────────────────────┘
```

Fig. 4.4 Job description form

within an entity are then drawn out to provide bench-marks against which the other jobs will be measured. For the key jobs the proportion of each of the six components that goes towards making up the wage paid to an employee carrying them out is established. The evaluation of a job is then made by comparing the weightings of the six factors with those of the base jobs. It can be seen why the factor comparison method causes difficulties, since an accurate representation requires a complex calculation.

There is a very simple method of job evaluation, which is to give jobs *straight rankings*. With this method jobs are ranked according to their relative importance to the organisation. This, on the face of it, appears to be the simplest way of comparing jobs and it is certainly the easiest method for employees to understand. Nevertheless, it can create problems in a large organisation where there are hundreds of different jobs in different areas, and seemingly unrelated work is placed in the same category. Some subjectivity must inevitably come into the comparisons, and however much a person appraising a job finds out about it by talking to those who do the work, it is not the same thing as having performed the task oneself for many years. Thus employees may not accept the classification of their work.

An example of a job evaluation form based on the weighted points system is provided in Fig. 4.5.

The job evaluation of clerical work

It is usually harder to apply job evaluation procedures to clerical tasks than it is to factory work because there is more scope for subjectivity in the process. Office work is one area of employment where there may be differing elements in the work although the job title is the same. For example, one word-processing operator may be dealing with the production of form correspondence while the other may be using the equipment to prepare some complex tabulations for accounting reports. Then many people in offices are subject to constant interruptions which make it difficult to measure their work output and establish standard units for their responsibilities. It is suggested that much clerical work requires some initiative, which is hard to evaluate as, indeed, is the loyalty that clerical workers are said to give their organisation. The question is: how should such factors be evaluated?

One classification is that of the Institute of Administrative Management, which has categorised clerical work into grades as follows:[9]

1. *Grade A* work concerns simple jobs which, although requiring no previous clerical experience, have to be performed under close supervision. Examples falling into this classification would include the sorting of documents, and batching these, perhaps for dispatch elsewhere.

2. *Grade B* work involves tasks which are simple to do and can be carried out by following limited but well-defined rules. These tasks require little training, after which they should be performed successfully. The people carrying out tasks in this grade have to be clearly instructed and supervised in their work, which requires checking after completion. The jobs in this category could include the use of basic office equipment such as the calculator or the photocopying machine.

3. *Grade C* tasks are also of a routine nature, and clear instructions are required for their execution. However, employees must have either a special aptitude, such as an ability to use more complex office equipment, or some experience which has, over time, made them proficient in their work. One of their functions may be to check the work of category B employees.

JOB EVALUATION FORM

DEPARTMENT	JOB TITLE	REFERENCE		

	NOTES	WEIGHTING	POINTS	TOTAL
ENVIRONMENT				
Danger		10		
Unpleasant		10		
Monotonous		10		
SKILL/EDUCATION				
Basic education		20		
Training		30		
Initiative		10		
Dexterity		10		
MENTAL/PHYSICAL EFFORT				
Concentration		10		
Strength		10		
RESPONSIBILITY				
Equipment		10		
Costs		10		
Quality		10		
Time		10		
TOTAL				
NOTES				
DATE	ASSESSOR			

SUGGESTED JOB CLASSIFICATION SCHEME

GRADE*	I	II	III
RANGE	160 — 130	129 — 80	79 and under
SCORE			

*Money values can be allocated to each grade.

Fig. 4.5 Job evaluation form based on a weighted points system

4.   *Grade D* work requires a considerable amount of experience. However, although some initiative in the work may be required, it is done following predetermined rules. At the same time, since the work in this category is generally repetitive, it does not require much supervision. Work will include having skills such as shorthand and typing.

5.   *Grade E* moves into the higher levels of work where more initiative is necessary, and in this kind of work discretion may also be required. Additionally, the tasks require some specialised knowledge, and responsibility for the work carried out. This category of work can include either the supervision of those in the previous groupings or jobs of a non-routine nature which are carried out without supervision.

6.   *Grade F* covers the highest levels of clerical work. The work in this category requires the use of judgement for certain aspects of the tasks, which may be complex, and full responsibility for the work. This may involve special skills such as knowledge of statistics, an ability to use computer software, or perhaps some technical knowledge, e.g. in support of the work of the chartered secretary, the professional accountant or the lawyer. Such staff will also need supervisory skills since they are likely to be responsible for a number of employees in a section. In addition, they will generally have close contact with management, thus providing a bridge between other clerical workers and management.

7.   *Grades G and H* require professional or specialist knowledge. Grade G covering those who have reached their last stages of study for the final examinations of professional bodies like ICSA or accounting bodies such as the Chartered Association of Certified Accountants (ACCA) or Institute of Chartered Accountants in England and Wales (ICAEW), and who may supervise up to 20 people. Grade H includes people holding professional qualifications, with responsibility for the management of a larger number of people.

Merit rating

Merit rating involves the appraisal of the work of individual office workers with regard to proficiency and performance, with some form of reward based on work achievement. As with other techniques to measure work performance, merit rating has its advantages and disadvantages.

The advantages of merit rating
One advantage of merit rating is that it gives recognition to an employee's ability and rewards him for good performance. The grading of employees can then be linked to promotion prospects, which will encourage ambitious employees to do their best. Merit rating also has the advantage of developing management's ability to appraise its staff. In order to carry out merit rating management must establish and maintain close contact with subordinates, which is likely to improve employee motivation.

The disadvantages of merit rating
The rating itself will bring in some subjectivity, i.e. the subjective views of a

manager about his staff. This problem may be overcome somewhat by training managers in the use of the technique, although not all managers will develop the skills required to make them completely objective when carrying out their appraisals. There may also be a reluctance on the part of the manager to rate his staff detrimentally. As mentioned, if a manager is to carry out merit rating properly he will have to maintain close contact with his staff, but because of the limited time available he may not be able to do this as well as he should. Thus there is the danger that the process will eventually become standardised, thereby failing in its objectives. For example, an employee's performance may deteriorate, yet he is not moved down the scale since there may be a reluctance on the part of the manager to downgrade him. Or the employee's work content may change, with a change in rating indicated, but this may not be picked up.

The process of merit rating

The first thing to consider is whether all the clerical workers will be included in a merit rating scheme or which groups will be singled out. The personnel department must discuss the proposed scheme with both management and employees – and if appropriate, with any union representing the latter – before implementation. There must be agreement at all levels about the scheme and its operation.

An appraisal form will be designed to cover the major factors to be rated, and all parties involved must agree on its format. Guidelines for the ratings that can be achieved by employees are frequently given on the form itself. An example of the form is provided in Fig. 4.6, with the guidelines for awarding points shown in Fig. 4.7. When completing the form, the manager should be encouraged to make comments as to why he gave a person a particular rating.

The process of appraisal should take place on a regular basis, usually at annual intervals. The disadvantages of having such periods between assessments is that the person making the appraisal, who is usually the immediate superior of the member of staff being appraised, may be influenced by recent events. The manager carrying out an appraisal should have knowledge of the person being appraised over the whole of the period under scrutiny, or at least have access to detailed records from his predecessor.

Opinion varies as to whether staff who have been through the appraisal process should be informed of the 'verdict'. Where some payment is associated with an employee's rating, staff will know from this whether they have been rated high or low; one school of though is that they should be told the reasons behind their rating if they are to know how they can improve their performance.

Once a merit rating scheme has been introduced and become well established, all too often it will be taken for granted. The manager will carry out his appraisals on an automatic basis, and the employee will accept any rewards he receives through the scheme as the norm, both of which defeat the purpose of the scheme. Once a good worker is receiving the top merit payment, he may

STAFF APPRAISAL FORM

NAME AND INITIALS	REFERENCE	
DEPARTMENT	STATUS	GRADE

	NOTES	RATING
KNOWLEDGE OF JOB Training Experience		
PERFORMANCE Output Quality		
ATTENDANCE Absence Late		
OTHER FACTORS Adaptability Co-operation Innovative		
TOTAL		

NOTES

DATE	ASSESSOR

Note. Suggestions for awarding points are shown overleaf.

KEY TO MERIT RATING

GRADE*	1	2	3
RANGE	60 and above	59–40	39 and under
SCORE			

*Merit payments can be allocted to each grade.

Fig. 4.6 Staff appraisal form for use in merit rating

tend to coast along. In this case staff should be encouraged to do even better by linking promotion prospects to the scheme if at all possible. Then some merit rating schemes turn out to be no more than a method of rewarding either the loyalty or the long service of employees, perhaps to reduce labour turnover, but it should be seen that there are better ways of doing this.

The problems associated with the introduction and operation of a merit rating scheme show that it is important to distinguish between average

FACTOR	POINTS RANGE		
	1 – 3	4 – 7	8 – 10
KNOWLEDGE OF JOB			
Training	Preliminary	Intermediate	Completed
Experience*	1 – 3 years	4 – 7 years	8 or more years
PERFORMANCE			
Output	Unsatisfactory	Average/Adequate	Exemplary
Quality	Careless/Slow	Requires checking	Reliable/Fast
ATTENDANCE			
Absence	10 – 7%	6 – 4%	3 – 0%
Late	Occasionally	Rarely	Never
OTHER FACTORS			
Adaptability	Slow	Average	Quick
Co-operation	Reluctant	Average	Helpful
* Experience will be awarded for years in the job, or related work, to a maximum of 10.			
Note: Points will be awarded to a maximum of 10 for each of the above aspects of the work.			

Fig. 4.7 Typical guidelines for awarding points in merit rating

performance and additional efficiency/extra effort, and to identify elements of reward for long service and loyalty separately.

The assessment of management's performance

The assessment of management performance is often done by superiors on a subjective basis according to personality traits, rather than by aiming for objectivity. Nevertheless, the assessment of management is important for a number of reasons. It may be done at the time when salaries are to be reviewed or promotion prospects are being considered, and a manager will usually be assessed by his immediate superior. The assessment can be carried out on a controlled basis using a check-list, which may be in the form of a matrix, or through a written appraisal with no parameters prescribed. When executive management is being appraised it is usual to have two or more senior managers carry out the task, and for the most senior people a committee may undertake the rating. Managers can be rated for the various attributes of management and leadership discussed in Chapter 2, and ranked accordingly.

Recruitment[10]

Recruitment of personnel requires that two factors be matched as closely as possible: the work to be carried out; and the potential of the candidate to do this successfully. Therefore, people responsible for recruiting staff must find out as much as possible about both of these factors. With the former, the job description provides a starting point, but somebody from the area of work in question should also be involved in the process since only he will have full knowledge of what the work entails. With the latter, knowledge can be gleaned from three sources: the completed application form; information from referees; and an interview. As a starting point, when sifting through the application forms or holding an interview these two factors will be matched, although others, such as the character and personality of the applicants, will come into the final analysis. Marvin Dunnette points out that 'People differ greatly. At the beach on any hot summer day, even the most casual observer is impressed with the amazing array of physical differences among people. But people also differ in a myriad of other less easily discerned qualities, such as intelligence, abilities, skills, motivation, and temperament. Indications of some of these differences can be observed in the ways people behave. Some are friendly, sociable, and outgoing; others shy and withdrawn. Some are forceful and dominant and leading; others meek, permissive and following. Some are constantly active, working or playing with great intensity; others are phlegmatic. It has been said that variability is nature's great joke, perpetrated on man to make more difficult his efforts to understand the universe . . . The different patterns of human behaviour are also clearly evident in the world of work.' He continues, 'Programs of personnel selection and placement in industry are essential.'[11]

The first step is to attract applicants for the job, which may be done through either internal or external advertisements. Advertisements cannot contain all the details, but should present the essential features of the job and state that people who are interested should apply for further particulars. The reply package will usually contain the job description, but may also include general information on the organisation, such as it size and conditions of employment, together with an application form. It is important to make available the job description and any further details of the employment because these should dissuade those who do not have the skills or experience necessary for the post. Thus a good job description can save a lot of time and effort in the recruitment process.

The application form

The application form will be rather like the personnel record form above – in fact, it will likely form the basis of the personnel record for people engaged by an organisation. It will contain personal information, and information about education and training, and past employment and experience. It may also provide space for applicants to disclose other interests, perhaps to say why they applied for the job and to provide a personal justification of their suitability. Much will depend upon the nature of the work and the level of the job. For very senior positions there may not be a standard application form; applicants may be asked to apply by letter and to enclose a curriculum vitae (CV). An example of a job application form (front and back) is provided in Fig. 4.8 and Fig. 4.9. Once it has been completed by the applicant, it provides information for the first stage of the matching process. If interviews are to follow, the application forms received will be sifted so that a short list of applicants can be drawn up. During the interview the application form will be helpful in providing material about the prospective employee, and he can be asked questions within this framework to explain, justify or expand on any information he has given.

EMPLOYMENT APPLICATION FORM

SURNAME	DATE OF BIRTH
CHRISTIAN NAME(S)	NATIONALITY
ADDRESS	SINGLE/MARRIED
....	CHILDREN
....	
TELEPHONE	

EDUCATION and TRAINING

SCHOOL/COLLEGES/COURSES	FROM	TO	DETAILS and AWARDS

PREVIOUS EMPLOYMENT

NAME OF EMPLOYERS	FROM	TO	POSITION and REMUNERATION	REASON FOR LEAVING

OTHER RELEVANT INFORMATION
(This may include information on experience, which would support your application.)

DATE	SIGNATURE OF APPLICANT

Fig. 4.8 A job application form (front)

DETAILS OF SERIOUS ILLNESS or DISABILITY				Absence through sickness within last 2–5 years		

FOR OFFICE USE ONLY

RESULTS OF TESTS:	ARITHMETIC		WRITING			
PASS	YES/NO		YES/NO			
DATE	ASSESSOR					

INTERVIEW

REMARKS:

DATE   BY

MEDICAL

X-RAY	YES/NO	DATE	INITIALS			

EXAMINATION NOTES

DATE   BY

EMPLOYMENT CLASSIFICATION		PERSONNEL		
DEPARTMENT			DATE	INITIALS
SPECIAL NOTES		REFERENCES		
		ENGAGEMENT LETTER		
		NI CARD		
DEPARTMENT		P45		
ACCEPTED	YES/NO	COMMENCED		
DATE OF COMMENCEMENT		INDUCTION		
NOTES		TRAINING ARRANGED		
		DEPARTMENTAL TRAINING		
		RECORD CARD		
DATE	BY	ENGAGEMENT PROCEDURE COMPLETE		

Fig. 4.9 A job application form (back)

The interview

Together with the application form and information received from referees, the interview will often mark the end of the selection process. However – especially with clerical work – there are many other things that can be done to ensure that the best people for the job are selected. For example, when completing application forms for a clerical position, the applicant will often type in the information requested. Yet the job may require some handwriting. In such cases the further particulars sent out should clearly state that the application form must be completed by hand. When the work involves the operation of machinery, and the advertisement for the job requests applications from people who can use it, those applying can be asked to demonstrate their proficiency. So the copy typist who claims he is good at tabulation work could be asked to type up some appropriate copy at the interview stage.

Most people at some time in their lives find themselves on the side of the selection process when they are interviewed for a job, and there are many sources of help in how to best present themselves. When a person moves to the other side of the table and interviews people with a view to selecting staff it is important that he has had some training in the process, which is often referred to as *scientific selection*. John Fraser writes, 'Interviewing must . . . be understood as an individual skill. It is not a particularly difficult skill, once a systematic approach has been grasped.'[12] He then goes on to show how people can develop interview techniques.

Preparing to interview applicants
Arrangements for an interview require careful planning. First the location of the interview must be considered. This may be a special interview room within the personnel area or perhaps a quiet office close to the site of the work. Another consideration will be who is to conduct the interview, and whether one person or a number of people (an interview panel) are to be involved. It is especially important to consider whether the person who is to be the immediate superior of the employee eventually selected for the job should take part in the selection process. The manager will be responsible for any people working for him and his performance will partly be related to their performance. Thus a manager should have a say in the selection of employees taken on for his area of responsibility. If any tests are necessary, they should be arranged before the interview if possible.

Any references for applicants should be obtained before the interview. Reading such references requires some skill, and it may be necessary to read between the lines. If a reference seems rather vague, a telephone call to the person who wrote it will often be more fruitful, since the referee may be more willing to chat about the applicant over the telephone and to say things he is not prepared to commit to paper. Also watch out for references that seem too good to be true. The candidate may be exceptional, but a glowing reference may hide the fact that the organisation currently employing him would be happy to get rid of him!

Conducting the interview
Interviews are rather artificial situations, with the interviewee often feeling

intimidated and uncomfortable, under stress, and thus understandably nervous. Therefore, the first rule in interviewing is for the interviewer(s) to make the interviewee feel at ease. He should be given time to settle down in what might be an anxious situation; otherwise he will not be at his best. The interviewer needs to be as objective as possible in his appraisal of the interviewee. A person's behaviour in an interview situation, which may be brief by necessity, may not be totally representative of what he is really like. So a person being interviewed may not express himself as well as might have been expected from the details on his application form, and where this appears to be the case the interviewer must try to draw out the interviewee. Sometimes a person's appearance will affect the interviewer's views about him, whether or not this is important to the job. Thus it must be remembered that first impressions can have a lasting effect and be over-influential, so at the end of the interview a more objective view of the interviewee needs to be taken. During the session the interviewer must avoid either side-tracking himself, or being side-tracked by the interviewee.

A major problem with an interview is that it will not tell the interviewer whether the person is likely to succeed in the work, although sometimes pre-interview tests, e.g. for dexterity, can help provide more information about the aptitude of applicants. The main function of many interview situations will be to get the interviewee to open up and so help the interviewer ascertain his attitudes to work and how he is likely to fit in with other employees. At the same time, the interviewer must avoid being unduly prejudiced by what the candidate may say about things unrelated to the work.

Interviews cannot be planned, whatever side of them you are on. So it is bad policy to try to plan an interview situation since to force it on course may restrict its development. Flexibility is the key and it is better to let things flow naturally, especially if the candidate is being put at his ease. Two other golden rules for interviewers are not to offer candidates advice, and not to argue with them.

The autobiographical interview

One interesting form of interview is the autobiographical interview. In this the interviewee tells the interviewer the history of his life, with interest being not so much in what is told but rather in the way it is told. The secret of an autobiographical interview is for the interviewer to remain passive and to listen carefully to what is being related – a difficult task if the interviewer gets interested in what is being said and would like to clarify points raised or ask for details.

Group selection

Sometimes interviews will take place in groups. This is especially so for senior positions or when recruiting management trainees. Group selection tends to lead to more informality in the selection process and group discussion can often draw out a lot more information about candidates. This method of selection can be especially important when the employer wants to see how candidates will fit into and adapt to the social aspects of the job. Some group interviews take place over a number of days. This form of interview has the advantage of providing the interviewer with more time to assess candidates and see how the members of the group react in various, perhaps contrived situations.

The final selection

At the interview itself the interviewer will have looked at the physical make-up of the person, his character and disposition, past attainments, general intelligence, special aptitudes, interests, and personal circumstances. But there is also the achievement potential to be considered and from the appraisal of these factors a final selection will be made – assuming that there are suitable candidates. Otherwise it may be as well to readvertise the post rather than appoint a candidate who falls short of requirements.

Whatever the post being filled, the final selection must not be taken too lightly. It is costly to engage the wrong people, especially since it is often difficult to get rid of them – even when a trial period has been stipulated. And if a person does not stay long there are the additional costs of having to start all over again. Recruitment is a time-consuming process.

Candidates should be informed of the results of the interview as soon as possible, with confirmation of success in their application perhaps being subject to a medical examination and provision of originals of birth certificates, educational documents, and so on. Failure will not fall so hard if time is taken to explain a candidate's areas of weakness.

In many countries employees must be given service agreements. In the United Kingdom these came under the Contracts of Employment Act 1972, until it was amended by the Employment Protection (Consolidation) Act 1978. Such contracts have to be in writing and provide the employee with information on his employment, such as how his remuneration will be worked out, holiday entitlement, pension arrangements – and, not least, what is expected from him. The contract must also give information on any disciplinary or grievance procedures within the organisation.

The post-engagement audit

Despite the problems associated with using interviews in recruitment, they remain the best means of ensuring that the right people are selected for employment in the entity's various jobs; at the very least, they should ensure that people who are unsuitable for the work will not be employed. Nevertheless, it would be sensible for an organisation to see how good its selection procedures have been, and whether they are more effective in some parts of the entity than in others. It is therefore a good idea to have a post-engagement audit.

In the post-engagement audit a report is obtained from the manager responsible for the recruit to show whether he has settled down in his post, adapted to the work and is performing his job to the satisfaction of their manager. The personnel department will also monitor whether any new employees leave the organisation soon after they have started. From the information gained in a post-engagement audit, questions can be asked about what can be done to improve the organisation's recruitment procedures and, even where these seem to be effective, whether they could still be improved.

Training

The education and training of employees can be divided into the basic groupings of general and specific training. General training is the education and training that a person receives, probably before starting work or in some form of apprenticeship, with much of the cost borne by the State or the person receiving it. Specific training involves learning the skills required by a particular organisation and relevant to the work to be undertaken. This form of training will likely be provided by the employer, although it may have been 'funded' by a previous employer. As well as classifying training into these two groupings, it is also common to divide it into 'types' of training; the categories generally used are induction, apprenticeships, job, supervisory and management training. (Management training is sometimes referred to as management or executive development.)

The benefits of training

Training has a number of advantages and provides an organisation with many benefits. The most tangible of these is that it improves a person's efficiency. Clear relationships have been found between the training that a person is given and his efficiency, especially in terms of speed and quality. Training helps recruitment in that many people, especially young people looking for their first job, try to find employment with an organisation that will give them some training. This also promotes the entity's image. When there are labour shortages, especially of skilled employees, training will help to prevent or reduce these. (However, some industries cluster around certain locations, and firms operating within these areas receive benefits from economies of scale by having a trained work-force to draw on.) Training helps to improve and maintain employee morale. The morale of employees is always highest when they can cope with their work without undue stress. As a result, the employee is more likely to develop a loyalty towards his employer, which in turn helps to keep the organisation's labour turnover ratio low.

The training of employees will also provide a source of potential managers and supervisors, thus enabling internal promotion – another plus in the motivation of employees. Training is often necessary to help in the introduction of new equipment or methods, and can be helpful in gaining their acceptance and also in reducing the time required for new machinery to become fully operational. If people are left to learn things on their own they will take much longer than if they had received some training; thus training reduces the learning period. The untrained person tends to create more wastage or is more likely to damage equipment – whereas with training there is a reduction in the wastage of materials. For example, the person who is told to produce photocopies without being shown even how to switch on an unfamiliar machine is likely to have to make a number of copies before he gets good ones, with an inevitable wastage of paper. The reasons for training are summed up in this statement by Michael Jinks: 'The essential elements in any commercial enterprise are materials, equipment and manpower. Training, allied to the other human resource specialisms within management, ensures a pool of manpower of the required levels of expertise at the right time.'[13]

The training policy

Organisations must formulate a training policy to suit their specific needs. This will be based on such things as: the number of people within the entity that will need training at some time or other; the level of the training and standards expected; the jobs requiring the most training; whether training is to be used to prepare workers for advancement; the methods of training, remembering that bad training may give negative results; and the type of training to be undertaken, e.g. whether it will be internal or through outside agencies.

When an organisation is planning its training policy, the costs of various forms of training and the resources that will be allocated must be considered. The place of the training function in the entity's organisational structure will also have to be considered. If there is a training manager or department, it will often come under the personnel department.

The entity may undertake to train skilled craftsmen or professional people if they sign a training contract. The training may be provided within the entity or outside depending upon whether it is worth the organisation developing the skills necessary to do this in-house, or 'on the job'. If it does carry out the training itself, it will be more effective when the various stages of the training can be broken down into small components. Then each of these can be dealt with over a period of time rather than exposing the trainee to everything at once. Sometimes it is both cost-effective and more efficient to let a local college carry out the training, releasing employees to attend their courses. The opportunities an entity provides to employees for training and the help (in the form of release or finance) will have both costs and benefits. When establishing a training policy the organisation will have to weigh both sides of this equation.

Evaluating an employee's training needs

The first point in the evaluation of employees' training requirements is to consider how people will be selected for training. For example, it would clearly be silly to start somebody out on a training programme which would eventually require an ability to distinguish between different colours and to find out later that the person was colour-blind. In this example there should have been a selection procedure to check for colour-blindness.

Often in the large organisation there will be notices of training programmes available to various categories of employees. These will state: what the training entails; how one should apply; what the selection procedures will be; what help will be given to people embarking on such programmes; and what is expected of them.

A systematic approach must be adopted when drawing up an individual's training programme. This should include: a statement of what is to be achieved; the method(s) to be used; the extent of the training; a specification of the programme in broad terms; and (extremely important in gauging the effectiveness of the training) information on how the trainee will be tested during and on completion of the programme.

Controlling and evaluating training
Control over and evaluation of training is important. There are two major costs to training: the disruptive effect on an organisation's work; and the costs of the training itself. It should be expected to recoup these costs through a well-trained labour force. William McGehee and Paul Thayer note: 'Evaluation of training in industry is in much the same category Mark Twain placed the weather. There are frequent references, both oral and written, to the necessity for evaluating training, but little evidence of any serious efforts in this direction.'[14] Nevertheless, some form of cost/benefit analysis could be carried out to show how beneficial proposed training is expected to be, and this should be checked after the event by ascertaining its actual value.

Induction

Whether the entity is large or small, some form of induction for new employees must be undertaken, however rudimentary. For the new employee has to be 'welcomed', and this in itself can have a significant effect on the way he settles down within the organisation. Induction for the new member of staff shows him how his work fits into the concern, what he is expected to do and, if appropriate, he will be introduced to the team that he will work with. This all helps to give his employment a good start by creating an image of a caring yet efficient organisation. Large entities which regularly take on a number of new employees will have a planned induction programme. This will be organised by the personnel department, although it will involve people from the work areas which are to receive the new employees.

An induction programme has a number of objectives. It will introduce the organisation to the new employees, perhaps providing them with a brief history of the entity and its development. Overall policies will be explained and organisational structure will be described, showing how the various components slot in together; the new employees may also be told about the major personalities involved. Special attention will be focused on the areas in which the new employees are going to work. Some of these aspects of induction can be done most effectively by using film or video recordings, touring the premises, or getting people from different areas to deliver brief speeches. The aim with this stage of the induction is to create a favourable impression of the organisation without undue exaggeration.

The entity's personnel policy should be described, with an explanation of the working environment, hours of work, and any rules or regulations that employees will have to follow. Information on any welfare and social facilities should be given, with an opportunity to meet union officials.

Sometimes the large organisation will produce an employee's handbook, which will include the information given at induction. A copy will be given to all new employees to reinforce the information they received, since they are unlikely to remember everything heard during the induction session. (If new editions of the employee's handbook are produced with much revised information, copies should also be given to existing employees.)

The new employee will then be introduced to his work place. He will be shown his working environment and meet the people with whom he is to work, and to whom he is going to report. He will be shown the job that he is expected to do and how this will be done. Any special rules of the area will be explained, especially with regard to safety regulations, and these must be spelt out carefully.

Induction should not aim to present too much information at one time. It is usually beneficial to spread it over a period. As each stage is completed there should be a check that the information has been assimilated, especially important matters like safety regulations. There should also be a post-induction training audit to see what has been remembered and how useful the induction programme has been to the new employee, with the emphasis on how the procedure could be consolidated and improved.

Supervisory training

In Chapter 2 it was seen that one of a supervisor's tasks is to get the best out of the employees he is responsible for. If he is not trained to do this effectively he should not be brought to task if he does not seem to perform as well as expected. The supervisor comes between the worker and the manager, which in itself poses problems for people employed in the supervisory function, and there is always the danger that they will appear to run with the hare and hunt with the hounds.

Great care is needed in the selection of people to move into a supervisory role. As a rule, before a supervisor is appointed he will have been trained in the relevant skills and worked in the area he is going to supervise. This is important, for if he is asked by an operative to help with a problem and he has no idea of what to do, it will inevitably reduce his credibility. In addition, he might be encouraged to study for the Certificate of Supervisory Management. The supervisor's training should help him to develop his powers of communication, since he will have to communicate with both the people he supervises and the management responsible for his area of operation. Supervisors must learn how to give orders without fear or favour, this being one of the ingredients of leadership. They must also know how to instruct other people, for a supervisor will usually have to instruct his staff in some aspects of their work and ensure that any safety regulations are observed.

Management education

The earliest form of 'management development' was with employees working their way up through the organisation. In many family businesses pride was taken in the fact that before a member of the family could take over the firm, he must have worked his way up from the bottom, even to the extent of sweeping the factory floor or cleaning the shop windows. Through this there would have been some job rotation, i.e. the person 'rotating' from one job to another and so gaining experience in most aspects of the enterprise's work, a wider understanding of its problems, and an overview of it if the rotation was sufficiently wide.[15]

If this approach is taken to management development, it is important to make sure that any job held for a brief period is worth while in terms of its contribution to the development of the holder. At the same time, he must be making a valid contribution to the organisation. An extension of this is to give a person with management potential a project to carry out. As well as giving him experience, this will also indicate whether he has management potential.

In the selection of people for management training, an organisation may consider its own employees who have come up from the shop-floor or special intakes of management trainees who, in the large organisation, are likely to be graduates. Management training will aim to give trainees a knowledge of management principles, practices and techniques, as well as the skills to enable them to solve problems and make decisions, and to plan and control, using the latest management techniques available. All in all the managment development programme will affect a broad range of the individual's abilities and behavioural patterns. It may enhance the trainee manager's social skills as well.

There must in addition be continuing training, either to 'top up' existing management skills or to introduce any new developments. Continuing training is also important as the manager moves higher up in the organisation, since it provides him with an insight into the other areas that interface with his own.

In recent years in the United Kingdom, business schools (the most prestigious ones being in London and Manchester) have grown up to provide specialist management education. Management development programmes are usually in the form of lectures or seminars, with the emphasis on contributions from the delegates to the programme. There are thus likely to be role-playing exercises, case studies and business games. T-groups may also be introduced into some management development programmes.[16] Videos are currently felt to be an effective means of conveying information to managers. Distance learning programmes (DLPs) are also used; Open University courses are prime examples of this method. Another development in this field has been the introduction of Computer Based Learning (CBL) techniques, where the teaching material is provided on a computer disc and used interactively; an example is the Plato series, which has management development programmes in such areas as accounting and finance. The advantage of such programmes is that the manager can learn when and where he wants and at his own speed, with the added facility of adequate repetition or revision until competence is achieved.

Manpower planning

Manpower planning is part of an organisation's corporate planning programme. For example, it is important to relate the size of the work-force to any planned expansion or contraction, especially in terms of the number of managers and supervisors needed at any future date. Manpower planning must also consider future staff requirements for office work, even if office services are planned to remain stable in terms of employee numbers. For there will inevitably be some natural wastage as people retire or leave for other reasons, and they will need to be replaced.

Both the quality (skills) of the employees and the quantity needed have to be considered. Skill requirements are always changing; for example, typists are increasingly being replaced by people with word-processing skills. As a result, the quantity of people is likely to be smaller but they will require enhanced skills. This is the sort of change that manpower planning must take on board. Where work is transferred to a more complex method of processing, the people recruited for it will probably need a better education and training in specific skills. The other side to this is that some machinery 'de-skills' work, meaning that it can be carried out using less-qualified personnel – another change which must be kept in view.

Briefly, the steps in manpower planning are to appraise the *current situation* with regard to the organisation's work-force, and to *forecast the future requirements* based on the production, sales and/or administrative objectives of the entity. These two can then be related; areas where change is indicated will be analysed and decisions made to carry it out.

Behavioural aspects of management[17]

The analysis of people's behaviour at work has grown in importance since the 1950s, although it goes back much earlier, with Elton Mayo's Hawthorne experiments probably providing the starting point.[18] Behavioural influences in this context concern people's attitudes towards their employment and the factors that motivate them. It has become increasingly necessary to consider all aspects of motivating an organisation's office employees. The personnel department can advise management on the factors involved and on ways of motivating staff, some of which will become part of the entity's formal policies – for example, where there are monetary rewards based on work performance. These policies will be considered under the headings of promotion, environment and participation, which all affect a person's morale and motivation.

Motivation

The question of what motivates workers has been tackled by a number of people. Perhaps Abraham Maslow, who developed a theory on people's *hierarchy of needs*, is the best-known writer in this field.[19] He claimed that people have a progression of needs, from very low-level needs to much higher aspirations, running on a spectrum from a person's basic needs through safety, social and status to his highest needs, which are associated with self-actualisation.

The *basic* or physiological needs are those for food, clothing and shelter; in the workplace these are fulfilled by the basic wage that the employee receives. The *safety* needs are those that secure the future, such as providing for it by storing food and wealth; in the workplace these would be covered by security of employment and a pension. The *social* needs refer to the need to belong, e.g. to the family or the club; these can be harnessed in the office since employees belong to formal groupings such as those provided by welfare facilities, or to informal groupings of colleagues. The next level, *status and ego*, can also be harnessed in the office, although it has been said that class structure in the United Kingdom can be demotivating. Examples of status would be the job title, a manager with his own office and secretary, or the provision of a company car – the sort of trappings that may cause a person to strive for promotion and/or recognition. The highest-level needs concern *self-actualisation*, which involves creativity; this is more difficult to tap in the workplace, although when a person creates a new office system he is fulfilling this need. Not all employees require or aim to achieve all levels in this hierarchy of needs.

Fredrick Herzberg continues on the same theme in terms of the workplace, saying that people at the lowest level of an organisation are motivated by what he refers to as the hygiene factors, which are related to the job satisfaction they get. For example, a rise in the salary of a person carrying out monotonous work will increase this satisfaction, but only over the short term; the effect of getting more money will soon wear off, with the monotony of the work taking precedence once more.[20] These are only two of the many views on what motivates people in the workplace.

The most obvious thing employees are motivated by is money, but they will also be motivated by such factors as security, status, a sense of belonging, the possibilities of improvement and enhancement, and the opportunities available for variation and self-expression. The mix of these factors and their effect on the motivation of an individual will of course depend upon the make-up of the person. Management must therefore ask whether any of these motivational factors can be harnessed to improve the attitude of workers and thus their productivity. Usually the employee's lower-level needs are adequately covered (if not this will be indicated by high labour turnover ratios), but the higher-level aspirations must also find some degree of fulfilment for the benefit of the organisation.

Incentives, such as opportunities for promotion or to earn more money through bonus or merit rating schemes, probably provide the most important motivational influence on employees, especially since rewards for merit also indicate a recognition of effort. A good work environment can provide additional motivation.

Promotion

Prospects for advancement within the organisation is probably the greatest motivational force that an entity can harness. However, the opportunities for advancement in an office can be rather limited (although in the administrative function as a whole this is not the case). Promotion motivates in a number of ways at the same time. It immediately indicates greater status and more money; for supervisory work or management jobs, it usually brings more varied work, and frequently senior jobs have greater security attached to them. Thus it is important for an organisation to have a clear promotion policy which, as well as providing for succession in the organisation itself, constitutes a great motivating force. A promotion policy should aim to give the people identified as being worthy of advancement gradually increasing responsibility rather than big jumps.

An organisation's promotion policy must take into account the balance between internal promotion and external recruitment to senior posts. It must also ensure that there are equal opportunities for promotion within the entity's various areas; introducing an assessment system to identify potential supervisors and managers can help here. Consideration should be given to whether the policy could be linked to education and training. In all this it should be seen that internal promotion is by merit – although many unions prefer it to be through seniority, on the grounds that this clearly provides an objective way of identifying people for promotion. Seniority also means experience, and people tend to prefer those who are older than themselves as managers since a younger person managing an older one may reflect on the ability – or lack of it – of the elder.

The advantages of internal promotion, apart from the motivational influence, include: familiarity with the strengths and weaknesses of employees; better morale within the organisation; recognition of the service of the person promoted; and increased loyalty to the entity – which should reduce staff turnover, especially among the more able employees. However, external appointment to senior positions also has its advantages, which include: the injection of new blood into the organisation; the introduction of people with different experiences; it can sometimes mean that the best person is given the job, or at least indicates how people performed at the interview; it avoids training costs, since the organisation from which the new employee comes will have borne these; and when there has been an external appointment to a senior post this can, in a different way, motivate any existing employees in line for promotion to strive even harder.

Environment

The environment as a motivational factor has three aspects. These are; the workplace's environment; welfare facilities as well as other forms of employee welfare; and concern for the health and safety of the employee.

In some organisations a welfare officer will be appointed and will advise management on the development of the entity's welfare facilities. The provision of such facilities will depend upon the resources at the organisation's disposal, the number of people it employs, and whether there is poor morale. The last may show up through absenteeism or a high labour turnover ratio.

Welfare facilities fall into a number of categories. These include: *economic* welfare, which provides pensions, holidays with pay, sickness benefits and medical facilities; *social* welfare, i.e. social clubs and sports facilities, services such as hairdressing and chiropody, and cheap mortgages; and *legal* welfare, which comes through State direction and covers health and safety.

Health and safety

There are certain legal requirements concerning the health and safety of an organisation's employees. Roger Henderson writes, 'The rules and regulations that control our use of office space are so numerous, so complex and so phrased in legalistic jargon that they are difficult to understand even by experienced administrators'. He continues that the Health and Safety At Work Act 1974 does three things: 'It gives greater legal emphasis to accident prevention; it defines accurately the onus of responsibility; and it aims to simplify previous legislation by bringing under authority a wide range of rules and regulations introduced over many decades.'[21]

Nevertheless, even if there were no legislation a good working environment makes economic sense, since a fit work-force is important. Thus the lighting where close eye work is required, proper heating and ventilation, and reasonably clean premises must all be considered. Facilities must also be available for the personal hygiene of employees. Often an organisation will provide some form of medical care for its employees; the large entity may have a sick-room and a resident nurse, perhaps bringing in a dentist and a chiropodist. The mental health of employees must also be considered, especially as stresses continue to increase. Valerie Ridgeway says, 'We hear about stress a great deal these days. Psychologists would say it describes the bodily reactions brought about by a variety of adverse environmental effects. Stressors (the events that cause stress) range from the accumulation of little upsets and hassles that face us daily to major "life events" such as the loss of a loved one'.[22]

Facilities to deal with accidents must be available, with staff trained in first aid procedures and records maintained for any accidents that have taken place.[23] It is important too for an organisation to train staff in the prevention of accidents; apart from any legal obligation to do so, it is a wise step since employees who have had an accident may be away from the workplace for a considerable time. Accidents also affect the morale of other workers, who feel that it might have been they or that management is to blame in failing to take adequate precautions.

A safety committee can be established to look into accident prevention throughout the organisation, and the large entity may have a safety officer. He will advise on the implementation of safety regulations and ensure that staff are instructed in safety matters.

Participation

Chapter 2 discussed some of the human relations aspects of management. Various management traits were dealt with and it was suggested, among other things, that the management style may be autocratic, paternalistic or democratic. Today most organisations feel socially responsible towards their employees. The aim should be to ensure that there is harmony between the owners of the entity and its managers and employees. One of the relatively recent developments in this respect is the recognition that the participation of employees in decision-making within the entity can be beneficial.[24] At one level participation may be through the communication of major plans to the employees and asking their views about them, through the creation of consultative committees, or even by the provision of suggestion boxes.

The organisation can benefit from participation in many ways. Generally, when a person participates he gains greater satisfaction in his work, which in turn improves his morale. It can also harness the creativity of the work-force by tapping their ideas to improve productivity. Successful suggestions can be tied into financial rewards based on the value of the improvement to the organisation, which should encourage even further co-operation.

One way an employee can participate and thereby have some direct control over his time at work is when a system of flexitime is operated. This is where the employee has an agreed number of hours to work each week but some flexibility in his attendance. Most entities have busy periods, say from 10.00 a.m. to 12.00 and from 2.30 to 4.30 p.m.; these periods will be designated as core time, during which all employees must be at their workplaces. Outer limits for attendance will also be established, say between 8.00 a.m. and

6.00 p.m. The employee can then decide upon his own working hours within these parameters and even build up free time, i.e. working additional hours and 'banking' them – although there will be a limit to the amount of free time that can be built up. This free time can then be taken off by prior arrangement with the supervisor. Flexitime provides benefits to both employee and employer. The employee has more control over the actual time at which he works, and through building up free time he can take days off in addition to his holiday entitlement. The employer has a more contented work-force. However, there can be a major disadvantage to the employer if, say, all employees choose to come in early and leave early, or build up a lot of free time and then take many complete days off. This can cause periods when the office is undermanned and/or weaken attendance during the core time. However, when reasonable numbers of employees participate in a scheme of flexitime because they tend to have different working habits, some preferring to start early while others work late, the system is generally beneficial to both sides.

Conclusions

As mentioned at the beginning of this chapter, the people who work in an organisation are its most important and most expensive resource. Therefore management must aim to get the greatest co-operation and benefit from them. Basically this concerns all aspects of the entity's personnel policy. However, in addition to the administrative aspects, ways to encourage and motivate office staff must be considered. Employees must be given opportunities for training and promotion, as well as a good working environment and welfare facilities. Especially important is the need to harness the employee's goodwill and loyalty – which can be done through sensible employment policies.

Questions and discussion problems

1.   (a) Explain what is meant by *labour turnover* in the office, and briefly discuss the benefits to management of a knowledge of *labour turnover ratios*.

      (b) A City firm has a number of similar offices, one of which has a much higher labour turnover than the rest. What could be the reason for this? Selecting two of the possible causes that you have mentioned, explain how their adverse effects could be overcome.

2.   As office work gets more complex it becomes even more important to obtain as good a match as possible between the abilities of an applicant and the job description.

      (a) Produce a job description form for those applying for an office job with which you are familiar.

      (b) Draw up an application form for those applying for the post for which you have written a job description, in order to ensure that as well as collecting basic information about potential employees, their ability to carry out the job can be ascertained.

3.   Write a report to your employer which explains merit rating and describes how it can be administered within an organisation.

4.   A supervisor controls an office in which 30 people work. How would you assess the efficiency of this supervisor?

5.   (a) What is an employment contract?
      (b) Discuss the main elements of an employment contract for office staff.

6.   Write a report to your employer describing the means of training office or administrative personnel that you have found to be the most effective, supported by reasons.

7.   'If an organisation does not maintain training records for individual staff, it does not take training seriously.'
      (a) Discuss this statement with particular attention to the benefits of maintaining such records.
      (b) What information must be maintained on staff training records and how would it be set out for (i) the clerical assistant; and (ii) the office manager?

8.   (a) Design a *training record card* for employees working in an office, with space for details of both their pre- and post-employment education and training. Show clearly the heading for each field and indicate the space you would allocate for the information likely to be contained on the card.
      (b) Discuss briefly the objectives of induction.

9.   Because new employees have joined your organisation in a piecemeal fashion, formal induction courses as such have not been arranged for them. However, because of an expansion programme which will require a large number of trainees in the office services department, in a few weeks' time 15 young people will be joining the staff. Management has decided to organise a two-day induction course for them on their arrival. Produce, in memorandum form, an outline programme for this induction course, based on an organisation with which you are familiar. (NB: Marks will be given for the style of the memorandum.)

10.   Draw up an induction programme for office employees joining a large commercial firm.

11.   Why does the office supervisor need to have a knowledge of the behavioural aspects of management?

12.   (a) Briefly explain what is meant by the term 'employee welfare'.
      (b) In what ways should management consider the welfare of the organisation's office staff?

13.   Fatigue and low morale are two of the major enemies of efficiency in the office. Explain fully the possible causes of *both* fatigue and low

morale, and discuss how they can be eliminated or their adverse effects mitigated.

14. In a medium-sized firm, management relies mainly upon selections from existing office staff to fill higher positions. Discuss the advantages and disadvantages you would expect to find arising from this policy.

15. Current legislation entitles an employee to safeguards and security in employment, and requires an employer to follow health and safety regulations in the workplace. Write a report to management which briefly outlines the legislation in these areas, and explains its purpose and the likely implications for your organisation. Your answers can be related to the regulations in a country of your choice, which should be clearly stated. (NB: Marks will be awarded for the form and style of the report.)

16. 'Participation of office staff in decisions about their work leads either to the development of organisational slack or to people's discontent in their work,' Explain whether you agree or disagree with this statement, and provide reasons for the view that you take.

17. (a) What do you understand by the term 'flexitime'?
    (b) Discuss the benefits of flexitime to both the firm and the employee. In your answer say whether you think that there are any disadvantages associated with its use.

18. In an organisation's office building housing more than 200 people, it has been noticed that absenteeism, especially on Mondays, has been on the increase. Explain how you would develop a system both to report and to deal with absenteeism.

5
Communications

Introduction

Chapter 1 looked at the 'information explosion' of the twentieth century, which has led to an ever-increasing need for information in all sectors of the economy from the government (central and local levels) and the private sector. Although the background of this information revolution was given in the first chapter, where data and information were defined, the book will now turn to aspects such as the classification of information and its communication. In addition to the broad background of these aspects, business documents – including letters, reports and forms – will be discussed, together with 'non-paper' methods of communication.

The characteristics and classification of information

An understanding of the major uses and characteristics of data and information will provide a better grasp of how the means of communicating them have developed. Such an understanding will also help in the analysis of communication problems arising within an organisation, where the chief aim should be to minimise them and to improve the entity's communications system.

Information may be used on a routine or *ad hoc* basis with the purpose of helping in decision-making, planning or control; using a matrix, we then have six broad categories as shown in Fig. 5.1.

Purpose ╲ Uses	Routine	*Ad hoc*
Decision-making		
Planning		
Control		

Fig. 5.1 The six categories of information

The words decision, plan and planning, and control have been defined as follows:

> DECISION. Act of deciding, settlement of an issue, conclusion come to or resolve made; decidedness of mind.[1]
> PLAN; PLANNING. Intention, way of proceeding; arrange beforehand.[2]
> CONTROL. Power of direction and restraining, right of supervision, means of checking or verifying the results.[3]

The routine type of information is that produced on a regular basis, for example for day-to-day control purposes and perhaps to help in decision-making, although at this level it is more likely to involve basic data. The use of routine information will probably come within the ambit of lower-level management and supervisors. *Ad hoc* information will often be for strategic uses and to help in problem solving; it will thus be used more by senior executives and top management.

Whether the information is routine or *ad hoc* it has to be communicated, and communicated in a way which will stimulate the people receiving it to act on the information. Indeed, if the communication of information does not have the potential to motivate its receiver into action of some sort, the question of whether really useful 'information' was communicated needs to be asked. Even a communication which is just for information should cause it to be noted. This potential to evoke response from the receiver indicates that there are motivational aspects to information, i.e. it has potential secondary uses in the development of initiative and job satisfaction.

Information also has a service function. This applies from its use at the lowest levels in the supervisory function to use by the chief executive of the organisation, who will be planning and controlling through the two-way communication of information – downwards and upwards, mainly using the principle of Management by Exception (MbE). Obviously, the information requirements and what is communicated will vary for different departments and levels within any organisation. Nevertheless, the functions and applications of the information communicated will be largely for the same or similar purposes. Therefore information facilitates the achievement of an organisation's strategic and operational objectives through the day-to-day administrative and management procedures necessary to enable the smooth running of an entity or a part of it. The communication function may be formal or informal, and both within and outside the organisation.

Classifying information

Information can be classified into a number of different groups. Within a grouping the classification will be mutually exclusive, i.e. it will fall under only one of the headings within that grouping. However, with classification between groupings there will be no mutual exclusivity: sometimes the same information will be classified differently for different purposes and so may fall into more than one grouping. The groupings into which information can be classified are set out below.

Repetitive or non-repetitive

Whether the information is repetitive or non-repetitive frequently depends on how it is produced and whether its production is on a regular or an *ad hoc* basis. Regularly produced information generally involves routine reporting, where the information is generated at regular intervals usually no more than one year apart. *Ad hoc* information is related to special studies or assignments which either have not been previously undertaken or arise irregularly over the longer term to provide information, usually in a non-repetitive form, to assist management in its decision-making or planning role. Obviously, the dividing line for the classification of some information will depend upon a subjective view of the classifier. And in some cases views about the classification of a certain piece of information may change over time.

Past, current or future

The main use of past information is for control purposes. For forecasts or plans the use of future information will be more appropriate – although the person making the plans is still likely to ask what happened in the past at some time during the analysis. Over time, of course, future sets of information will usually move into the current classification and eventually become past information.

Active or passive

Active information is that which activates the recipient and so causes some action to be taken, whereas with passive information probably the only thing the recipient will do is make a note of it or file it. Even in this case, some activity will have occurred in the decision of whether to note or to retain the information for future reference. One might go so far as to say that the greater the degree of activity generated, the more successful the information and its communication have been.

Internal or external

The internal and external classification of information depends upon whether it is ultimately directed at people within the organisation or towards an outside group, such as a firm's consumers or shareholders, the financial Press, the government, the electorate, and so on. When information is made available to the general public it is said to have been published. Much of the information produced by an entity is likely to fall into both categories.

The same information may have many applications. For example, the information in a routine report provided for control purposes, such as a cash control report, will fall into a number of categories since it will be repetitive, historical and internal at one and the same time. It will also be active because it should cause appropriate control action to be taken by management.

The value of information

One of the most difficult things to assess in relation to information is whether it is sufficiently valuable to justify its collection, processing and communication. Frequently it will be hard to measure the benefits of generating and communicating information. This problem is not peculiar to the information function of an organisation, since it is often difficult to ascertain the value of other service areas. Research and development (R & D), advertising effort, and perhaps even some personnel services such as training are examples of this. Nevertheless, an attempt should be made to appraise the value of any information generated (even if only informally), especially in the case of repetitive information. The cost of generating the information is known or can usually be obtained. However, the value of information cannot always be quantified. In some cases, perhaps with information on the reduction in the number of rejects in production or to help in the control of working capital, its value can indeed be computed. But because of the difficulties associated with information, any work involved in the collection of data, turning it into information and communicating it must be done in the most efficient possible manner consistent with obtaining effective results.

Communication

Communication of information is a two-way process because the communicator can rarely force his communication to be received and so must help motivate the recipient to take heed. Thus the clarity of the communication and sometimes an enthusiasm or flair on the part of the communicator will all help here. Attitudes of mind at both ends become important ingredients. Feedback can also be used to find out whether communications are being received in an acceptable and beneficial way. It will be helpful if the recipients in the communication process have the opportunity to participate in it.

As already noted, business information and its communication have the function of achieving goals by harnessing the abilities and skills of personnel. Unfortunately, problems can arise here, making it necessary to consider the factors which help in the production of effective communications and the methods best suited to particular needs.

Problems in communication

Frequently things go wrong in an organisation because communication between management and employees is poor. An individual will often act in the belief that he has communicated something and becomes annoyed because the recipient acts incorrectly – i.e. not according to the initiator's wishes. If the recipient believed the message to be something quite different and acted in good faith he will perhaps feel wronged, more because of the annoyance of the communicator than anything else. The fault is of course in the inadequacy of the communication which cause the wrong reaction.

Communication problems fall into two main categories: *semantic*[4] problems, which involve words and social mix, especially where specialist terminology or jargon is used by the communicator; and *technical* problems, arising from the medium through which the information is transmitted. Figure 5.2 provides a general representation of communications systems and problem areas.

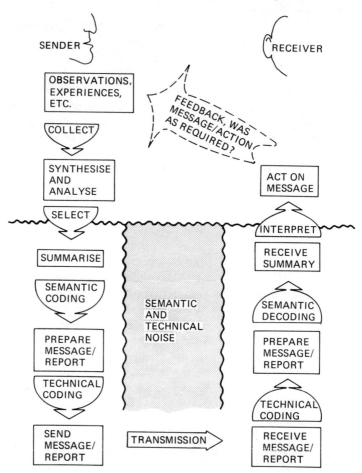

Fig. 5.2 The process of the communication of information and its problem areas

If both the communicator and the recipient are aware of the problem areas likely to arise and focus on their possible adverse effects, it should be possible to mitigate their brake on the system, even if not to completely eliminate the adverse effects. If the likelihood of misunderstandings can be reduced, the maximum possible benefit can be gained from an organisation's communication processes.

Basically Fig. 5.2 can be explained as follows. A person who wishes to communicate information or instructions to another will compile information from his observations and experiences. After having analysed the data and synthesised the information, he will select from this to produce an appropriate summary of the factors he wishes to communicate. This summary will be turned into the written or spoken word, i.e. it will be coded semantically in preparation for transmission. Careful consideration must be given to the most appropriate form of communication, which may be through a written report, a meeting or over the telephone, since this will influence the coding process. The information will then be transmitted and the recipient will receive a summary which he will have to interpret. The sender will expect there to be some congruence between the message sent and what he wanted to be received, and the action taken. How good this process has been will be demonstrated by how closely the recipient acted in relation to the way in which the sender, who had the benefit of the complete information, would have. The sender can use feedback to ascertain how close the actions taken following his communication were to his original intentions.

Obviously, both semantic and technical problems can arise. The former concerns whether the receiver uses and understands the same language as the sender. This does not of course merely arise where either party uses a foreign language; it can also involve the terminology of a trade or profession. When such problems occur it is referred to as *semantic noise*. The other communication problem involves *technical noise*. For example, when a telephone line is bad, one person finds that the number of a third party given over the line turns out to have been received incorrectly. A photocopy which is faint or blurred may cause figures to be misunderstood. Both the sender and the receiver must be aware that problems can arise through semantic and/or technical noise, minimising these possibilities by ensuring that they speak the same 'language' and that the technical means used to relay the message lead to it being clear.

Good communication[5]

When all the people involved in a particular communication process have thought about it carefully, there is likely to be good communication. They should consider Rudyard Kipling's six serving men of communication, namely the why, who, what, when, where and how of the communication.[6]

One major problem, however, is that the communicator will be under work pressures and so may have difficulty in finding sufficient 'thinking time' to enable him to consider his communications carefully; thus he may not make them as clear as he should. Nevertheless, time spent doing this will generally save time and, more important, possible misunderstandings and headaches later on. When thinking out a communication the sender must consider the objectives behind it and remember that communication is a linking process. It joins both the sender's and receiver's minds, and anything that confuses, distorts or makes this linking process fuzzy will have an adverse effect on the communication. Consideration of the following points will be useful. Once the basics have been grasped, it will be seen that they have strong inter-relationships.

Why
Perhaps the most important question to be asked in respect of information gathering and the communication process is one of necessity. As already noted, the communication of information is basically to elicit some sort of response, or provoke action on the part of the recipient. If the response is to be passive the communication may not be necessary, thus saving its costs. It can now be seen how this factor influences or governs the others.

Who
Consideration of who will receive the communication is also extremely important. As noted above, the spoken and written word have little relevance to anyone who does not share the language, a similar situation arising with the use of jargon. The same may apply to a particularly articulate wordsmith trying to communicate with someone with a limited vocabulary. Thus the register (vocabulary, construction and content) adopted for any communication must be the appropriate one to enable the recipient to understand immediately.

What
From the why and the who will come the 'what', for these should influence what it is necessary to communicate. Obviously, the more information communicated the greater will be the cost. These costs do not merely involve the sender's collection and processing costs. The receiver also has to bear the costs of the time needed to process the communication through its assimilation and any ensuing action. Therefore, what is communicated should be kept to a minimum that will allow the 'why' to be achieved.

When
Another important aspect of communication is timing. Generally, timeliness is all-important in the communication process. Information received too late for its purpose will have no value at all.

Where
Where the communication is to take place will depend upon a number of factors. It may be in the office or between offices, and probably will be increasingly between people working from their homes. Today it is also possible to communicate 'on the move' with telephones being installed in cars, trains and aeroplanes.

How

The means of communication will depend upon the previous four factors. For example, two people who do not share a common language may be able to have some elementary form of communication through the use of sign language or drawings. Circumstances will dictate how communications are made. If speed and a hard copy are essential, a telex could be the appropriate form of communication or the telex may be stored on punched tape and transmitted during cheap-rate periods; under different circumstances, a letter may suffice.

Methods of communication

Methods of communication may fall into the basic classifications of being perceived by sight or sound, sometimes referred to as visual or oral/aural communication. From this subclassifications can be made for methods of visual and aural communication. A knowledge and consideration of the methods of communication available will help in the selection of the most advantageous way for a particular purpose. Visual communication can be through the written word as in letters, memorandums, forms and reports or, increasingly, by means of VDUs. Sound communication involves the use of the spoken word, which may be instant or recorded, and other forms such as bleeps or bells. (When the telephone rings or buzzes it provides an initial communication, indicating that somebody wishes to communicate further.) Both visual and aural communication will include words and/or figures, although visual communication has the obvious advantage of being able to provide a conceptual representation of some information in the form of pictures, graphs, charts and so on. Communications can, in addition, take on an extra dimension through the use of mechanical devices such as the telephone or television, or indeed with the increasingly sophisticated electronic devices.

Selection of the method of communication

The selection of the method of communication to be used for a particular purpose will be determined by precedence and specific need. Anthony Cox writes, ' "Effectiveness" of the communications system is as important as "efficiency". One may have the most efficient system or network money can buy but still have ineffective communications. Too many organisations, in fact, fit this profile. To be effective, any technology relies on people to make the best possible use of it'.[7] Therefore careful thought must be given to the most effective way of communicating information, especially the first time a class of information is to be communicated. The factors that have to be considered when selecting the method are outlined below.

Speed

Here, the question to be answered is whether the transmission must be instant or will allow some delay between origination and receipt, and if so how much delay is acceptable? Similarly, after what lapse of time will the information cease to be valid or of use?

Convenience
The question of whether the method of communication used is convenient to both its originator and the user is an important one. Clearly, it is no use sending information on a VHS videotape to a person who has a video recorder which uses the Betamax format, since he will have no facility to see and hear it. Complex data which would be better presented in a tabular form will lose impact and create confusion if embedded in the text of a long letter.

Confidentiality
It is important to know whether the information is confidential or not. Personal details of an employee demand and deserve confidentiality, and should not be sent through the post on a postcard!

Distance
The distance to be covered may limit the methods that can be used. Obviously, it would not be cost-effective to use pneumatic tubes for communications between the branches of an organisation situated in a number of different countries. But it would be as well to weigh cost benefits when urgency needs to be brought into the analysis.

Record
Whether there should be a record of a communication and how long it must be retained generally depend on its significance.

Accuracy
The method of communication will affect its accuracy. For example, messages noted down over the telephone are likely to be less accurate than those received via a telex machine. The visual display of architectural drawings on a TV monitor will be less accurate than the original drawings. Sometimes accuracy will be the ultimate goal in the communication.

Safety
The safety of important documents will require special consideration, and a number of aspects not necessarily related to confidentiality will be involved. For example, if the loss of a document would cause problems it would be prudent to keep a duplicate in a different place.

Personnel
What staff are available to help in the communication processes and their abilities, skills and levels of competence will often influence the choice of the communication method.

Entity
The size of the entity, its organisational structure and its location will influence the methods of communication employed and will determine the resources available for the communication process.

Cost
This is one of the *most important* factors in communication, especially when it is brought into the selection of the most appropriate method where there is a choice of satisfactory ways available, and when related to the benefits expected to accrue from the communication. The benefits expected should more than cover the cost of generating, assimilating, and communicating if it is to be justified. However, since the cost of communicating information is not always immediately apparent, or because the unit cost of the transmission seems small, this is frequently overlooked.

Technical means of communication

It is difficult to classify the technical means of communication as isolated elements, especially since the methods of visual and aural communication tend to be inextricably interwoven. Here they will be discussed together in general terms.

The great advantage of the use of sound to communicate in the form of the spoken word as a direct communication is its immediacy. The direct contact can enable an immediate reiteration of the message or a clarification of any points made through subsequent questioning by the recipient – the response being in 'real time'. This should lead to a greater understanding by the people on both sides of the communication process, who achieve this with the minimum of fuss or delay. A development of this, which enables people using aural communication to be in different locations, is audio-conferencing;[8] where a number of telephones are linked together and those participating hold their conference at a distance. The spoken word is also the natural way for people to communicate, especially when combined with the visual dimension of face-to-face discussion[9] where, through the use of facial expressions, there is an added advantage of being able to convey meanings in a clearer manner. Aural communication can be divided into: face-to-face discussions, meetings, etc.; communication by line through the telephone; the use of waves through radio and television, especially over satellite; and stored oral communication through the use of audio tapes. The major disadvantages of communication by sound arise when it is combined with a mechanical device, especially where long distances are involved and there are technical noise problems. These can limit the ability to communicate effectively using the spoken word. When the spoken word is used on an impersonal basis using some form of technical equipment, it can also have an inhibiting effect; an example of this is the number of people who hang up when they hear a telephone answering machine on the number they have dialled.

Mechanical methods are also used for visual communication. These include various forms of written communication and those used to produce and copy text. The text can be copied using carbon paper, simple duplicators, photocopiers or complex computer-controlling printing equipment.

Telex and television enable transmissions over long distances, which overcomes the problem of communications between people who are at different locations. Communication through closed-circuit television (CCTV) can have a number of advantages. If it is installed where dangerous processes are involved, CCTV enables monitoring with the minimum risk to the controllers. Then there are impersonal devices like the telephone answering machine, as well as cables and telegrams; and document transmission using facsimile equipment referred to as facsimile telegraphy.[10] Electronic mail is another possibility. Barry Goodman writes, 'Electronic mail is an alternative to facsimile, with the advantage of producing quality print at the other end travelling at incredible speed. Data can be transferred from a word-processor or similar terminal via the public telephone network to a compatible terminal at the other end.'[11] Others take the view that facsimile is one component of an electronic mail system, Stephen Connell and Ian Galbraith writing, 'The concept of electronic mail is rapidly gaining acceptance in the business community as an efficient, cost effective communications alternative. Faced with declining mail service, escalating costs and an increasing emphasis on time as a precious business commodity, more and more organisations are investigating electronic mail as a stepping stone to improve office productivity. Not only existing services like telex and facsimile, but such newer technologies as communicating word processors, Teletext or packet-switched networks, can be the building blocks of an electronic mail system.'[12]

The radio bleep system, although offering limited communication facilities, does enable immediate contact to be made and thus triggers off further communication over the telephone between the parties concerned. A development of this form of communication is cellular radio. Its name comes from the division of the country into a number of cells which have a low-power transmitter sited within them to enable a large number of units to be used on a small group of radio frequencies.

There are also pneumatic tubes to enable bulky documents to be transmitted over short distances, the rapid development of courier and messenger services in large towns and cities, and the use of postal services on a national and international basis.

Nevertheless, 'paper' correspondence such as letters, memos, reports or forms is probably the most common type of communication currently used by organisations. This is especially true with the advent of word processors and facsimile transmission. Improved copying facilities enable economies of scale, making their use more attractive. Not surprisingly, all this has added to the sheer weight of paper information generated. Thus the way in which reports are written, statistical information presented and forms designed becomes all-important because it can promote efficiency in the compilation, receipt and comprehension of communication, especially with regard to the time individuals may spend assimilating the mass of documents received.

The organisation of data and information as text

A fundamental concern in any communication by text is how the information is organised, presented and finally communicated. Jonathan Sharpe points out that 'Writing has frequently been described as a craft. In other words, if one is to acquire a reasonable fluency and felicity of expression, it needs to be learnt and developed by continual practice; a truth that applies to those whose task is to compose business letters no less than it does to other forms of authorship.'[13] Elsewhere he writes, 'Any business man who wishes to become proficient in letter writing could do worse than cultivate the habit of reading as widely, though not too indiscriminately, as possible. In time his critical facilities will begin to exert themselves, he will become more selective, and a definable style will begin to take shape in his own writing. Reading and re-reading has an influence on our ability to express ourselves, and it is more subtle than we are sometimes aware.'[14] This section will distinguish between letters and memorandums; in subsequent sections the preparations of reports and forms, and the presentation of statistical data will be dealt with in greater detail.

The letter and the memo both provide a vehicle to communicate information as text. Similarities include the need for clear, simple and concise language, and layout that should enhance readability and comprehension. The major difference between these two forms of written communication is in the purposes to which they are put. As a generalisation, the memo is used for internal communication, whereas the letter is intended for people outside the organisation. Thus the memo tends to be more impersonal than the letter, although there are degrees to this. The level of informality and friendliness depends upon the purpose, who the sender and recipient are, and the relationship between them.

The memo is felt to provide a more efficient and effective method of communication, and will sometimes be written on special 'memo' forms often printed in pads. Where a reply is required the 'ping-pong' memo, so called because it provides space for query and reply on one sheet, is useful. Basically, this is a memo which produces a copy of the information sent and a record of the reply as they are written, perhaps using NCR (no carbon required) paper. The originator keeps the top copy and sends two copies on to the recipient; the latter writes his reply and returns it on the second copy, keeping the third for his records. An example of a predesigned memo form is provided in Fig. 5.3.

```
┌─────────────────────────────────────────────────────────────┐
│                            MEMO                               │
├───────────────────────────────┬───────────────────────────────┤
│ FROM                          │ TO                            │
│ DEPARTMENT                    │ DEPARTMENT                    │
│ SUBJECT                       │ DATE                          │
└───────────────────────────────┴───────────────────────────────┘
```

Fig. 5.3 Internal memo form

The report

The executive or manager, whatever the functional area he operates in, will find that much of his work is influenced by and involves the preparation of reports, both as a recipient and an originator. A person in his role as a recipient of reports must frequently wish that those he has to read were more understandable. Thus there is a need for both clarity and brevity. Obviously, reports should not go to such extremes as to make them useless or ineffective; therefore one of the keys to good report writing is balance.

A written report can be defined as:

> A written method of communicating information to people, or groups of people, from which conclusions or recommendations will either be explicitly expressed or may be implicitly drawn.

This definition brings out three major features of a report:

1.   It is a *communication* between people or groups of people.
2.   It provides *information*, such as past performance, information to help in decision-making, etc., or information required for control, appraisal, comparison or other purposes.
3.   It leads to *conclusions* and/or recommendations.

When the latter are not explicitly stated they will frequently be implied from the way in which the report has been written, as often happens in the case of a control report. The conclusions and/or recommendations may lead to no action being taken, or in some cases to the suggestion that further reports will be required before a decision can be made. Therefore, all reports will be either *active* or *passive*.

The classification of reports

Reports can be classified as *routine* and *special*, with the *technical* report a subclassification of the latter. All of these may be in the form of published or unpublished reports.

The routine report

This is a report which contains information collected on a regular basis. Examples are the collection of statistics for the government or information from the various operating areas or departments within commercial or industrial enterprises, where they may be routine to produce information for production scheduling, progress chasing, sales achieved, cash budgeting purposes, and so on.

One of the difficulties in deciding whether to classify a report as routine concerns its time-scale. For example, a company's annual financial statements must, by law, be produced on a regular basis. But can these really be defined as routine reports?

The special report

The special report is often used at the higher management levels within an entity to communicate detailed information to executives which would otherwise have taken each of them time to obtain. Therefore, within a large organisation special reports will be 'commissioned' by senior management from other staff and these will provide information to help make decisions about complex issues. Examples would be special reports about potential investment in new plant or a marketing campaign.

Frequently, special reports will be commissioned by the government. At the highest level such reports in the United Kingdom will concern the establishment of a Royal Commission to look at some complex legal, economic or social matter, and detailed investigations will take place with the collection of appropriate statistics and information. The opinions of experts in the field will be sought and interested parties and pressure groups consulted. The findings will be compiled in the form of a special report, which will be used by the government to help decide what action is to be taken.

The technical report

The technical report could fall into the category of a routine or a special report, with the latter sometimes being published. The name 'technical' merely indicates that the subject matter and the information included in the report are of a technical nature.

The published report

Published reports can be of either a routine or a special nature. Reports are published by many bodies, including: the government; trade unions; political parties; trade associations; consumer associations; and dozens of other economic, political, legal and social organisations. The published reports that most people will come into contact with are those produced by the government, including White, Blue and Green Papers and routine statistical reports such as census; and the annual reports and financial statements published by public limited companies (PLC). The fact that such reports are published and therefore of wider circulation distinguishes them from unpublished ones. However, 'published' does not necessarily mean that the report has been printed in a glossy format; publication is rather defined as having been made available to the general public.

Reports in communication

Reports provide both an important source of information and a method for communicating it, and their usefulness to the manager cannot be overstressed. As already noted, business communications, including those via reports, may be sent in a number of directions. These are summarised in Fig. 5.4.

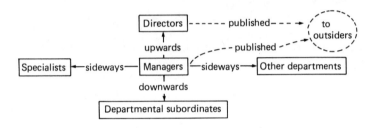

Fig. 5.4 Directions of communication

Fig. 5.5 provides a matrix which indicates the possible classifications of reports and the directions in which they can be used to communicate information.

Direction of communication / Classification of reports	To insiders			To outsiders
	Upwards	Sideways	Downwards	Published
Routine				
Special				
Special (technical)				

Fig. 5.5 Report classification and the directions of communication

Reports are one of the most important lubricants of the management system through their provision of information to decision-makers. But, as with a mechanical system, it is important to be careful in the choice of lubricant, making sure that the one used is the best for the purpose.

Report writing

The same basic principles can be applied to the compilation of all types of written reports. Although these principles will be discussed here, some additional points on the routine and the special report will be considered later in the chapter. Two basic factors to bear in mind when writing a report are the cost and the timeliness of their production; both affect the amount of information contained in a report. It is also important to ask whom the report is being prepared for and for what purpose it is to be used. Whether the communication is to go *upwards*, *downwards* or in a *sideways* direction, or some combination of these, may have a bearing on the style and the content of the report. However, as in all forms of communication the most important principle is why the report is required – and whether it is really necessary. Some essentials of report writing have been developed and should be applied when reports are compiled and written. The most significant of these are set out below.

Objectivity

Only data which are objective should be used to compile a report, although it is inevitable that any conclusions drawn from the data will be affected by the writer's own views and by the amount of information and the manner in which it is presented.

Language

The language or register used to write a report should be appropriate to its potential readers. Jargon and technical terms should therefore be avoided if at all possible. If they must be used they should be explained, or at least defined, in a language that all readers of the report will understand.

Simplicity and clarity

One objective of report writing should be to present the report in the simplest possible way and not aim to impress readers by including every detail or with literary flair. An extension of simplicity is clarity, and writers of reports should be clear to themselves as to what message they wish to convey. They must make sure that they write nothing which is ambiguous or likely to be interpreted in a different way to that intended. Uncomplicated, easy-to-read language will best achieve these aims; short sentences, careful punctuation and headings will all help to make a report easier to read and assimilate.

The form and style of reports

The presentation of a report will generally follow certain basic rules, although obviously there will be variations to fit the circumstances. The objective and content of a report will frequently affect the way in which it is presented. The following provides a structure for the presentation of all types of report. The way in which the flesh is put on to this skeleton in routine and special reports will then be discussed.

Title

All reports *must* have a title – even routine reports compiled on standard forms – which should indicate the purpose of the report. If the report is made on a form it may have a reference number which will likely become familiar to users, and thus will probably become the title of the form in general usage.

Originator and reader
The report should clearly state to whom it is addressed and by whom it was compiled.

Date
A report *must* be dated. Time passes quickly and it is difficult to put a date on an old, undated report.

Terms of reference
The terms of reference established for a report should be clearly stated at the outset. These will usually refer to the original instructions authorising the report, the date of which should also be given. Even a routine report on a form will have implicit terms of reference. Sometimes a report will be drawn up by a person on his own initiative. In such cases a statement of the reasons for compiling the report should be given in place of terms of reference.

Arrangement
To ensure that a report provides the maximum impact it should be well presented, and ordered in a logical manner. Like items should be grouped together under appropriate headings wherever possible. Numbered paragraphs will make for easier reference during any discussions or communications on the report. Detailed data are likely to divert the reader's attention from the main purpose of the report, especially statistical information, lists of addresses, etc. These should be included in an appendix, with the advantage of easier reference to any detailed information in the report.

Statistical information
It is often beneficial to illustrate statistical information through the use of visual aids such as graphs, charts and/or diagrams. These help to provide an immediate picture of information in a reader's mind and frequently make it easier for this sort of information to be understood. However, good graphs, charts or diagrams require time and probably some inventiveness to prepare, and so are likely to cost more than information in tabular or written form. As usual, the costs have to be weighed against the benefits expected to ensue. Examples of the use of graphs, charts and diagrams to present statistical information are provided later in the chapter.

Conclusions and/or recommendations
A report should present conclusions, and sometimes recommendations are required. These can be made at either the beginning or the end of the report, or perhaps summarised at the outset. When the last approach is taken, a detailed

discussion of these will also be needed at the end of the report. In many routine reports the recommendations are implicit in the data; in such cases the conclusions will have to be drawn by the reader.

Appraisal of a report
Once a report has been produced its value can be assessed according to whether it is clear, correct, complete yet concise. If it satisfies these four criteria, it should achieve its communication objectives.

The routine report

One of the ways in which a routine report can be produced is by using a standard form. Forms for this should be as simple as is practical, although not to the point of compromising the objectives of the report. Any boxes to be completed should be sufficiently large to contain all the data required, carefully grouped and ordered so at to allow the convenient collection and use of the data.

Figure 5.6 is an example of a routine cash control report. It has been designed as a standard form to enable the easy collection and assimilation of the information needed for cash planning and controlling purposes.

		F/128
CASH CONTROL REPORT		
Department: YARTOFT BRANCH 8 weekly period ending		
	Budgeted	Actual
OPENING BALANCE	1,000	1,021
RECEIPTS		
Cash sales	500	682
Collections from debtors	20,000	22,193
Other	65	65
TOTAL RECEIPTS	20,565	22,940
TOTAL CASH AVAILABLE	21,565	23,961
PAYMENTS		
Cash purchases	100	108
Payments to creditors	10,000	12,619
Wages and salaries	4,500	4,730
Miscellaneous	600	600
TOTAL PAYMENTS	15,200	18,057
CLOSING BALANCE	6,365	5,904
PREPARED BY ——————————— DATE———————		

Fig. 5.6 The cash control report – a routine 'form' report

The special report

Although compilers of special reports should also follow the basic principles of report writing, there are several additional factors to take into consideration. These are as follows.

Selection of the special report writer

The people who are selected to compile special reports must be competent in the following:

1. *Knowledge of the subject area.* A report writer needs sufficient knowledge and awareness of the report's field – for example, of the industry or the operation of the line departments they are to become involved with.
2. *Ability to collect data.* He must be able to collect information, through interviews if necessary, and to translate their observations into words. Sometimes information will be collected at source, or library research may be required. Frequently in the collection of data the compiler of a report will have to gain the co-operation and confidence of the people from whom he is obtaining information, in which case his status will have to be considered.
3. *Analysis and synthesis.* Once material has been collected the report writer must have the ability to carry out some analysis and synthesis of the raw data that have been obtained. This will be particularly true when the study includes a significant volume of material.
4. *Logical and orderly presentation.* The aim of the report writer is to put the data into orderly groupings and to present it in a logical manner. Depending upon the information under scrutiny, he will need the time and ability to do this.
5. *Conclusions and recommendations.* After information has been collected and analysed, the report writer may be required to draw conclusions and make recommendations. He must therefore have the ability to consider a situation and the data and information on it objectively, so that personal feelings, views or preferences do not intrude into his conclusions and/or recommendations. When the report has been compiled he will have to communicate the results to the commissioning authority, bearing in mind that this should stimulate action.

A poorly compiled and written report, even if it contains beneficial conclusions and recommendations, is likely to be ignored, whereas one that has been well written and presented is more likely to stimulate action. Thus it is important to exercise great care in the selection of the reporter.

Preliminaries to the assignment

Attention must be given to a number of points before investigations for material and any other work are carried out on the special report. This is particularly true of the report's *terms of reference*. These should be stated clearly and precisely, preferably in writing. The terms of reference of a special report should include details of the following:

1.   *The compiler.* There should be a statement of *who* is to undertake the assignment. It may be carried out by an individual or a group of people, perhaps set up as an *ad hoc* committee. If a number of people are to be involved, the person who is to act as group leader must be clearly designated.

2.   *The objective.* The *purpose* or the *aim* of the report must be defined. Perhaps the objective is the introduction of new technology, or to provide information to help management make a decision or solve a problem. If the reason for the report is clearly stated in its terms of reference, there will be no ambiguity as to its objective.

3.   *Constraints and parameters.* The parameters of a report will *define the limits of the investigation* and the areas to be affected by recommendations made. People preparing a special report should not become side-tracked. If they come across areas which are outside the boundaries but feel that reporting these would be beneficial, they should suggest consideration at a later date.

4.   *Timing.* The *completion date* for the report should be stated in its terms of reference. Otherwise, the area of investigation might be expanded indefinitely and thus extend the time of completion. There has to be a trade-off between the detail required in a report and the time allowed for its completion. The longer the time permitted to carry out an assignment, the more detailed will be the data and information accumulated by the compiler(s). Similarly, the analysis and synthesis of these data will become more intricate and increasingly time-consuming. As a result, the reader will take much longer to assimilate the material. Sometimes complex reports will be required, but frequently in commercial and industrial situations the basic facts will suffice, and these can be collected in less time and at a lower cost. And a special report containing every possible piece of information useful to a decision-maker arriving too late to permit action is much worse than a basic report on time.

5.   *Cost.* The costs of the preparation and use of reports must be appraised with care. They must be weighed against the benefits expected to accrue from the information provided. Once a special report likely to involve a complex assignment has been commissioned, a budget should be drawn up and controlled.

6.   *The user.* The terms of reference for any report should state to whom it is aimed. The users will be responsible for seeing that the report's recommendations are implemented if they agree them, or they may draw their own conclusions as to the appropriate action. Thus a knowledge of the 'audience' to whom the report is addressed, as with

any piece of writing, will have an important bearing on the way in which it is compiled, written and presented.

7.   *Briefing*. The authority commissioning a special report should discuss its terms of reference with and then brief the compiler about what is expected, to ensure that possible ambiguities are ironed out before the work is commenced.

If a number of people are involved in the preparation of the report they in turn should be briefed by the team leader. The objectives of the report must be clearly stated to them. The methods of investigation to be used and the ways in which this will be done must be explained. Finally, working plans need to be established to show who will deal with a particular area, and any critical timings should be highlighted. This should all be written up in the report.

If there is to be discussion with or observation of managers or employees in the area covered by the report, they must also be briefed and told how they will be involved. This should encourage co-operation, which will not only help those involved in the reporting process but will also improve the quality of the information obtained.

Investigation and collection of information
Information must be collected in a logical order. Each stage in its collection should lead on naturally from the previous one. This is particularly important if something has to be available before another stage in the process. As information is collected, related batches must be co-ordinated using an efficient filing and retrieval system.

The team leader must supervise the collection of information and provide advice to members of his team. He should also ensure that the assignment's timetable is adhered to.

Conclusions and/or recommendations
A report's conclusions must be presented in a clear and unambiguous way. Where appropriate, a statement should be given as to how these were reached. If any subjective statements have been made when drawing conclusions, these must be clearly identified. In cases where there are several possible and/or feasible alternatives, they must all be given together with information on their expected outcomes. Ranking can also be used to show which courses of action are likely to be the most beneficial, with the rationale underpinning them provided.

Often in a long report a summary of the conclusions and/or recommendations can be given at the outset. This approach has three benefits: first, it helps the reader of the report to know what to expect; secondly, it provides a convenient reference to the report; and thirdly, it is especially helpful to busy executives who may have time to look only at the report's conclusions and recommendations. However, where the conclusions of a report are given first they may condition the reader's thinking and give him a preconceived idea as to what conclusions should be drawn from the body of information following.

Writing the special report

The basics of report writing apply to the special report. A major aim in presentation should be to activate users. Once the point is reached where the report is to be written up, these stages should be followed:

1. *Analysis and synthesis of data.* As the information is collected it should be carefully recorded and filed under appropriate headings. The aim should be easy retrieval for review and reassessment, especially for the construction of the report. With a special report, the material will likely require one or more revisions before the final copy is produced.

2. *A first draft.* A first draft of the report should be prepared. Even in outline form, it should indicate the form of the final document. In a formal report the language will be in the third person, and reported speech might be used.

3. *Editing and presentation of the final draft.* The first draft will be edited and any necessary alterations made to improve not only order but also content. The final layout of the report must be sharp and attractive. There should be section and paragraph headings, numbered and referenced to help readers. A long report should have a table of contents and perhaps an index to help users find their way in the document. The width of margins and whether the report is to be printed on one or both sides of the paper must be considered, and will partly depend upon whether the users of the report are likely to want to make notes. Finally, any relevant points of 'house style' must be followed.

4. *Duplication/reproduction of the report.* The method of reproducing copies of the report must also be considered. Prestigious documents, e.g. for distribution on a multinational basis to key personnel or for external distribution, may warrant being professionally printed. On the other hand, if distribution is to be limited or only among working colleagues, carbon copies, stencil duplication or photocopies may be adequate. Cost will be an important factor in this decision.

Examples of layout for special reports.

Figure 5.7 provides an example of a short special report produced in the form of a memorandum. It is taken from a report compiled by the training officer of a large department store at the request of his managing director, and concerns the training of the store's department managers.

Figure 5.8 is an example of a framework for a more detailed special report, taken from a report prepared about a scheme for a newspaper cutting file.

Report writing must not be looked upon as a necessary evil, but rather as a useful tool to help management in its communication processes. And the compiler's reputation can be considerably enhanced on the production of a good report.

To: The Managing Director

From: The Store Training Officer

Date: 2nd January 19XX

Subject: REPORT ON THE TRAINING OF DEPARTMENTAL
           MANAGERS

1. Reference your memorandum dated 4th December
    19XX on the above subject.   TERMS OF
                                                         REFERENCE

2. The Departmental Managers' duties are   DEFINITIONS
    clearly defined in Administrative Memorandum
    1432 and Job Description JD/DM/4.

3. At the moment there are no training schemes   INFORMATION
    for either the induction or the continuous
    training of Departmental Managers.

4. A programme of training for Departmental
    Managers should be arranged to include:

    (a) imparting a sound knowledge of goods
         sold by their department;

    (b) providing them with experience in
         related departments;

    (c) the provision of a continuous training
         programme on sales techniques;

    (d)   RECOMMENDATIONS
         enable them to undertake on-the-job
         training of sales assistants;

    (e) training in the administrative
         procedures necessary to enable
         part V of their work, as
         stated in their Job Description
         reference JD/DM/4, to be carried out.

    This training programme should be implemented
    by a combination of: on-the-job training;
    periods in the store's training school; and
    through release to attend courses at the
    local college, as appropriate

Signed   _____
               (Store Training Officer)

Fig. 5.7 An example of the layout of a short special report in memorandum
form

```
Page

Frontsheet    TITLE


1.            TABLE OF CONTENTS


2.            INTRODUCTION
              Including details of terms of reference,
              definitions, etc.

3.            CONCLUSIONS AND/OR RECOMMENDATIONS
              In summary form.

4.            INFORMATION
              Details of methods used, including a
              synthesis of replies to questionnaires
              sent to possible users, etc., and an
              analysis of the findings.

5.            CONCLUSIONS
              Drawn from the information, together with
              outline recommendations.

6.            A SUGGESTED SCHEME
              Including details of location, equipment,
              publications used, indexing system,
              procedure for cutting and filing, use of
              files, security of files, etc.

7.            APPENDIX
              Copies of the questionaire sent out,
              other specimen documents, appropriate
              statistical tables and other information,
              target names and addresses, etc.
```

Fig. 5.8 Framework for a detailed special report

Forms

It has been said that the form provides the foundation of all paper-based recording systems. However, the concept underlying the form can be extended to other methods of records management, including computer-based systems. Forms have the objective of recording information in an orderly manner and communicating it in a way which is easily assimilated.

Today vast quantities information, some vital and some routine, have to be recorded; it is important that this be done in an economical manner, yet in a way which allows efficient retrieval and presentation whenever required. The form used to do this can establish a precedent and a routine to make it easier to add to any existing record. However, the fact that information is recorded by form, on paper or a VDU, inevitably has an influence on the system; thus the effect of using a form must be carefully examined. It is all too easy for forms to proliferate, with a new one added to the range of those available without consideration of whether it is serving a new function or duplicating another. So the form needs to be controlled and monitored. This section will consider the design, production and control of forms.

Principles of form design

There are two main factors to be considered in form design: first, the form must be designed to suit the work, not the other way round; secondly, it should streamline things, providing economy in the collection and use of the information contained on it. Although there are principles of form design, much can be learned about the technique from observation and experience. A number of factors must be borne in mind: the information that is to be recorded; the number of copies required; and the paper that will be used, in terms of size, quality, colour, etc. Other influences on the cost of the form include those of its completion, storage, retrieval, and any other necessary handling. All these factors should in turn be related to the purpose of the form.

Elimination
The first question when a new form is proposed or the design of an existing one is to be reviewed is whether it is really necessary. Perhaps the existing form can be eliminated by combining it with another. It may be possible to reduce the number of forms in existence by consolidating the information from a number of them on to an all-embracing standard form.

Copies
For forms in use, the number of copies made and whether they are all necessary should be appraised.

Size
The size of the form and the number of pages it is to have are important. The production of an entity's forms in standard sizes, and the equipment the form will be used with, e.g. mechanical aids or filing cabinets, should all influence decisions about the appropriate size. It is also important to make sure that the *fields*, i.e. the boxes on the form, provide adequate space for completion.

Handling
How frequently and by what means (i.e. manual or electronic) the form will be handled must be determined. Look at the environment it will be used in. These factors will have a bearing on the type of material the form is to be produced on – whether paper, card, or in electronic form.

Arrangement
The arrangement of the fields on the form is an extremely important

consideration. This must be examined in relation to the easiest way of filling in the form. The order of the fields should help in the completion of the form, perhaps by relating this to other documents as appropriate. It must be remembered that time, a valuable commodity, is necessary to complete a form and has its cost – which will be higher if the form is difficult to complete. In addition, complicated forms may create frustration and anger in their completion.

Simplicity and aesthetic qualities
The form should be both attractive and simple. The type size and face used to produce the form will be important considerations. If it has a pleasing appearance this will have a positive influence on the attitude of the person completing it.

The form's purpose
The form's purpose is of paramount importance. The form must be designed to fulfil this purpose, which is basically the recording of information, sometimes in conjunction with other systems or equipment, in the most economical manner. When considering the purpose of a form, the following questions must be asked:

1. Is the form for internal or external use? If for distribution outside the organisation, considerations of prestige may come into the design and production of the form.
2. Are any legal considerations involved? Sometimes a form has to be completed to provide information required by law.
3. What is the life cycle of an individual form, and how frequently will it be handled?
4. What environment will it be used in? If in a factory it may get dirty and oily; if outside, consideration needs to be given to likely weather conditions. These points affect the selection of the material on which the form will be produced.
5. Does the form have a relationship with other documents? Will it be transcribed from them or its information entered elsewhere? If so, the related documents should be made as compatible as is feasible and have their fields in the same order.

Aspects of using forms
Ease of identification and how entries will be made must also play a role in determining the form's design and production.

Identifying a form
Forms must be easy to identify, especially when an entity uses a large range. The form should have a title – the shorter the better. However, the identification of a form does not necessarily stop there. Identification is sometimes

easier if the form is provided with a reference number, perhaps using a classification code based on a system such as the Dewey decimal system. Often large organisations identify their forms using a code, and indicate the dates when the form was issued, last revised and printed. There should also be a prominent field to enable the identification of a form in a series, e.g. for the name of an employee on a training record form. Sometimes forms will be colour-coded, or identified with large letters, numbers or symbols to help in their initial sort before classification and storage. For other purposes, serial numbers may be better.

Instructions
The layout of the fields should be guided by the rationale behind the form. For example, a form used to collect information from applicants for a job automatically indicates its purpose through its title and from a cursory glance at its fields. If the instructions for the completion of each field can appear in or near the relevant field, it will be helpful to the person completing it. Instructions should, at least, be at the foot of the page or on the page opposite the fields they relate too. If there are many instructions they can be printed on a separate sheet of paper.

Entries
Sufficient space must be provided on a form for the amount of information to be entered. The fields should be grouped into principal sections, with related ones together; bolder typeface is used for section headings. It will help in the completion of a form if there are rulings on it, for example around and within fields to keep entries in line, with vertical lines for columns of information such as figures. Where there are many horizontal lines the fifth one can be made bolder to act as an additional guide to entries and for reading the information.

Some forms have preprinted entries, where the items shown have to be deleted or ticked off. The main methods are to delete some of the alternatives or to tick the appropriate entry. There may also be part-printed entries, e.g. printed but with quantity and price left blank. This is often done when only a few items are sold. If the price to all customers is the same and does not change very often, these can be preprinted as well.

The method of entry will also have to take into account the numbers of copies of the form required, and whether these will be reproduced using manifold, carbon paper, or by photocopying. The colour of the form should not be too deep otherwise the entries may not show up. Certain fields can be accentuated by shading or blocking them to give emphasis to them and their entries; however this process must not obscure the entry itself!

Producing the form

The main considerations in the production of a form are its purpose and cost. Sometimes it may be unnecessary to provide an elaborate form printed on the best-quality paper if a simple duplicated version would suffice. The basic factors to consider are: the paper to be used and if it can be of standard size; size and style of the typeface; method of printing; and last but not least, the cost of reproducing the form.

Materials
When considering the material on which the form is to be produced there may be internal constraints, e.g. the life of the form; the frequency of its use; the environment in which it will be used; how the entries are to be made; and the number of copies required. There may also be external considerations concerning the method of printing to be used, which may be related to the grades and size of paper used; paper can range from very thin paper for airmail use through to heavy card. With some forms, no carbon required (NCR) paper may be used to provide copies automatically.

Type size and face
In the production of a form the typeface and type size used are important considerations. They can enhance the presentation of the form, determine whether it is easily legible, and help in its completion.

Printing
Forms can be produced internally by duplication, photocopying or printing, or externally by employing a printer. The decision of how to produce the form in bulk should be based on how many copies are required and the internal facilities available for their reproduction.

Cost
The costs of the production of a form in bulk are not the only ones to be considered. The major cost will generally be that of completing and using the form. Thus, although printing costs may be reduced by making the form smaller, this could cause an increase in the entry costs. The aim should be to balance the various costs of the production and efficient use of a form.

Steps in the production of a form

The first draft
A first draft of the proposed form should be made after consultation with its compilers and users, taking into account the factors discussed above. Once it has been prepared, the form's overall appearance will be considered and any editing changes made. It is sensible to try the form out with pilot entries, especially if the form is complex, to see whether the fields provide sufficient space for entries and that the completion instructions are clear.

Ordering the form
With the final draft approved, the form can be reproduced in quantity. The

instructions to the printer, whether internal or external, must be made clear and precise. The draft will provide the printer with a visual impression of what is required, especially for field space. The type of paper, ink and typeface must be specified, as well as any special finishing such as folds, punched holes or perforations (or whether the form is to be made up as pads, perforated books or continuous stationery). For a complex form it is sensible to request a proof. However, it must be remembered that changes, other than printer's mistakes, can be costly. So it is essential that the design of the form and the specifications given to the printer are correct in the first place. When using outside printers, an estimate from two or three will ensure a competitive price. Sometimes a form will be designed for ordering other forms and will provide a check-list for the instructions to be given to the printer. If forms are produced regularly this will ensure that nothing is overlooked.

Control of forms

Forms and the records on them have life cycles which must be controlled. If an entity has a form designer he will usually also control the forms used. Even when nobody is employed solely for this purpose, there must be some control mechanism. The life cycle of a form encompasses its design, introduction, any revisions and modifications, and its final redundancy. The objectives of form control are: to classify forms; to control any new issues or changes in existing forms; to control production costs; and to supervise quality and quantity.

The classification of forms
Efficient classification will help the control of forms. Sometimes the classification system will grow up on an *ad hoc* basis, making later modification difficult. Classification should be based on a short title and a reference number. However, the system must, above all, be simple and easy to implement. There can be a primary classification for groupings of forms, e.g. for sales, purchasing, accounts and production, etc., according to the tasks of the organisation. To implement form control it is necessary to obtain a copy of each of the organisation's forms in existence; both a blank and a completed sample should be made available. These should be listed in a 'forms register' with a section for each classification, and with titles, reference numbers, dates of revision, etc., included.

Control over new issues and changes in forms
Once form control has been introduced, any new issues or changes in existing forms must be catalogued. Proposals for new forms should go through the control authority, which is in a better position to determine whether an existing form can do the job required.

Records of forms being planned, in print and in use must be maintained. When changes are made, all copies of the obsolete version must be destroyed together with the obsolete printing plates. New issues should be dated, as should changes.

Cost control

Forms are sometimes produced indiscriminately, with factors such as labour costs, a proportion of overheads, etc., all being overlooked. The production costs of forms should be recorded. If the forms can be produced by either internal or external means, the cost of both must be closely compared. The costs of storage, handling and redundancy also need to be taken into account.

Some firms 'charge out' the costs of forms to users; when revisions are made, blank copies which have become redundant are also charged to the department which asked for the revision, although this residual cost will sometimes be reduced by the value of the paper if it can be used as scrap. The cost of forms to user departments may be controlled as a stationery issue.

Quality control

The form control department should consider the qualitative aspects of the forms produced, including the method of production, quality and thickness of the paper used, and so on. When money is saved by reducing the quality of a form, it is important to be sure that this does not distract from its use. For example, thinner paper may mean that the form will tear more easily and so take longer to run through processing equipment; or it may not last over the record's life cycle.

Quantity control

This concerns the stock control of forms. It involves balancing the length of print runs with the cost of stock holding, with the volume of use and the possibility of obsolescence coming into the analysis. Stock holdings should be based on average consumption of a form, with possibly some minimum stock for contingency purposes. In determining the stock of forms, factors for consideration will be: finance costs and storage space available; avoidance of stock outs, i.e. making sure forms are in stock when required, especially for priority users; economy of print runs (bulk orders should reduce procurement costs); and wastage when out-of-date forms are replaced by new ones.

Introduction of form control

It is often convenient to place forms under the control of the O & M department. However, when form control is initiated the entity's employees should be advised so that when the register of forms is compiled, all forms in use from every part of the enterprise will be included.

The functions of form control can be summarised as follows: producing forms by the most economical means; standardising forms and eliminating unnecessary ones; making sure that forms are well designed and that they fulfil their purpose effectively; ensuring that entries made will be at the lowest cost possible; considering ideas for amendments to forms and the production of new ones; making sure forms go only to authorised users; reviewing forms on the register periodically; specifying the retention period for completed records and the method of their ultimate disposal; and carrying out spot checks to ensure that procedures are followed.

Examples of forms will be found throughout this book, especially in Chapter 4.

Statistical information

The basis of many reports is statistical research, so that a knowledge of the presentation of such information is important. It may be presented as a table of figures; however, this section will deal with the presentation of statistical information in a way that makes it eye-catching. Some people are put off if they have to wade through information in the form of large tables, where they have to try to remember what has gone before while assimilating the next row or column of figures. And it is often difficult to discern patterns from the figures presented in the form of a table. However, if the presentation can be conceptual, perhaps in picture form, the 'pattern' of the statistical information will often stand out. This does not mean that the detail of the figures need to be overlooked. It may be possible to incorporate actual figures on the graph or chart being used; nor does this secondary representation preclude the user from returning to the primary figures to obtain more detail.

The classification of statistics
Statistics can be classified as *descriptive* or *manipulative*. If the man in the street were asked to explain the word 'statistics', it is probable that he would base his definition on the former classification and say that they described things, such as the number of people who live in a country, their average income, how many people own television sets, and so forth. Statistics can also be 'manipulated', i.e. they can be formulated in a way which will help draw conclusions from them. The value of these conclusions will depend upon a number of factors, especially the confidence limits that can be placed upon data, which show the probability of the conclusions being correct. The data collected may concern *primary* or *secondary* data. Primary data are collected for a particular purpose; secondary data will have been collected for another purpose, but subsequently additional uses are discovered.

Uses of statistics
Statistics have many potential uses, but it is not proposed to list them all here. All the functional and service areas of a firm have a use for them at some time or other. In production they can be used to help in quality control, often described as statistical quality control (SQC), and as such they can also be associated with the quality of work carried out in an office. In marketing they

can provide a time series to help make forecasts of sales. They have many uses in the accounting and finance area, e.g. when used to carry out the appraisal of investment possibilities, especially in the form of discounted cash flow (DCF) techniques. In the office they have uses connected with personnel, work throughput, the costing of office work, and so on.

Terms used in statistics

Perhaps more than in most areas, statistics has a language of its own. When a report writer or user finds statistical applications in a report, he must learn the jargon used. While it is not the objective of this section to provide a course on statistics, it would be useful to mention some of the more frequently used terms.

The word 'average' when used in statistics has a specific meaning in a range of definitions. *Simple average* is the summing of a number of items and dividing them by the number of items totalled. In this process equal significance is given to each item in the sample, and even when an item occurs more than once it is only counted once. On the other hand, in finding the *mean* or the *weighted average* of a batch of figures, the importance of each item to the sample is considered. The mode and the median have nothing to do with averages. The *mode* refers to the figure occurring the greatest number of times, whereas the *median* is the number of the middle of the data after ranking in order of magnitude. An extension of the use of the median involves *quartiles*. In a series of figures the upper quartile is the item midway between the median and the highest number in the series, whereas the lower quartile is the one midway between the median and the lowest number. If the series is divided into 100 parts, the value of a one-hundredth part is referred to as the *percentile*.

How far the items spread out from the lowest to the highest number in the series is referred to as the *range* of the readings. How the items in a series are distributed around the mean is referred to as the *dispersion*; and the distribution or deviation around the mean is referred to as the *standard deviation*. If the distribution is *normal*, this means that the statistics produce a 'bell-shaped' pattern. Deviations around median and quartiles can also be found.

Sources of statistics

There are many sources of statistics both within and outside the entity. The external sources are numerous, some statistics being available in published form for general use (e.g. the statistics collected by government agencies). To obtain statistics from other external sources it is sometimes necessary to belong to the body that derived them, as with statistical information compiled by commercial, trade or professional organisations. In some cases the statistics will be confidential and access to them may require some input, as in the case of many Inter Firm Comparison (IFC) schemes.

The presentation of statistics

In the presentation of statistics, as in any other procedure, it is important to select the method best for the purpose. Thus if the various ways to present statistics discussed below are to be used, the questions asked should again be the why, what, where, when and how. Basically, the presentation of statistical information can be classified into presentation using graphs or charts, and the latter may be in either block or pictorial form.

Graphs

Most people are familiar with the use of graphs to present statistical information. The major forms of graphical presentation are: the line graph; the band graph; the distributive graph; the semi-logarithmic graph; and the cumulative percentage frequency curve. Graphs have the advantage of accuracy, but they do not provide as pictorial a representation of the statistics as do some forms of charts, and they are not as easily digestible for those unfamiliar with their plotting and application.

The line graph

This is the most common form of graph. It presents the two variables, the *independent* variable along the base, or horizontal axis, and the *dependent* variable on the vertical axis. The area establishing the parameters of the graph is referred to as *the field*. If more than one graph has fields which use the same scales, their representations of information can be superimposed upon each other, perhaps using different coloured lines or ones which are dotted, broken or with different thicknesses, to permit comparisons.

When establishing the axis for a graph it is important not to give a distorted view through the manipulation of the scales, e.g. by truncating. An example of a line graph showing the annual sales of a motor manufacturer is provided in Fig. 5.9.

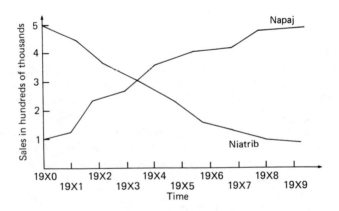

Fig. 5.9 The line graph: sales of cars

The band graph

This provides the components of a table of figures in bands. Thus it represents the *aggregate* of a number of items in a single line on the graph. For example, a time series of the sales achieved for a firm's different product groupings could be shown in this way; or a firm's profits could be shown divided into the amounts being paid to shareholders, retained by the firm, and used in the payment of tax. This approach can be less confusing than having a separate graph for each piece of information since it immediately provides an overall picture. However, it cannot be seen as an accurate representation of specific detail. An example of a band graph showing the division of a company's profits is given in Fig. 5.10.

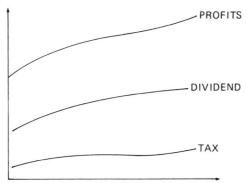

Fig. 5.10 A band graph: the division of a company's profits

The distributive graph

The distribution of statistical information in graphical form can be shown on a distributive graph. An example showing the variance around the standard production costs in the manufacture of calculators is provided in Fig. 5.11.

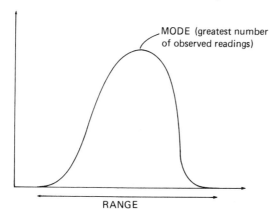

Fig. 5.11 The distributive graph: distribution around the standard cost of producing calculators

The semi-logarithmic graph

This is drawn to overcome the problem of depicting *rates of change* on a graph. Whereas the line graph shows changes in absolute terms, the semi-logarithmic graph provides relative comparisons of the changes that have taken place. Although it retains the dependent variable axis of the line graph, the independent variable is calibrated in logarithmic form. An example shows the effect of this. A firm has been doubling its production every year for a number of years. The line graph would depict this as a steep curve, whereas the semi-logarithmic graph would show it as a straight line which represents the changes more correctly by an equal gradient. Figure 5.12 provides an example of a semi-logarithmic graph depicting rates of change in production over a period.

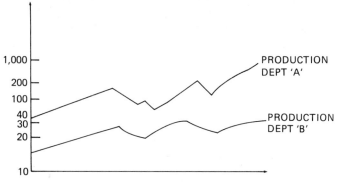

Fig. 5.12 The semi-logarithmic graph: rates of change in production

The cumulative percentage frequency curve

This curve, which is sometimes referred to as the *ogive*, draws out the cumulative position from a set of figures – e.g. for the population's age distribution or for the market share of the firms in an industry. An example of a cumulative frequency curve for the height of a group of adults is shown in Fig. 5.13.

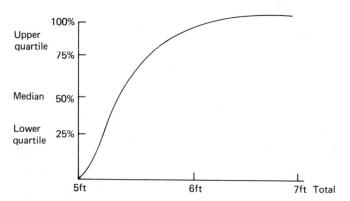

Fig. 5.13 The cumulative frequency curve: heights of adults

Charts

Statistical information may be charted in block form or through a pictorial representation of the statistics. Forms of charts include: the bar chart; the pie chart; the Gannt chart; the Z chart; the pictogram; and the diagram.

The bar chart

This chart uses bars to indicate the frequency of an item. Each bar may be divided up into components, e.g. in the various classifications of manufacturing costs of a product over a number of years, where the bars can be split into their components of labour, material and so on. The bars may be extended vertically or horizontally. There may also be *cumulative bar charts*, which are drawn up to show information on a cumulative basis. Figure 5.14, with upright bars, is the presentation generally found; the less usual presentation, where the chart has it bars extending horizontally, is shown in Fig. 5.15. Both feature sales by product groupings. Figure 5.16 provides an example of a cumulative bar chart with upright bars. This shows how the sales of an organisation build up over the year.

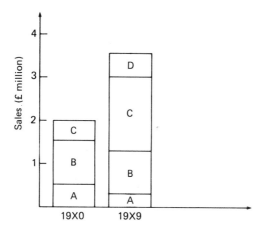

Fig. 5.14 The vertical bar chart: sales by product grouping

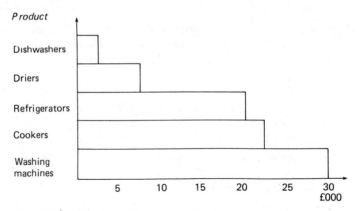

Fig. 5.15 The horizontal bar chart: sales by product grouping

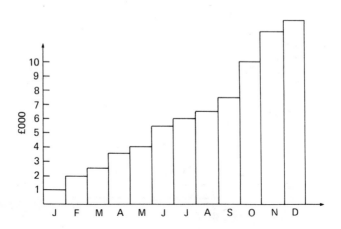

Fig. 5.16 The cumulative bar chart: cumulative sales of X during 19XX

The histogram

This is a special form of bar chart that illustrates frequency distribution. An example would be the 'history' of the population in terms of such things as how many people are to found in defined age bands. As with other bar charts, although its bars may run vertically they can also go horizontally. Figure 5.17 gives an example of a histogram showing the age distribution of a country's female population.

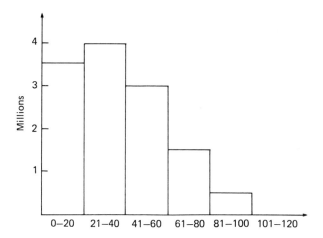

Fig. 5.17 The histogram: females in Exodia by age group at 31 March 19XX

The pie chart

This chart owes its name to its circular representation of information in the form of a pie or cake. Each 'slice' refers to components of the pie. Although the chart relates to a specific period, a number of these charts side by side can show any changes in 'shares' of slices between periods quite dramatically. However, it does not provide a good representation of changes in the whole, although sometimes circles of different sizes are used to represent changes in overall size over a number of periods. This can however, be misleading. An example of a pie chart showing the employment categories in an industry is provided in Fig. 5.18.

The Gannt chart

This chart is widely used by production planners. It represents time as a *constant space*. Differences in the production for a period are shown by lines of lengths based on the production achieved. Thus although the columns on the Gannt chart are of the same width and show the figures for the planned and actual production of the period, in addition, the actual production is represented by a line. Any excess or overplanned production extends on to a new line to emphasise this; shortfalls are also obvious from the fact that the line does not extend across the column. The cumulative figure of actual production is represented by a line as well, with any over- or underproduction to date clearly highlighted if the line either under- or overlaps a period. An example of a Gannt chart is given in Fig. 5.19.

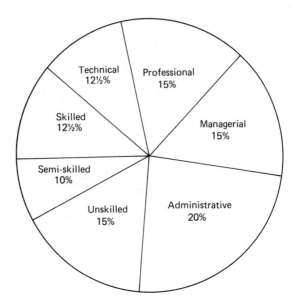

Fig. 5.18 The pie chart: percentages of employment categories in an industry at 31 December 19XX

PERIOD	January	February	March
Planned	1,000	2,000	500
Actual	1,500	1,000	1,000
Monthly actual			
		Jan. Feb.	
Cumulative			

Fig. 5.19 The Gannt chart: used in production planning and control

The Z chart

This chart gets its name from its shape in the form of a Z. It is used to depict current and cumulative figures and the moving annual total (MAT). The current figure comes out more or less horizontal, the cumulative figure runs as a diagonal from left to right, and the moving annual total is also more or less horizontal. Information on the MAT comes from the last reading for the period being considered. For example, when periods of one month are used over a year, the first month of the new period plus the last 11 are used to compute this. The MAT provides a good indication of trends without having to wait for annual figures. An example of a Z chart used to show the sales of a firm is given in Fig. 5.20.

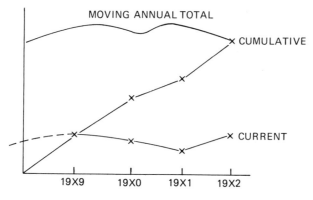

Fig. 5.20 The Z chart: sales over a four-year period

The pictogram

The pictogram is sometimes referred to as an *ideograph*. It represents information through appropriate pictorial symbols. For example, information on the production of motor cars could be depicted by a symbolic representation of cars. However, there is the danger that the size of the pictures may be taken as an indication of the extent of the information, whereas unless very large numbers of a symbol are used it will rarely have any relationship to this. An example of a pictogram showing the sales of knitting yarns over a two-year period is provided in Fig. 5.21.

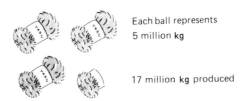

Each ball represents 5 million kg

17 million kg produced

Fig. 5.21 The pictogram: sales of knitting yarns

Diagrams

Diagrams can also be used to depict information. The map is a well-known example of this form of representation. Sometimes the diagram is used to provide a conceptual representation of information, for example the diagrammatic map depicting the London underground railway system. The diagram may also be useful to show relationships between the managers of an organisation, as in the organisational chart (see Chapter 2). The diagram in Fig. 5.22 depicts information about the distances between places in Great Britain in a conceptual way, although the actual mileage is provided to make this factual. Yet the very nature of the method of presentation helps people to assimilate the information, especially whether the places shown lie to the north, south, east or west of one or another city.

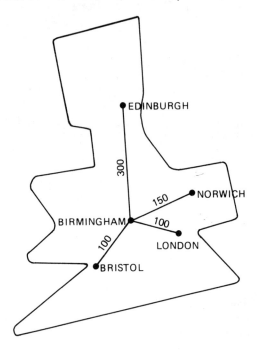

Fig. 5.22 The diagram: location of a firm's depots

Conclusions

Effective communication is crucial to the efficient running of an organisation. The originators, communicators and recipients of information must give careful thought to the overall processes involved. Today's entities depend on information for survival and success; however, the cost of obtaining and transmitting it is usually high. The relevance of the information collected and the way in which it is to be communicated must be examined if an organisation is not to sink under the quantity and cost of generating it. To avoid this, management must be aware of rapid developments to help in the communication process.

A knowledge of the concepts which underlie information and its communication is important to all involved in office work or other forms of administration. This chapter has shown that communication can be in many forms, including visual and aural and by human or mechanical means. In its transmission information can be subject to semantic and technical noise which can distract from the effectiveness of the communication. The written word (although today it may be electronically transmitted) is still the major form of communication, so it is essential to master effective written communications, especially when writing reports. A knowledge of the principles involved will help in the production of sound, informative reports, which will not only make the writer more effective, but will also enhance his potential for advancement within his entity. The way that any statistical information is presented in a report must also be carefully considered.

Finally, the form provides an economical and functional vehicle for collecting and communicating information in many circumstances. Forms are often closely related to office systems, and sometimes the success of the system depends upon the appropriateness of the form and its availability. The form should be designed to fit a system which itself has been designed to carry out some specific task.

Questions and discussion problems

1. Many of the major problems arising in management situations can be traced to poor communication. Analyse the basic principles of good communication and relate these to efficiency in the office.
2. Distinguish between data and information, and discuss how they are dealt with in a management information system.
3. Write a report on how an organisation could get report writers to improve their reports. (NB: Marks will be given for the form and style of the report.)
4. (a) Distinguish between a report, a letter and a memorandum.
   (b) What principles determine the writing of an effective memorandum?
   (c) Draft a brief memorandum to section managers expressing concern about the increase in personal telephone calls made by staff. The memorandum should make recommendations on means of controlling abuse in this area.
5. Discuss the use of forms in the provision of routine reports. Describe the principles of form design.
6. Discuss the problems that are likely to arise if careful attention is not paid to: (a) the instructions; and
   (b) the sequences and fields, in form design.
7. Discuss the advantages of the control of forms, and explain how this can be done.
8. Because of the need to increase the range of forms used in an organisation, you have been recruited to be responsible for them. As your initial task, you are to write a report to the managing director briefing him on the principles of form design. (NB: Marks will be awarded for the form and style of the report.)

9.   What points would you consider in the presentation of statistics in a report so that they would:
      (a) be accurately depicted;
      (b) be visually appealing; and
      (c) highlight any underlying patterns and trends.

10.   Since the late 1970s there has been a growth in the provision of personal messenger services in large cities. Discuss the advantages and disadvantages to an organisation in the use of these. In your answer, bear in mind such factors as the function, size and location of the organisation.

11.   Postage and telephone charges continue to show marked increases. How could the use of the post and the telephone be contained?

12.   Discuss the various services that an advanced telecommunications network can provide to help in the operation of an office. In your answer explain the advantages and consider any disadvantages which each of the services you cover may have.

13.   'The new communications suppliers can deliver much more than just quicker or cheaper versions of established services. They can provide managers with the means of transforming how they do business – provided those managers have an understanding of the new offerings, and the will to accept them.' From 'Telecommunications: Liberalisation of Managers' by Sandy Skinner, *Administrator*, March 1984.
      Discuss the major transformations which have taken place in the telecommunications industry in recent years, and relate these developments to communications between offices.

14.   'Videotex – in Britain – is the generic term to describe television text systems, whether they are transmitted as part of the broadcasting service (viz. Teletext) or relayed by wire – effectively connecting the viewer to a distant computer.' From 'Cheap and Friendly', *Administrator*, October 1984.
      Required:
      (a) A detailed explanation of the function of Teletext;
      (b) A discussion of the possible uses of video text in the office and the benefits that such systems can provide in the execution of office work.

Note: Questions from other areas will frequently be found to be on the lines of 'Write your answer in the form of a report', stating that marks will be awarded for the report style of the answer. It is important to carry out these instructions if the marks for the report style are to be gained. For example, see the following questions in other chapters: Chapter 4, questions 9 and 15; Chapter 6, questions 3 and 9.

6
Control of office activities

Introduction

The control of office work has many aspects. Some concern the speed at which the work is done, the quality of the work produced and the cost of the work. To an extent, effectiveness in these respects will depend upon how efficient the supervision of processing is. The overall costs incurred in running an office are one aspect of financial control, and the office manager's role here generally involves budgeting. In addition, he will usually have responsibility for his office's petty cash. Another function in the office is related to insurance, and the office manager needs to be familiar with its basic principles. When a new aspect of work is allocated, the office manager must be able to look ahead and determine the best way of performing it and, after carefully examining the possibilities, to plan how the processing will be done. Control charts can be used to show how either the proposed or the existing flow of processing does, or could, take place. An attempt can then be made to measure the clerical work. This may be done for a number of reasons, among them to help introduce a merit rating scheme to motivate the entity's employees.

An important consideration in the office when new work is to be introduced or the methods of processing for existing work are to be changed is planning, especially for staffing. This means either obtaining suitable staff and training them in the appropriate skills, or considering the best way to gain the acceptance of existing staff for the new work or methods and arranging any necessary retraining. One important aspect in the introduction of any new procedures is a follow-up to see whether the new system or methods are working as proposed and whether the results are as effective as was first envisaged.

The all-important service of Organisation and Methods (O & M) provides benefits in this respect, and its use to improve methods of processing office work must be considered. Thus a knowledge of the techniques of O & M, how these are applied, and their benefits will be valuable to anyone who manages an office. An appraisal of the efficiency and effectiveness of the processing of office work should include an office audit, one aspect of a management audit. This chapter will deal with all these aspects of the control of office activities.

The control and quality of office work

As already noted, the office manager, supported by supervisors, is responsible for the control of office work. This is sometimes referred to as the inspection function. There are five aspects to this: whether adequate information has been supplied by the person who commissioned the work; whether the person undertaking the work has made an accurate judgement about what is expected in the final result; and following from these, accuracy, appearance and timeliness in production of the work.

The adequacy of instructions
When work is distributed to the person allocated to deal with it, there may be either too many or too few instructions about what is expected from him; both can have an adverse effect on the final product. Too many instructions may mean that irrelevancies are explained, which may confuse the issue or make the worker think that the supervisor is patronising him, especially if he is experienced. But too few instructions may mean that the work produced will be incorrect, or that the person carrying it out will have to ask repeatedly for more information about what is required. This can make the worker look incompetent when in fact it is the lack of instruction that is at fault. Rules must be followed by a supervisor when allocating work. He must consider the overall experience of the staff being allocated the work, whether they have carried out the task previously, and how complex the work is. The supervisor must try to ensure the best match between his staff and the work to be done in his department.

Office work often comes in from source external to the office processing the work, for example where an office service has been centralised. In this situation it is useful for the person requiring the work to complete a simple form indicating whom it is for, detailing any special processing and specifying the completion date.

The operative's judgements
With most clerical work an office worker has to make some judgements about the best way of doing it and about the results expected. When office staff have to make such judgements they must be carefully monitored at first, and even as they gain more experience they will have to be checked at random to ensure that they are maintaining standards and that any judgements made do not conflict with the entity's policies.

Accuracy
Some office work demands complete accuracy while other tasks do not; with

the former, quality control becomes important. However, this will be left to the discussion of errors in office work below.

Appearance

The final appearance of the work should always be appropriate to its purpose. An elaborate appearance is not always necessary and may be costly in relation to the resources used to achieve it, especially in terms of the employee's time. The environment in which the work is carried out and the equipment used to process it can affect appearance. For example, an old photocopier may not produce clean copies; or operatives may have a printer which keeps going wrong, getting ribbon ink on their fingers every time they put it right – with the ink transferred to the paper fed into the machine.

A rule of thumb in the processing of office work is that when neat work has been produced it is more likely to be accurate, since the operator has taken a pride in his work. Where untidy work has been produced, the worker is more likely to be prone to error.

Less care is often needed in the appearance of work for internal consumption than for external. Sometimes work being distributed within an entity, especially if prepared on a regular basis, will benefit from production in a standard format, perhaps using preprinted forms. These may give a rather bland appearance to the work but will ensure that all the information required has been provided. The form also helps the person using the information on it, especially when he can locate its components automatically.

With work produced for external consumption, appearance will be one of the things influencing the image of the entity in the eyes of the outsider. So it can affect an organisation's reputation and the goodwill shown towards it.

If the operative producing the work signs his name to any slips returned to the person who commissioned it, this may encourage him to take a pride in his work since it has his personal tag attached.

Producing the work on time

The timeliness or promptness with which office work is produced can be important. This does not mean that all work will or even should be processed the moment it is received. Some work will be sent along well ahead of time. As noted above, work can be sent for processing with a slip attached giving information about requirements and completion date. If this approach is taken, the office supervisor can fit work into schedules; work that is not urgent can be done during slack periods. Some people commissioning work will be notorious for always wanting it returned 'the previous day'. Work scheduling will be dealt with later in this chapter. The main point here is that work scheduling is one of the functions of the office supervisor, who must ensure that work is completed on time.

The error aspect of quality control in office work

One aspect of the control of the quality of office work relates to errors in processing. G. E. Milward writes:

> Many errors are made for four principal reasons, which are not exclusive types of mistake. In practice all of the following may well be involved: The methods employed are clumsy using operations which are conducive to error, or materials of poor quality. Staff are badly selected or insufficiently trained and instructed. The clerk or machine has failed to carry out instructions, or maintain an expected standard. This failure may itself be caused by a poor working environment. There has been faulty distribution of duties and work.[1]

Errors in office work can be discovered in several ways, e.g. they may be: brought to a firm's attention by a customer; thrown up through some self-checking procedure; discovered during a routine check; found during a spot check; or highlighted during an office work audit.

As with the production of goods in a factory, office work needs a system of *quality control* to ensure that its quality is maintained at the standard required. One aspect involves an analysis of errors to show when and where they came about and, if possible, why and how they occurred. This can be done using an error log or error dockets. These provide a method of recording errors by staff or supervisors which can be analysed periodically.

An analysis of errors will generally indicate that the same sort of error occurs on a regular and perhaps frequent basis. When this is the case steps can be taken to reduce or eliminate it. The error that occurs infrequently is more difficult to eradicate.

One of the major requirements in the design of a system to process office work is that it should be foolproof and minimise the possibility of errors. Another important consideration is that it should be able to highlight areas where possible errors have occurred, for examination and corrective action if appropriate. An example can be found in word-processing software. In the use of Microsoft's WORD there is a spelling check which looks for possible spelling errors in a document.

However, it is not always possible to introduce a system to discipline the way work is carried out and help avoid the occurrence of errors. It therefore becomes necessary to develop procedures to check for and correct errors. For example, after a document has been written, someone other than its writer can check it before finalisation; or where calculations have been made by one person, another should check these for accuracy. The amount of effort to be spent checking for errors will to some extent depend upon the likely effect of the error. For example, a spelling error in an internally distributed document may raise a smile but probably nothing more, whereas if the text were sent outside the entity this may influence the recipient's opinion of the sender. Or if an unfavourable miscast on an account is not picked up it will lose money. In decisions about the effort to be directed to picking up errors, the cost of the resources involved must be compared with any savings likely to be made through finding and dealing with them. This raises the question of whether the quality control system will pay for itself. A simple example would be where the cash in a department store cash register was a few pence short. The cost of supervisory staff's time in balancing this would more than outweigh the benefits of so doing – although if such discrepancy happened regularly it might indicate that a member of staff was misappropriating funds; such an error would be well worth looking into.

Arithmetical checking can often be carried out by self-balancing through the use of *square balancing*. This lists numerical information on a matrix and provides an automatic check because the balances of the figures on both sides of the square should come to the same amount, for instance where analysis columns are used. (Square balancing will not show up any errors caused through omissions or compensating effects.) Another method of checking figures is to use an adding machine with a listing or tally roll, with one person calling the figures listed back to another. A variant is for the figures to be listed twice by different people; or if only one person is available, he can list the figures twice but in a different order. These methods are referred to as *blind* checking.

Where text is prepared by typewriter or word processor, one operator can *proof-read* the text keyed in by another. Or the proof (the copy of the text) can be returned to the person who originally drafted it for checking or amendments.

Action which can reduce errors

There are several ways of ensuring that errors in the processing of office work are kept to a minimum – remembering that errors come mainly from systems, machinery and people. Badly conceived and inadequately designed processing systems lead to more errors than does the well-designed system. The environment in which the system and the machinery are used can affect the performance of workers and the quality of their work. If equipment is old or poorly maintained it can cause errors. The careful selection of staff will also help to reduce errors. In Chapter 4 it was seen that employees must be matched to the job they are expected to carry out. Once the right staff have been selected they need to be trained. If they are thrown in at the deep end, apart from not doing the work very quickly they are also likely to make errors.

Many errors occur because instructions are ill-conceived, incomplete or not clearly stated. This can be overcome by ensuring that managers and supervisors have been trained to formulate their commands carefully and to communicate them clearly and precisely. Finally, staff can be put into a situation where they are genuinely overworked. To avoid this the supervisor must ensure that employees are only given a volume of work that they can reasonably be expected to complete during their working hours.

Correcting errors

When an office worker makes a certain error for the first time, the initial reaction may be to reprimand him. However, this is only likely to cause ill feeling and will not help either the morale of the person who made the error or their work performance in the future. The other extreme is to ignore the situation, which is no help either. Whatever the error it must be pointed out to the worker who made it, and the reason the error occurred should be established. It is also useful when an error is found not to point it out but to ask the operative to find it. In the process of doing this the operative might discover why it happened and how to avoid making the same mistake again. When an error arises from carelessness the person who made it should be told in no uncertain terms to be more careful in the future. If it came about because of poor supervision, then the supervisor is to blame and the operative should be shown how to correct the error and given the necessary training or instructions to ensure that it is not repeated.

Financial control in the office

Most office managers will be required to have an understanding of financial control. Generally their knowledge need only be basic and limited to control over the office's petty cash and budgeting, especially the cash budget. Although financial control mainly involves ensuring that budgets are followed, it also provides a powerful tool to deter and check fraud in the office. Dr C. A. Horn says that 'The subject of theft by employees is one which receives very little frank discussion'. He continues, 'Prevention is, of course, better than cure. While this may not be entirely possible, sensible policies based on a compromise between the requirements of security and financial accountancy can be effective providing there is obvious equality of treatment and consistently high standards are enforced rather than intermittent purges.'[2]

Petty cash in the office

Offices are often supplied with a float of petty cash so that small payments can be made for urgently needed supplies not available from central stores. The office's petty cash system will usually be an imprest one, where an amount is established for the petty cash float, say £50. Every time money is drawn to make a purchase a receipt must be obtained and the amount written up in a petty cash book. Then, whether at regular intervals or when the amount of cash remaining in the float has fallen below a certain level, the vouchers are listed and returned to the chief cashier or the finance department, and the office is reimbursed with the amount spent – thus taking the float back to its original amount, in this example £50.

It is important that somebody, usually the office manager, be responsible for authorising any expenditure from petty cash and ensure that purchases are supported by vouchers. When a purchase of an unknown amount is to be made, adequate cash will be booked out from the petty cash, with a check after the transaction to ensure that both the voucher and any change are returned. At prescribed intervals, according to the accounting control period used within the entity, the petty cash book will be balanced.

Occasionally the organisation's internal auditors will make spot checks on petty cash to ensure that the vouchers and remaining cash equal the amount originally allocated.

The budget

Budgeting provides a tool to help the office manager plan the expenditure needed to maintain his office. Taking this a step further, budgetary control helps him to see whether the actual expenditure and the budget targets are in line. The stages in the use of these techniques are: to establish a budget, which sets the expenditure limits for the area; to record the actual expenditure made; to compare the two (any differences between the two figures are referred to as variances) and analyse them to monitor performance against the budget; and to take control action where any deviations highlight this necessity. Budgetary control thus allows the technique of Management by Exception to be used, for management will be able to look for any exceptional differences, or variances, between a budget and the performance of an area.

An office budget can be defined as:

> The financial and/or quantitative statement in money terms, prepared and approved prior to a defined period of time, for the expenditure of an office to enable its processing objectives to be achieved during that period.

Budgetary control in the office can be defined as:

> The establishment of an office budget and the continuous comparison of the expenditure targets established with the actual expenditure of the area, ascertaining what, if any, differences there are between the two and, when differences arise, to analyse these and so establish why they occurred and to take necessary and appropriate action to bring the budget and actual expenditure into line in future periods.

The master budget for an entity is the sum of the budgets derived for each of its areas of operation. However, the immediate concern of the office manager will be the budget which covers his area of operation. He should have a say in the establishment of it and ensure that he gets sufficient resources, including staff, to enable him to carry out the work envisaged for his area. Frequently a number of items in an office budget will be dealt with centrally; for example, after discussions with the office manager, senior management is likely to allocate him space with the costs of occupying it allocated to the office expenditure as part of the organisation's overheads. Then a staff establishment will be allocated to the area. Even when resources are allocated to an office manager, e.g. for expenditure on new equipment or supplies, he may still have to go through some central purchasing agency within the entity to order or draw the supplies. In the end, although all offices will have an expenditure budget, generally the only cash actually handled by them will be petty cash, with all other expenditure centralised.

The cash budget

If the office manager is involved in all the cash payments for the resources his area uses, he needs to know about cash budgeting since this is an important tool to help with cash planning and control. The first stage is for the office to be allocated a cash budget showing the amounts involved and the timing of the receipt of this cash, which should be sufficient to deal with the office's needs. It is important to note that in cash budgeting the cash movements will not always follow the pattern of the transactions from which they flow. This is because many transactions take place using credit facilities. For example, stationery may be purchased using account facilities offered by the supplier, who requires payment at the end of the month following purchase. Thus the cash will not be shown as 'flowing out' at the time the goods were acquired but only when payment is made at a later date.

The big advantage of establishing a cash budget is that it enables the office manager to know what resources will be at his disposal and to ensure that the cash inflow in any given period are matched. If his cash budget indicates that there will be some periods ahead when there will be insufficient cash to meet the expenditure envisaged, he can plan action to deal with shortfalls that could otherwise cause embarrassment.

Insurance in the office

Although the office manager is not required to be an expert in the field of insurance in the office, he does need to know about the basic principles of it for this area. Chris Vecchi points out, 'Insurance is something which touches everyone's lives whether at work, at home or at leisure. Whenever trouble strikes such as bad weather, a fire or theft it is to insurance that the businessman and the private householder turn for help.'[3]

Insurance is defined in *Everyman's Dictionary of Economics* as: 'The means by which risks are shared between many people or institutions who face them, so that in the event of a contingency befalling an individual he is compensated for his loss out of the premiums paid by all insured against it'.[4] The major principle underlying insurance is the sharing or pooling of the risk of loss contingent upon loss in an event such as accident or fire. This is why insurance is frequently referred to as one aspect of *risk management*.

A number of entities wishing to guard themselves against the possibility of their offices being destroyed by fire can take out insurance cover related to this risk. The entity or party wishing to cover itself against this possibility is referred to as the *insured*. It will approach an insurance company, called the *insurer*, which will have made statistical calculations as to the likelihood of any offices being burnt down and from this information decide upon the amount that an insured party will have to pay into the insurer's pool of funds for that risk. This amount is called the *premium*, which will be related to the likelihood of a claim being made. Thus where the risk is high, perhaps even indicated because of many past claims, the premium will be high since the pool must be sufficient to cover potential losses. A *proposer*, the person wishing to take out the insurance, will complete a proposal form and if acceptable to the insurer, a contract of insurance (called the *policy*) will be issued. This will show in what respects the insured is covered should the event insured against occur.

There is a distinction between insurance and assurance, as explained by the following extract from *A Handbook of Management*:

> A contract of insurance is one whereby the insurer (generally an insurance company) undertakes in return for a premium to idemnify the insured against the financial consequences of the contingency insured against, up to the maximum amount stated in the insurance policy, whereas the term 'assurance' is sometimes used for those contracts where the contingency (e.g. death) is one that is bound to occur at some time.[5]

Important principles of insurance

As well as the concept underlying insurance discussed above, there are some important principles associated with the operation of insurance. These include: insurable interest; utmost good faith; indemnity and contribution; subordination; and reinsurance.

Insurable interest

This important principle of insurance describes the concept that people can take out insurance only on something in which they have a bona fide interest and where, if a loss does occur, only the person sustaining a financial loss from the event can have it put right by the insurer. This principle is based on the assumption that a person with an interest in something will not want to see it damaged or destroyed. Otherwise people could insure other people's property against fire with the intention of burning it down. This also means that you cannot take out insurance on another person's life except that of a close relative or a business partner in whom there is a close interest; otherwise there might be the temptation to dispose of him. (It is interesting to note that until some 200 years ago in the United Kingdom, when the Life Insurance Act 1774 made it illegal, it was possible for somebody to take out insurance on the lives of public men or even strangers.)

Utmost good faith

This makes it necessary for both parties to an insurance policy, the insurer and the insured, to make a complete and full disclosure of any material facts related to the insurance contract. This is specifically to avoid the possibility of a proposer not disclosing all the material facts about the situation he is trying to insure against, and he is the only one with this knowledge. If one party to the contract does not disclose a material fact then the party who is offended by any such non-disclosure can make the contract voidable. One example would be a life assurance policy where, under a question on the proposal form such as 'Are you in good health?', a proposer omits to inform the insurer that he has recently had a serious illness. If he dies shortly after the contract has been completed and the insurer finds out about this omission, the policy is voidable.

Indemnity and contribution

The major insurance contracts concern *contracts of indemnity*, where the insurer will only make good any loss that the insured has suffered. This principle, like the insurable interest one, is based on the concept that it should not be possible for the insured to make a profit from an insurance contract. Otherwise, there would be a strong motivation to buy an asset, insure it for much more than it was worth, arrange for it to be destroyed and claim the higher value of insurance. The exceptions to this are personal accident insurance and life assurance, since there is no market through which to value loss under each of these.

This brings home the point that it is not sensible to *over-insure* anything, since the insured can gain no benefit and will pay a higher insurance premium than he need. Thus if an office building worth £100,000 is insured against fire for twice this amount and is destroyed, the insurer will pay the insured only an amount which will put him into the same position he was in before the fire occurred, i.e. £100,000. If the insured had insured the building for £100,000 with each of two insurance companies, he could not claim £100,000 from both. If one company had paid him the full amount of the loss, the principle of indemnity would again apply and the other company would not have to pay anything – although usually through a question on the claim form the proposer is asked 'Whether the loss is covered with anybody else as well'; where this is the case, the companies can get together and apportion the payout between them, the principle of *contribution* applying.

The principle of contribution is also applied in cases where the insured is *under-insured*. If a claim is made in such a situation the insured party will usually be recompensed only on the proportion of the loss to that of the value of the property that he insured – since it will be assumed that the insurer was prepared to bear part of the risk. For example, if an office worth £150,000 was insured for only £80,000 and subsequently a fire caused damage to the extent of £75,000, although the insurance was for more than the damage the maximum that the insurers would be likely to pay would be £40,000, since this was the proportion of the damage to the proportion of the total cover held.

Subordination

The indemnity principle states that although a person fully insured against a possible loss is entitled to complete indemnity for any loss suffered, he must not be able to make a profit out of it. Building on this the principle of subordination is brought in, where, if in a loss there are rights against a third party, the insurer is entitled to these. Therefore if an office was destroyed by fire, the insurer would have any rights to the salvage value of equipment or to damages that may be obtainable through suing a third party who may have caused the fire through negligence or arson. Under the principle of subrogation most insurance policies require that the insured add his name and so join in with the insurer to make any claims, perhaps by litigation against the third party.

Reinsurance

This is where the insurer who has given cover for a large amount feels it puts him at too great a risk and asks for the help of another insurer to provide cover for part of the original amount involved – i.e. he reinsures some of the risk with one or more other insurers.

Insurance and the office manager

There are several classifications of insurance related to the office and which can be insured, such as: the staff or visitors to the office having an accident; the theft or burglary of items; and damage in the office caused by fire or other disaster. The entity should also consider taking out loss-of-profits insurance, under which the insurer will pay the normal running expenses of the office which are still incurred while it is out of action after any disaster. For example, if the office is destroyed by fire the insurers will cover staff salaries and any other necessary payments until a return to normal functioning. There is another important aspect to insurance in the office: if valuable records are lost they may have to be recreated, a potentially expensive exercise to carry out, so there may need to be insurance cover for this eventuality. Thus the office manager must make sure that his office is covered against all the likely and even unlikely contingencies.

In a small organisation the office manager may be responsible for all aspects of his organisation's insurance, such as: property and stock insurance; fraud insurance;[6] the insurance of vehicles;[7] accident and private medical insurance for employees; third party claims and other areas; and even insurance against professional negligence.[8]

Many companies have personnel who have to travel overseas in the course of their duties. It is often the responsibility of the office manager to arrange the insurance cover necessary for their trip. This insurance will cover the eventuality of an accident and any related medical expenses, and many other contingencies such as cancellation and curtailment of travel, personal public liability, and loss of baggage.[9]

The investigation of office work

Although the job of investigating office work is one of the functions carried out by O & M personnel, the supervisor of an office also needs to know its objectives, especially in terms of whether work is being done in the most efficient and effective manner. This will help him decide on the scheduling of work and the setting of targets for the individuals under his authority in relation to quality and volume. This in turn can lead to the establishment of performance standards for office work which can be used for merit rating schemes, thus helping to motivate office employees. One of the first steps to be taken when an O & M assignment – or an office audit – is being carried out is to identify and analyse the current methods used to perform the work.

The reasons for investigating office work

There are several reasons why office work should be investigated, and these will be influenced by how long the system or method under scrutiny has been in force. An investigation of office work will show what the elements of the work are; any weaknesses in the way it is being done should then be highlighted. At the same time, the different outputs of operatives for the same kind of work can be noted, and will provide information to help in devising a system of merit payments. An analysis of the work will also give cost information, which will help in estimating the future costs of carrying out some particular clerical function. For a full investigation, several questions must be asked about the work.

Why is the work done?

This is the first and most important question. It asks whether the work is really necessary and how useful it is; also whether it is necessary at its current scale or if there could be some reductions in the level of operations. For work may be overtaken by events, and although a particular function may still be needed, its methods may have become obsolete. Thus the work may no longer be fulfilling a useful purpose or even its original purposes.

If the answer to this question is that the work is in fact necessary, then some subsidiary questions on the what, who, how and where, which are all interwoven, can be tackled.

What work is being done?

This question will have an important influence on who does it, how they do it and where it is done. The concern here is to know what the final output is and for whom it has been completed.

Who does the work?

An early question that needs to be asked is who carries out the processing. For example, are all the elements of a job completed by the same individual or group of people, or do a number of groups contribute towards the completion of a particular task? The answer to the question of who does the work may highlight the fact that it is not being done by the best person for the job. If so, then there will be a need to redeploy staff. The answer to this question may also indicate that when a number of related tasks are being carried out, they would be better grouped together and allocated to a team. The answer might also show that the best work flow is not being employed to facilitate the performance of work.

How is the work done?
This question leads on to whether the methods used for processing are the best possible in terms of cost-effectiveness, the quality of work produced and the speed at which it is completed. The answers may indicate that there are better ways of doing the work.

The location of the work
The question looks at where the work is being carried out. A supplementary question is whether this is the best place in terms of cost, convenience and control. For work located in an office building, the answers could provide some useful information about the flow of work. It may be found that an assignment of work moves from one office to another and then back, whereas a rearrangement of the flow might reduce the extent to which it has to be transferred between locations.

An important point related to this question concerns speculation about the move of office work into the worker's home. The benefit to the commissioning entity is that it reduces occupancy costs. At the same time, there is the disadvantage of less control over work carried out in the home, especially for output targets related to time and the quality of the work. The benefit to the worker is that he does not have to travel to a place of employment and can schedule the work to fit more conveniently with his own time requirements. Today, the answer to this question tends to point to relocation where much clerical work in involved.

The volume and timing of work flows
The volume of work to be done and the time for completion will have a bearing on speed and quality. The location and supervision of the work influence these aspects. Even if the quantity of work cannot be ascertained exactly, management will want a general idea of the volumes, both in relation to the timing of the inflow of work, so that it can be scheduled to meet any output deadlines, and its eventual completion. There may be peaks and troughs in work input either on a short-term basis (daily, weekly or monthly) or over longer cycles (e.g. quarterly or annual). Sometimes the records of previous periods will indicate what the work-load is likely to be for future periods.

To help measure input and output, office work can be divided into basic categories. Work schedules can then be established.

The cost of the work

Finally, the cost of undertaking the work has to be evaluated. In addition to the direct unit cost of doing the work, the indirect or overhead costs must be considered and generally will be allocated to the unit cost of carrying out a particular job. Cost is one of the factors that must be taken into consideration when comparing the different ways in which a particular piece of work can be done, although the final decision will also bring in quality and speed factors.

The relationship of speed and quality

It is important to be aware of the speed at which the work is completed, in terms of both the departments and the individuals doing it. Quality and speed are related: if an office is working at full capacity, corners may be cut as far as quality is concerned in order to achieve the volume of productivity required. Yet these two factors are usually separated out because when there is spare capacity and all the available work has been completed there will be waiting time, which may hide the fact that some employees work faster than others. The speed at which office work is completed can be measured in a number of ways, including: the number of staff employed to ensure that the tasks are completed; the volume of office supplies consumed in a period; the quantity of the finished product, which may or may not bear an exact relationship to the amount of materials consumed; and the cost of carrying the work out, although this measure assumes some relationship between time and money.

Both the quantity of the work produced and the speed at which it is carried out can lead to the establishment of standards for the completion of the work. When using such standards, however, the work environment and the machinery employed, whether modern equipment is available and the calibre of the staff must all be considered.

The time of day and week will also influence the speed at which work is carried out. On a daily basis, the tendency is for work rates to be low when people arrive and until they get into their stride, and then to pick up soon after arrival. However, towards the end of the day things will start to slow down as people become fatigued. On a weekly basis, when employees arrive on a Monday morning they should be fresh; by the time Friday afternoon comes around they may have become jaded and will be looking forward to the weekend's relaxation, so their work performance is likely to drop. Standards will need to be based on some average for these factors.

Methods used in the investigation of clerical work

A number of methods can be used in the investigation of office work. One important consideration is the likely effect on the behaviour of those whose work is under examination. Thus it is important to inform the supervisor and employees of an area of what is to be involved. What should not be done is to investigate the work of an area in secret since this can only produce hostility and raise barriers against the study.

There must be clear terms of reference for the proposed investigation. First it is usual to make a brief survey of the work and then select the best method of investigating and measuring it. Precise boundaries must be established for the assignment. The investigation must also cover all representative time periods associated with peaks of work and where there is slack in the system. The process of the investigation must not disrupt the work or cause workers to perform in an untypical way. The work investigated should be divided into suitable elements which make measurement as easy as possible. It should be followed through from its receipt in the area being studied to its dispatch after completion.

The investigation

Several decisions should be made before an investigation begins, for example about what the tasks are, who is to be responsible for carrying them out, how the investigation is to take place, and how any measurements are to be made.

The people carrying out the investigation can influence the way in which the operatives perform their tasks. The work should be considered in relation to any previous and subsequent tasks to be carried out on the work. For example, the printing of a document will be dependent upon a previous stage, that of preparing the text; similarly, any collating and binding of the reproduced text will be affected by the way in which it is printed. This may highlight the fact that more of the work would be better carried out in the same area, using the same staff to see through a series of related tasks.

The measurements of the work will be based on some concept of average. During the investigation, therefore, average situations must be measured (although this is not always possible); the value of the averages selected can affect the final results. For example, are they weighted to take into account work done by either good or poor performers, or whether workers observed were at the median, the upper or the lower quartile? Thus it is important for the staff measured to be representative, for if the final results are not based on representative samples this will cast doubt on the value of the investigation. An example of the misuse of average would be if the work of the reception area of a holiday camp in the British Isles were investigated during the peak holiday month of August, with the results multiplied by 12 to indicate the annual work-load of that department.

When jobs are broken down into their components and the times that it takes different people to do each of these measured, it is important to note that the summation does not necessarily give an indication of the time that the whole task will take. It is also important to make sure that when the investigation takes place, the situation under scrutiny is not unduly influenced by the presence of the investigator, thus making the situation somewhat artificial. For example, the supervisor who knows that an investigation is about to take place at a time when the work flow into his area is slack may hold back work to ensure that there is a steady flow for this period of the investigation. He may also discourage visitors to the office during the investigation because they interrupt the work; yet normal visitors will have an important influence on the work throughput.

Two large behavioural problems are likely to arise during the investigation of office work. The staff of the area being investigated may work that little bit harder during it, yet they would be unable to keep up this performance for any length of time; or if they feel higher standards may be set in the future based on their study performance, they may slow things down. This is why it is extremely important to communicate the reasons behind the investigation to the staff of the area and explain that they must operate normally throughout it.

Sampling techniques used in the measurement of office work

In the measurement of any work it is usually impossible to measure the complete volume of it, so the investigator must resort to the use of sampling techniques. There is a clear distinction between sampling and approximation, and it is important to bear this in mind. *Sampling* is a statistical technique in which one or a few items are selected as being representative of the group as a whole, referred to in the jargon of statistics as the world or the universe – which must have been carefully selected without bias. An *approximation* is quite different; it usually involves the rounding off of numbers into a figure which is easier to deal with and so saves time when making calculations. For example, an approximation could be used when counting the number of words in a piece of text by finding out how many words there were to, say, ten centimetres of a page of text and multiplying the count by the number of centimetres or pages of work.

There are problems in the application of sampling techniques to clerical work measurement, the main one being the difficulty of obtaining representative samples. Another is that if employees find out they are part of a sample, they are likely to work differently from normal. The main form of sampling used in clerical work measurement is *activity sampling*. Here it is useful to test the results from the sample for some obvious aspect of the work, the results for which are known for the group as a whole.

Samples must be selected on a *random* basis and made as representative as possible in terms of the time period and the operative chosen. Staff should not know when the selection of the sample is to be made; and when it is to be made, if conditions appear significantly different from normal the choice should be postponed – for example, if a number of staff were away through a flu epidemic or during a holiday period.

The use of control charts to appraise office work flow

One of the methods used to help in an analysis of office work is charting. This is not a measurement technique; rather it shows the processes of the work and the order in which they are carried out. There are several ways of charting office work, including the use of specimen charts, procedural charts, flow charts and diagrams. Normally the charts of office work use standard symbols to indicate the major operations involved; this allows the individual familiar with them to see at a glance what work is involved. An example of the type of symbols used to chart office work is provided in Fig. 6.1.

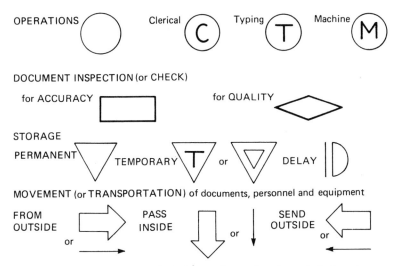

Fig. 6.1 Examples of symbols that can be used to chart clerical work

Specimen charts
The specimen chart is not really a chart but a collection of the documents associated with the work being investigated – hence its name from these 'specimens', which may be papers, forms, etc., gathered up in the order used. These are displayed on a specimen chart, usually a pin-board which is sufficently large to take the documents and any notes on their completion in the order they are used. Sometimes string will be attached to indicate the flow of the work. It is useful to produce two batches of these specimen documents, one blank and the other showing a sample of completed work. An example of a specimen chart prepared to show the documents associated with a sales enquiry is given in Fig. 6.2.

This specimen chart can be described as follows: 1 indicates the receipt of an enquiry by the post room, which may have been in the form of a letter; 2 indicates that the sales office will prepare a typed reply and produce one copy of this; 3 indicates the customer's original letter, together with the copy of the reply filed by the sales office; 4 shows the reply sent by the post room to the customer.

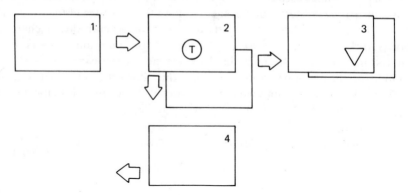

Fig. 6.2 Specimen chart for a sales enquiry

Procedural charts
As the name of this technique implies, the procedures involved in the work are charted. This goes further than merely producing another job description for the work. It is charted on a special form using standard symbols to indicate the tasks involved at each stage. This allows the person familiar with them to see the number of tasks involved, whether they be procedures or movements of documents, at a glance. The major advantage of this approach is that it emphasises any possible omissions in the recording of the work and also highlights any unnecessary tasks being performed. An example of a procedural chart is provided in Fig. 6.3.

Flow charts
The flow chart is the most common method of charting office work. Flow charts come in a number of guises, including outline process, flow process and multiple activity charts. However, they will be discussed in general terms here.

The approach taken in the flow charting of office work, again using symbols, is to show the processes involved and the movement of documents at a glance. Stages of the work are charted in the order that they are performed so that the stage of completion is demonstrated. Often an outline chart will be produced as a first step in the process to provide a general overview of the total work scheme. This is then developed into a comprehensive flow chart to show all the activities performed in further detail. An example of such a chart, showing how a sales enquiry received from a customer is displayed, is given in Fig. 6.4.

Diagrams
Diagrams may be produced to show the way in which office work is processed. Used to measure linear work flows, they are sometimes referred to as *flow* or

METHOD ANALYSIS FORM		
DEPARTMENT: *SALES OFFICE*	PROCEDURE FOR: *ANSWERING CUSTOMERS ENQUIRY*	
DOCUMENT/FORM USED: *LETTER IN REPLY ENVELOPE*	ASSOCIATED WORK/DOCUMENTS: *CUSTOMER'S ENQUIRY*	
SYMBOL	OPERATION DESCRIPTION	TIME PER:
⇨	Post Room receives customer's enquiry	
⇩	Sales Office	
Ⓒ	Insert typing & copy paper with carbon	
Ⓣ	Type reply	
Ⓒ	Staple carbon copy to customer's enquiry	
⇩	Copy to Sales Office Files	
▽	Copy and Enquiry	
Ⓒ	Insert envelope into Typewriter	
Ⓣ	Type envelope	
Ⓒ	Insert reply in envelope & seal	
⇩	Reply to Post Room	
⇦	Post to customer	
DATE: 24/2/71	ANALYSIS CARRIED OUT BY: *wffHarvey*	

Fig. 6.3 Method procedure chart for a sales enquiry

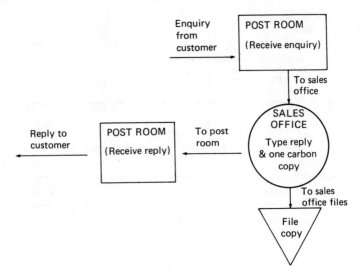

Fig. 6.4 Flow chart for a sales enquiry

string diagrams. These are useful in depicting the location of work and the flow of work between locations. They usually represent the work area on a diagram which has been drawn to scale. Symbols can be used to show the processing points, with arrows or pieces of string to show the directions in which the work actually moves. When a scale diagram is involved, the advantage of using string is that it allows some measurement of the distances the work has to travel between stages. Different-coloured string can be used to examine the possible effects on the processing of rerouting the work. Different colours can also be used to represent the various types of work, or work which comes from different sources outside the office. Thus a conceptual picture of what is involved is built up. Figure 6.5 shows a flow diagram, which again uses the customer sales enquiry as an example.

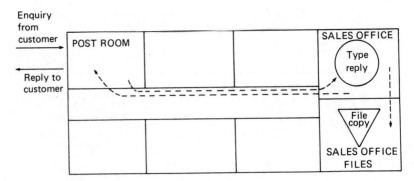

Fig. 6.5 Flow diagram for a sales enquiry

A comparison of the approaches using the specimen chart, the procedural chart, the flow chart and the flow diagram for a sales enquiry can now be made.

Methods of measuring clerical work[10]

There are five major methods that can be used in work measurement. These are: by the observation of the operator; through the amount of work allocated; through the amount of material consumed; from the money value of the work produced; or by asking the operator. However, before using any of these, the job description and any charts or manuals showing how the work is carried out should be obtained and examined.

Observation

Probably the most obvious method of finding out what is involved in office work is to watch what the workers do. The great disadvantage of this approach, already mentioned, is that the behaviour of the operative may not be normal once he realises he is being observed. This requires great skill on the part of the person making the observations. The investigator must explain frankly to the operative what is involved in the investigation and how important it is for the routine observed to follow the normal pattern.

The observer must be familiar with the nature of the job before starting to consider the people doing it. This does not necessarily mean he has to become an expert in the work but he must, at the very least, know what it involves and what is required. He must also become known among the workers before starting to make measurements for his analysis; this can be done by having a few dry runs without the workers realising that this is the case. The observer must also learn to gauge whether things are proceeding normally at the workplace, whether undue influences are at work, or even when workers are genuinely having a bad day. Forms or log sheets may be used to record this type of observation.

The allocation of work

This is a simple way of measuring the work that a person does. The investigator finds out how much work is allocated to a worker and, assuming that it is completed in a specific period of time under normal conditions, this automatically provides a measure of the work. The major difficulty occurs when the worker being measured works faster or slower according to what he feels will be most beneficial to him in the outcome of the investigation. The allocation of work to be measured can be in small or large batches and can cover short or long periods. However, with small batches or short periods there is the danger that breaks, which must come into the analysis, will be taken between batches. Also, there can be spurts of activity with short periods which would not be sustained over a longer period. One advantage of this method is that the quality of the work produced can be ascertained through examination after its production.

By materials

The measurement of materials may be through those consumed or those that end up as completed work. The former can be measured either by allocations from the store after adjusting for desk stocks, or by looking at the materials consumed at the workplace. For this method to be successful the units of material must be homogeneous; for example, when work is measured by the number of sheets of paper typed up as letters, there is the assumption that all have about the same number of words. When this is not the case any exceptional items should be withdrawn from the batch and measured separately.

A crude approach to measuring materials that end up as completed work is to use the container measure method. Here the containers have had the volume they will hold measured. For example, it will have been established how many files a full container will hold. Another method is for tickets to be attached to each batch of work and collected to 'measure' each worker's output.

Money value

Office work can be costed out and the result used as a measure of the work completed, although this really means that the other factors have been converted into money terms. An advantage here is that different types of work can be compared because they are all in terms of the same measuring rod – money. However, there is a major problem concerning what is to be included in the money measure. Will it be the cost of the materials used, the worker's salary, something for the use of equipment? And what about the general office and a contribution to the entity's other overheads? Also, should there be a 'profit' element for the value added by the processing? The cash measure can also be applied to cost out an individual job.

One big advantage of a money measure is that it can be compared with the cost of having the same work done by an outside agency. Costing office work also shows the users of the service what it has cost to produce their work. This might surprise them and perhaps make them ask if any economies can be made in their processing requirements. There is often a tendency to ask for a few more photocopies than the exact number required and if the cost is known, the number actually needed might be specified in future, especially where cost is charged to the user.

Costs can also be compared with the benefits gained from the work. For example, the cost of chasing up a small debt where the person who owes the money will never be supplied again may be more that the amount that could be easily recovered. So if the psychological aspect of not wanting somebody to 'get away with it' can be overcome, it might be decided to forget about minor debts.

Using the operator

It is possible to ask the operator to measure his own output by recording the timing of the receipt of the work and noting when it has been completed, perhaps on a special form. This has the advantage of eliminating the observer's physical presence from the workplace and the disadvantage that it can interrupt the operator's work flow since he has to stop and record the information required. This problem can sometimes be overcome by incorporating the measurement in the work itself. For example, if documents are numbered serially it is easy to check how many have been processed in a period. Or the work may be entered as part of the employee's work activity, as in the case of the post room clerk who has to record outgoing mail and so provides an automatic record of the volume of his work.

A refinement of this is to record the work sounds – for example, the number of times a cash register opens. The worker can even be asked to speak a code at crucial points in the work, a process which will cause little disruption to his work. This will be recorded and the codes analysed by the person investigating the work.

The establishment of performance standards

Performance standards are difficult to set for clerical work, yet this should not discourage an attempt to establish them. Work standards include work measurement and the quality of the work, which sometimes must be absolutely accurate but less so at other times.

Timing devices

One aspect of clerical work measurement involves the use of some form of timing device, usually a watch or clock; in some types of work the measurement required is so fine that a stop-watch will be used. However, with most office work the finer divisions of time are not usually appropriate. Time stamps can be used to show when documents are received in an office and when they leave it, or forms can be designed with a field specially created to record progress through the entity; but these generally provide a measure in terms of days rather than minutes or even hours.

Measurements of quantity

The quantity of office work produced can be measured in several ways. This is usually done by making a simple count of the items to be measured, as with the number of copies of a document produced or the number of keystrokes made on the word processor.

Sometimes the count is done automatically using counting devices or through the serial numbering of documents, or where the date stamp for incoming mail also registers the number of times it has been used. Then documents can be batched into groups of a known number with perhaps coloured dividers, or topping and tailing, say, every ten documents.

As noted, work measurement should take place when the office environment and its activities are normal. It should not be done when there has been a breakdown in the central heating, after a peak period of work inflow, or using the expert worker in the field. The standard performance can be set as the time to carry out a task or to process so many units of work. Allowance must be made for any relaxation requirements and other contingencies which might slow things up. The standard eventually established should be that which a reasonably average worker could be expected to achieve. Merit award schemes based on standards could then be implemented.

Scheduling office work

One of the important functions of an office supervisor is to schedule work; the establishment of performance standards can help here. Assuming that the supervisor has an idea of how long it will take for each type of work to be completed and of the resources available, the next stage is to forecast the amount of work expected to come into his area, the timing of its arrival and the time of its completion.

The forecast

The amount of work that flows into an office is usually outside the control of an office manager or supervisor. However, it is possible to look at past work records and extrapolate from these to give some indication of likely future work-loads. If the situation is likely to change, appropriate adjustments can be made. When scheduling the work, adjustments may have to be made for improvements in work systems or upgrading of machinery used to process it.

Past work-loads can be plotted on a graph and linear regression analysis used to extrapolate the expected future situation if circumstances remain constant. However, seasonal trends which create peak-load periods require moving average techniques. Once the office manager has an idea of the expected work-load for his area a budget can be established, especially for the number of staff needed to carry out the work.

Short-term work programming

The forecast for the annual work-load has to be broken down into forecasts for shorter operating periods, e.g. weekly expectations. This can be done using a *work control sheet*. On a sheet such as that illustrated in Fig. 6.6, the work is broken down into smaller units and entered, showing the performance standard in time for each task. The supervisor can then allocate the work to appropriate members of staff. However, there needs to be some flexibility; for if somebody finishes the work allocation faster than expected, it must be possible to make reallocations.

Another use of the work control sheet is to monitor whether the work is proceeding to schedule. Colour coding can be used here, with one colour used for work which is on schedule and others for work which is ahead or behind. The form can also be used to show the times at which the work was completed, thus providing information useful in the future allocation of smaller work.

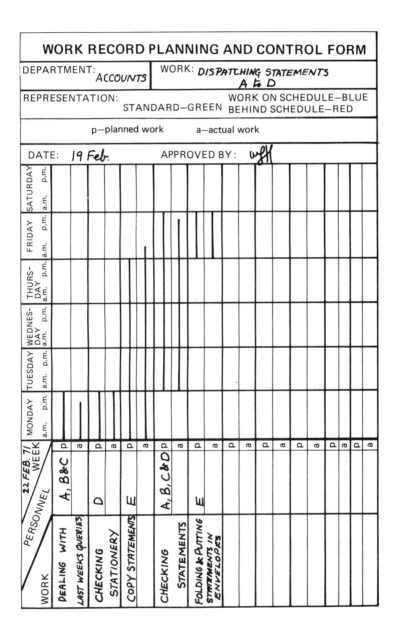

Fig. 6.6 Work record schedule and control form

Organisation and methods

Organisation and Methods (O & M) is an extremely important area in relation to the efficiency of office work. The British Standards Institute defines O & M as: 'A management service – the objective of which is to increase the administrative efficiency of an organisation by improving procedures, methods and systems, communications and control and organisation structure'.[11] *A Handbook of Management* states that O & M may be defined from a technique viewpoint as: 'The application of work study to the detailed administrative, clerical and office operations of an organisation in order to improve the methods and procedures in use'. It continues, 'It is therefore a study of the problems affecting the development, management and operations of offices'.[12] From these definitions it can be seen that O & M covers a wide area.

O & M is a systematic investigation into office work, asking why the work is done, who does what and where, and how it is carried out in the allocation of tasks. All the while the O & M specialist is asking whether there are any better ways of doing the work. From this recommendations will be made to management as to whether the processing should be carried on as before or done in a simpler, more effective way which will reduce its cost.

The organisation and the methods parts of the work continually interact with each other. From the definitions above it can be seen that O & M concerns *work study in the office*. It is not a new development; the concept of bringing experts in to study office procedures with the aim of suggesting improvements was first introduced in the 1920s. However, it was probably only in the 1940s that it gained force in the United Kingdom, used initially by the Civil Service because of the shortage of manpower resulting from the Second World War. It was then generally introduced and entities began to establish special O & M departments. Some small entities carry out O & M, not realising that they do this, when they apply the technique under the heading of *office work simplification* or *clerical method study*. Yet as long as they make a conscious effort to formalise a study of office work, they are effectively operating in the field of O & M.

Some of the techniques used in O & M have already been dealt with under the headings of work measurement and flow charting. Sometimes an entity's form design becomes a branch of the O & M department's work because their techniques can make an important contribution.

This section will deal with a number of aspects of O & M, including: why there has been increasing interest in the technique; whether O & M should be carried out by offices for themselves or whether there should be a special department for the function; in what areas O & M techniques could be applied beneficially; the objectives of O & M; and finally the cost of the function.

Why O & M?

For a number of years there has been increasing interest in the application of O & M, for reasons which include the following:

1. The increasing costs of carrying out office work does not simply mean that the unit costs of office work in entities have increased, but also that more paperwork has been generated in most organisations for the reasons discussed in Chapter 1. Therefore, any means of reducing these costs will be beneficial to the entity. In the case of private-sector firms this will mean higher profits, while public-sector entities will be able to do more with the revenue allocated to them. Such saving may come from increased efficiency or reduced costs, and although these two factors are closely related there is indeed a clear distinction between them.

2. Larger offices have come about through the factors mentioned above. Most organisations are finding that an ever-increasing volume of their resources is spent in the processing of paperwork, and a higher and higher percentage of many organisations' total work-force is employed in this function. Many entities now have hundreds or even thousands of staff to carry out the 'office work' function.

3. The extension of office services has come about for reasons also discussed in Chapter 1. To recap, these include: the general increase in economic activity; reduced spans of control, meaning that more executives make demands on the function; collection of information to help maintain a firm's competitive situation; and often office work is not adequately controlled.

4. The increasingly complex technology used has imposed its cost burdens on the function – in terms of higher capital and maintenance costs, and often because the operators of the new technology require specialist skills and therefore command higher salaries. As a result, getting the most out of the resources budgeted for office systems or simplifying them to help reduce the expenditure on office work becomes important.

In the past the possibilities of greater efficiency and reduced costs were concentrated on the production function, and techniques such as work study and value analysis developed to promote this. So although there had been cost reduction programmes for production for many years, it was not until the 1950s that they were applied to office work in any significant way. Trevor Bentley notes that 'Cost reduction is an attitude of mind which makes everyone conscious of waste and makes them seek ways to eliminate it'. He continues, 'Unfortunately, it is not an attitude of mind that is commonly met, except when people are looking after their own money'.[13] No doubt the fact that in manufacturing industries the units of production were more standardised, whereas in the office they were not, contributed to this delay. Also, since the need for office work had not increased to its current levels and the cost of employing office workers was not great, there was not the dynamics to encourage the development of cost reduction techniques. However, since then the volume of office work has grown dramatically and office staff costs have increased substantially, so that interest in cost reduction was inevitably transferred from production to clerical work. It should be remembered that cost reduction techniques, even in the manufacturing area, did not become sophisticated until quite recently, and ways of looking at the efficiency and effectiveness of office work are improving all the time. At the same time increased standardisation in office work has been achieved, especially with the development and application of the computer and the use of batch processing.

Should there be a separate O & M department?
The O & M function can, as with the office audit, be performed using people employed within the entity or bringing in outsiders. However, with O & M the choice is usually between two groups of insiders, the manager of the office himself or the organisation's own O & M specialists. The size of the entity must be one of the criteria, and with a very small organisation where it is not possible to employ even one O & M specialist, the office manager will have to carry out the role (and will thus require some training). Nevertheless, he is less likely to be impartial or as objective as somebody from outside his office would be. There is also the problem that if the manager of one office is put in charge of the O & M function within an entity, it may be difficult for him to be impartial when applying the function to his own unit. If an O & M department is established, it will more likely be able to carry out the function at arm's length and be objective, especially if its manager is recruited from outside and so has no close relations with anybody inside the organisation as yet. If somebody is newly appointed to the function from outside, he is also able to bring in new ideas and enthusiasm, and since he has no experience of past methods used is not in a strait-jacket.

A separate O & M department will more likely be able to take an overall view of the entity's office work, i.e. to put the work of one area into the context of the organisation as a whole and ask what will be beneficial to the entity rather than what is beneficial to a unit within it. The O & M group will have an input of ideas from elsewhere. It will also gain wide experience of a number of areas within the organisation and so can consider the application of a good idea in one area to another. The major cry from a manager who is asked to try to improve the efficiency in his area is 'I do not have the time for this', what with schedules to meet in completing the work of his department. It is all too easy to be concerned with the pressures of the present rather than the future, which is another disadvantage of using an individual with personal bias. The O & M department is set up especially for this purpose, however, and its time is spent carrying out O & M assignments as its routine work. The members of the department should also bring vision and insight into future plans when considering new processing methods or systems, using a longer time horizon when analysing a particular problem.

One of the major advantages of having a separate O & M group is that it can comprise people who have developed expertise and who can specialise in learning about the latest technology and methods in the processing of office work. Thus the department must allocate some of the members' time to becoming informed about the latest developments, asking manufacturers and suppliers for demonstrations of new equipment and attending office exhibitions and seminars to learn about current trends.

The department will also be able to obtain a working knowledge of the office equipment and machinery used throughout the organisation. All in all, through experience gained members of the O & M department will be better equipped to find solutions to the problems they encounter and to relate a number of feasible alternatives to the office under examination. This is particularly important when no general solution is likely to be applicable and one has to be tailored to suit the circumstances – NOT the work and purpose being made to fit the solution! As a last resort, if the department cannot solve a problem it should know where to go for help.

The O & M specialist should be kept closely informed about the entity's overall policies and objectives, making sure that any new procedures developed do not conflict and are compatible with long-term plans. For example, if O & M knows that there are plans to provide a computer network within the organisation, then when investigating an area with records management problems it should make proposals which will hold things together until computerisation, perhaps designing short-term improvements which will fit in with this.

In most organisations, when changes are made in one area of work there may be a ripple or cascade effect elsewhere. Possible knock-on effects require careful consideration before one section implements changes which, although beneficial to one area, might have costly effects elsewhere. Consultations must take place between areas affected to find out how the original proposals need to be modified so that final suggestions will be beneficial to the organisation as a whole.

Often it will be found that the why of some aspect of office work has not been reviewed for some time. As an outsider the O & M man will more likely be able to perceive what has become irrelevant or no longer has a useful function. Thus O & M would take a cost/benefit approach and would more likely know what benefits any sector of office work gives to the entity as a whole, whereas local departments probably know only the costs of their work, not having assessed its benefits. Another aspect is the behavioural reaction on the part of the recipients of an O & M investigation. The O & M department's members will be trained to deal with this aspect of the work and also to 'sell' the results of the solutions they propose.

Areas where O & M can be applied

This point can be dismissed in one sentence – where there is office work to be done! However, it must be remembered that today this does not simply involve the traditional areas of office work but also the sub-offices that spring up around organisations, such as costing and sales offices. As will be seen later, it is often the senior management of an entity that designates the areas to undergo an O & M survey, although this does not preclude the O & M department from making its own suggestions, especially when these are derived from an investigation which highlighted the need for an investigation in another area.

The main factor in the consideration of areas to undergo an O & M investigation is the potential cost savings. If at any time there are several areas that could be investigated these need to be ranked, not in terms of absolute cost savings but the cost saving likely per unit of O & M effort expended on them, or perhaps in terms of the O & M hours put into the investigation.

Areas which often benefit from an O & M survey include: communications; office layout; form design and control; records management, with particular attention to the way records are stored and retrieved; accounting procedures; stores control, especially stock management, receipt and issue procedures, and the general security of stores; and machinery, in terms of the type used for particular functions and whether it should be used centrally. Another area is the use of credit cards to cut cash handling costs. David Zerdin writes:

> At a time when companies everywhere are taking a critical look at admini-
> strative overheads, anything which helps to cut cash handling costs and
> improve cash flows has to be taken seriously. Not all the traditional overhead
> areas – rent, telephone, stationery, heating and lighting – can be cut without
> adversely affecting company efficiency. There is, however, one very simple –
> and often overlooked – route to reducing administrative costs: modifying your
> system of expense reimbursement.

He goes on to explain the benefits of providing employees with credit cards rather than keeping a cash float to pay them back for any expenses they may have incurred.[14]

Higher-level O & M projects include the following:

1.   When there has been a take-over or a merger between firms or a change in departmental structure, with the question of how the office function should be carried out in future.

2.   Where a complete or partial administrative reorganisation is to be carried out, or a reorganisation related to a particular purpose such as the standardisation of a procedure throughout the entity.

3.   In problem solving and trouble-shooting, where O & M may be called in on an *ad hoc* basis to deal with problems.

The objectives of O & M

Earlier in this book the types of authority within an entity were discussed, these being control, functional, service and advisory authority (see Chapter 2, pp. 51–53). The authority of the O & M function is normally only advisory. Thus an operational unit that does not approve of the recommendations made for it through an O & M study can reject them – although senior management could put pressure on it to accept. When higher management is favourably disposed towards O & M work, this effectively gives some form of authority to O & M's recommendations. Nevertheless, it is always better for O & M to try to put forward proposals likely to be accepted. This does not mean watered-down recommendations; rather there should be close consultation as the study proceeds, to explain what would be beneficial to the area and to find a form of recommendation that will be acceptable to the manager and staff. Sometimes a slight compromise in the recommendations will be better than either having them rejected or obtaining support from top management. O & M must remember that the line manager implementing any recommendations will be accountable for their outcome, since he can never be absolved of the responsibility of running his department.

The objectives of O & M are as follows:

1. To reduce the cost of office work, either through the obvious route of finding different ways of processing the same work using fewer resources, or using the same resources to carry a larger work-load.
2. To design more efficient procedures for carrying out office work.
3. To look for ways of simplifying office work.
4. To see whether errors in the work can be reduced.
5. To improve methods of controlling the output of the office in terms of quality and speed.
6. To look for innovations in the work being examined.
7. To make sure that the resources of an office, including space, machinery and people, are used to their full capacity.
8. To consider ways of measuring office work in the area under survey.
9. To improve security in the office, e.g. with petty cash, supplies, equipment, confidential documents, etc.
10. Most importantly, to ensure that any suggestions formulated are presented in a way that will be accepted, preferably with some enthusiasm.

Costing of O & M

One of the factors the O & M department should not overlook is the cost of its own activities. It is important that O & M makes a positive contribution to the entity commensurate with the costs of running the service. Thus some form of cost/benefit analysis must be applied to the O & M function. Sometimes, at the start of an assignment, this may be more of an act of faith; yet an attempt must be made to list the costs and ascertain the likely benefits of the assignment. One way of making users aware of O & M costs is for the services of the department to be charged out to them. This will ensure that those asking for the service will be careful in their consideration of the amount of help they ask for. Of course, this may also inhibit the use of the service.

As in any form of costing system, control is necessary. This will be based on records of the number of hours worked on a project and materials or services used. Before commencing an O & M project it is sensible to prepare budgets for the cost and time aspect of the project, focusing the minds of the people who requested it on the resources to be used. As the investigation proceeds a progress record must be maintained. Finally, a record of the total cost of the project and details of the recommendations must be kept, together with a statement of whether the latter were implemented and if a follow-up took place in order to ascertain the benefits in terms of money and quality.

When a budget for a project is drawn up, the manager of the area requesting the service should be brought in to agree the amount of time to be spent and resources to be used. Perhaps a general overview survey will be made by an experienced member of the O & M team to gauge what will probably be involved in the assignment and the benefits likely to result. If O & M is to be costed to users, it is easier to get an agreement on the amount to be spent on the assignment *before* the work has been commenced.

The place and status of O & M

If an O & M department is established in an entity, the normal considerations associated with a specialist function will apply. The manager must be carefully selected and a balance struck in the recruiting of staff between the experienced and those who are untrained but enthusiastic. An important consideration is how the staff will react to having to 'sell' their function and whether they have the ability to do this with tact and diplomacy. The advisory authority of the function will likely be reinforced by the informal status it can achieve through offering sound advice, and its position can be enhanced if the group is under the direct control of a very senior executive or a committee of senior people. The question when making a senior executive responsible for O & M is whether he will be able to support the function when undertaking investigations in his own area. This problem can be overcome by having an office services committee review potential assignments and monitor the reports produced.

The O & M manager

The O & M manager will be a critical force in motivating staff and ensuring that their recommendations have a good chance of being accepted. His personal qualities and expertise in the field must therefore be evaluated. Personal qualities will include an enquiring mind and a desire to make improvements. The manager must also be observant, and will frequently need patience, tenacity, tact, imagination, great energy and the ability to do some original thinking. Once the information has been gathered he should be able to criticise constructively. His ability to communicate, while important at all stages, comes into its own at the recommendation stage. Finally, perhaps the most important characteristic for an O & M departmental manager is the ability to lead and to enthuse the members of his team.

In the realm of expertise, the O & M manager should gain knowledge of the sector in which he works and of his entity in particular. It will also be helpful if he has had experience in a number of fields, since a knowledge of methods improvement elsewhere can be beneficial; frequently ideas, together with a little imagination, will be transferable. He needs knowledge of the principles and practices of management and supervision as related to different entities and different parts of his organisation, must know about office systems and methods, and will require up-to-date information on office equipment. This does not necessarily mean that he has to be an expert in all of these. Nevertheless, a good all-round knowledge and a willingness to visit office exhibitions and attend conferences to learn more are important. And when there is something he does not know or when he requires help, he must know where to turn.

The O & M team

The rest of the O & M team should have qualities similar to those of the O & M manager, although different members will have different strengths and weaknesses. Thus a balance of these qualities should be sought in the members of the team, although the personal qualities of tact and communication are important to all members. The basic considerations will be: a broad practical office work experience, preferably in a number of organisations or at least in departments within an organisation; an open mind; and probably an age of at least 25 in order to have the broad experience required. If this is to be their first employment in O & M they will probably need to be under 35, since people older than this may have become set in their ways. It will be helpful if the team is composed of people with a wide variety of backgrounds, since their experience can be applied to diverse problems. A large team will probably include accounting technicians and production personnel as well as former office staff, and the bright trainee manager on secondment from elsewhere within the organisation can be a useful member.

Training for O & M

The newcomer to O & M needs a sound training, and those established must have continuous training to keep them up to date. This training may be in-house, but it will more likely be beneficial if it is provided outside the entity, for example at colleges and public courses where delegates are exposed to people from different organisations. However, experience will be gained on the job. When a newcomer joins the team, especially if he has no experience of O & M, it will naturally take a little time before he is able to make major contributions to the work. During the early stages he will require much supervision and guidance in carrying out the tasks he is set. Because of this the team must be composed of people who intend to make a career in the area. Nevertheless, staff with special expertise on secondment from other areas can make welcome contributions to special assignments.

People within a large O & M team can be allocated areas in which to specialise, such as records management, word processing, etc. Each department can be allocated to a team member for his special concern, with the advantage that he will get to know it well (although in the interests of objectivity he should not become too friendly with its members).

The O & M assignment

Acting as a brake on the O & M function is any hostility or distrust from workers in a department facing an O & M study. Therefore, when O & M is introduced into an enterprise for the first time, the first assignment must be chosen carefully. If an area can be selected where the manager is willing to co-operate, perhaps because he is convinced of the good that O & M can produce or wants special assistance with a problem, this will help launch the project. If a successful investigation can promote the O & M function, it will lead to others wanting to make use of the service. O & M will thus be able to extend its activities and will be welcomed by new areas that want to benefit from the function.

Once established, O & M must still exercise care in the selection of a project in a section where it has not been applied before. It may be that the section has been running for years and members feel it operates successfully. In particular, the manager may believe that he has everything under control by dint of his experience. That management has seen fit to have O & M will seem to be a slur on his competence and efficiency, so it is a good idea if the first project can be limited, and one that will highlight obvious benefits.

The investigation should be carefully but openly discussed with the manager of the area. However, managers of host areas should be encouraged to deal with minor O & M problems themselves.

Selecting the assignment
When the team is fully established and the idea of O & M is accepted throughout the entity, it then becomes a matter of developing a rolling programme for O & M assignments. The major consideration is one of probable profitability, i.e. the projects likely to provide the greatest pay-off in relation to the resources needed to undertake them. A study must be justified and not be undertaken simply because that area has not had one for some time. Studies should also not be undertaken in an area in which there is particularly low morale or unrest, since this could aggravate the situation. Some form of cost/benefit matrix should be used to look at the resources and the time likely to be needed for each study on the list and to indicate their potential gains. The office work committee, composed of senior people from a number of departments, can set priorities; and the departments represented are less likely to

oppose investigations in their areas since they will have participated in the selection process. Good starting points include areas with bottle-necks, heavy peak loads or extensive slack periods, and where there are many errors or complaints about the work.

Materiality inevitably comes into the selection process. For example, if one office costs £5,000 a week to run and another £500, the total savings to be made when O & M assignments are first introduced are likely to be greater for the former than for the latter. A 10 per cent saving in the first department would obviously be of more benefit than a 50 per cent saving in the second.

The stages in the study are as follows: establishing the terms of reference; the briefing; the study; the analysis; consideration of alternatives; the report; introducion; and review.

Terms of reference

The O & M assignment must have its objectives and terms of reference stated clearly and carefully. This will indicate to the host area what is to be expected during the survey and to the study team what is required of it. At the end of the assignment it will help in assessing whether the objectives have been achieved. The limits of the study, the resources to be used, how information will be collected and how long it should take to complete must also be stated. It is usually necessary to inform the staff of the host area that it is not the intention of the study to cause redundancies. One of the best ways of promoting confidence in this respect is to provide examples of other areas where investigations have led to successful results and where staff reductions occurred through normal wastage or voluntary transfer to other areas. It will help if the manager of the area is genuinely interested in improving efficiency and reducing costs within his area. Another point to remember is that it is easy to go by the letter of the terms of reference and to forget the spirit of the study.

The briefing

The group leader should brief both the members of his team and the manager and appropriate staff of the host department. Sometimes this is best done by getting both sides together. As a start it can be helpful to make a brief study of the areas to be examined to provide a general impression of what is likely to be involved, although this may already have been done in agreeing the assignment and its budget. This will help the team leader decide how the investigation should be undertaken and what roles are to be allocated among the members.

The study

After briefing the main study can proceed. It is during this stage of the investigation that the workers of the area may feel 'dehumanised'; therefore the O & M man needs to be particularly discreet and tactful. He must also beware of stating his likely recommendations too early, although it may be useful to float some ideas to gauge reactions. A test run of work measurement techniques will help ensure that the most appropriate ones are used. In all this there should be open discussions with managers, supervisors and employees, and what they say about their work should be listened to carefully, especially in relation to any difficulties they have and their ideas about improvements. The workers' own description of their work must be checked through observation at a later date since, with the best intentions, their view of their own work may well be coloured.

It can be helpful to issue a questionnaire to workers to obtain information on the following: the objective of their work – what is to be achieved and who the ultimate users are; the necessary skills; where the work is carried out; the work environment; the layout of the workplace; how the work flows through their processing stage; whether there are any constraints, such as time limits on processing, security requirements or financial considerations; and where any bottle-necks in processing arise or if there is any slack in the system, especially if they cause periods of idle time. Examples of any forms used in the processing should be collected. Samples of the work may also be useful, but investigators must guard against collecting information merely for the sake of it.

The analysis

This is the stage where the data are sifted, sorted, grouped and analysed. It must be done away from the area of investigation so there can be no influence, even unknowingly, from the people carrying out the work. The information will then be collated, grouped and synthesised. There may be some duplication in this process, or the need for additional information may be highlighted; if this lies within the terms of reference it should be sought.

The alternatives and choice

Having referred back to the terms of reference and having obtained the existing method of carrying out the work, the O & M team must now consider all the *feasible* alternative ways of achieving the work objectives. Some of these may mean only minor modifications to the existing system, others a completely new system using different equipment. Two important points need to be borne in mind: the purpose of the work must not get lost; and the processing must fit the work, not the other way round. The primary source of the work should be identified, especially in relation to how it is collected for transfer to the processing stage being investigated.

In the selection from the alternatives, cost will be a major factor. Where new equipment is envisaged, the capital and operating costs require careful analysis. The fastest method and how work can be standardised must also be considered. Once a decision has been made, details of the system to be used must be worked out.

The O & M report

The findings and conclusions of a study are usually presented in the form of a special report. However, the reports for small routine investigations can be submitted in standardised format. And since the authority of the O & M department is generally advisory, recommendations must be 'sold' if they are to be accepted.

Selling recommendations is one of the skills a good O & M man develops. The problem is that people tend to be conservative and do not like change or the new – in other words, the unknown. Another difficulty is that the department in question may have designed the existing system and feels defensive about it. If the old system is condemned too strongly, there may be immediate opposition to the proposals. It will be helpful if a good relationship developed between the investigating team and the host area's staff during the assignment, so that each side respects the other. The broad areas where changes will be beneficial will have been identified, and views on the suggestions, how they are likely to work and what problems they will probably cause can be sought. The O & M team should not be too dogmatic in its recommendations, and in any event may find that an incorrect appraisal has been made when floating a proposal with the manager of the area. If the systems being proposed are similar to those in use elsewhere within the entity, the operating staff should be sent to see the work and the advantages it brings, for example through mechanisation of routine boring work. The report may benefit from a brief initial summary of its recommendations.

Installing the new system

Once recommendations have been accepted, it can be advantageous for the O & M team to oversee their implementation. The first step is to draw up a procedural statement to describe the new system and what will be involved in each of its stages of processing. Then a flow chart is produced. Any new equipment needed will be ordered and any special requirements in its installation prepared for, such as making sure there are sufficient power points. Necessary supporting stationery or documents should be designed. The system should be sold at desk level by describing the new system and explaining its objectives to staff. Staff should be given blank and completed examples of any new forms or stationery to be used, new equipment should be demonstrated, terminology explained and any necessary staff training arranged. It must be remembered that the responsibility for the successful operation of the new system will fall on the office manager.

An installation schedule may be necessary, with the old system still run parallel to the new in case there are any teething troubles and to ensure that productivity is maintained. The installation schedule may call for a staggered introduction to make installation easier, reduce any disruption during the change-over period and minimise any adverse effects of teething troubles. It may be necessary to have extra staff during the change-over period, especially if initially there is to be parallel running of the old and the new. Staff should be kept informed of what is to happen at each stage of the installation.

If staff are no longer required or are to be replaced, this must be done as humanly as possible. This is important not only for social responsibility reasons but also to help in the acceptance of new methods elsewhere within the entity at a later date.

The follow-up review

This is usually the most neglected stage in the procedure, especially if the O & M team moves on to another investigation elsewhere. Nevertheless, it is extremely important to review any new systems and ask if they have been installed as envisaged and are achieving their aims. Thus the O & M team needs to return at intervals (which should be further apart as time goes on) to check how things are proceeding and make any necessary adjustments. One of the main things that bears watching is whether workers have modified any of the new operations to suit themselves or, at the extreme, drifted back to the old system. It is important to listen to what people operating the system have to say about it since some changes they suggest may be beneficial; if so, they should be officially written into the scheme. The follow-up will also show whether the new system is advantageous and whether it may have a learning effect for future O & M surveys.

The office audit

The management audit has become a classic tool with which to examine any aspect of an entity's work. Because the word 'audit' is used many people assume that the technique is to do with accounting. This is not so, although in the process of many types of management audit it is inevitable that the cost aspects of the work must be considered. In his classic book *The Management Audit*, first published in 1932, T. G. Rose points out:

> It should not be forgotten that the financial audit, important and valuable though it may be, can only present the true facts of the financial position of the company at a given moment. It can make clear that a trading loss has been incurred, but the audit itself (apart from any personal communication from the auditor, due to his friendly relations with the concern he is auditing) will only reveal something which is already past history. An audit for management, on the other hand, may reveal a state of affairs which, though not at the moment causing a trading loss, may before long bring about that loss if steps are not taken to rectify what the management audit shows to be at fault. In other words, the management audit can prevent financial loss before it occurs, whilst the financial audit can only establish the fact that a loss has been made.[15]

Roy Lindberg and Theodore Cohn write that 'The auditor should investigate clerical operations quite closely because they are amenable to analysis, they are seldom well controlled, and such waste as exists is usually repetitive and therefore costly in the long run.'[16]

One definition of a management audit is that it is 'An audit of a company's policies, objectives, techniques, and processes resulting in a set of conclusions on managerial effectiveness and efficiency, and recommendations on possible ways of increasing performance and profitability.'[17] A general management audit can be carried out, or there can be a management audit of a particular line or staff function, such as a marketing audit or a personnel audit, or of a particular aspect of an area, e.g. for the former an advertising audit and for the latter a training audit. There can also be an audit of office work generally or of various aspects of that work. In many ways an O & M study of an existing area of office work covers some aspects of a management audit.

The way in which the management audit has been discussed so far may give the impression that the technique is applicable only to profit-making enterprises. However, the management audit can also be used in the public sector. For example, there could be a management audit of a hospital or a school, which is similar to the recently developed concept of the *value for money* audit. At a conference held in 1985 David Bishop said, 'Value for money is turning into the key phrase . . . in the 80's', continuing that it concerned 'Both giving value for money in the provision of . . . services and enabling operational departments . . . to get value for money from their own internal resources'. He added that value for money was 'embodied in the terms effectiveness, efficiency and economy', and that ' "effectiveness" is defined as the clear setting of objectives, measurements of progress towards achievement of those objectives and consideration of alternative means of achieving them; "efficiency" is defined as achievement of objectives using the minimum amount of resources or "inputs to the programme"; "economy" is acquiring the right quality of resources at the right time and at the least cost'. From the combination of these results he concluded that value for money may be defined as 'the best results for the minimum cost'.[18] He went on to show how this technique could be applied to the public sector.

Within any large entity there should be internal control; and an internal audit, both in the financial and the management sense, should take place, the former to prevent fraud, the latter to look at the way in which the work is being carried out. With financial audit there will be follow-up by the external auditor, who will ensure that an entity's financial statement presents a 'true and fair' view of its operation in financial terms. The external audit is carried out for both private- and public-sector entities.

Undertaking an office audit

Management and supervisory functions in an office include making decisions and being responsible for the planning and control of the work. Frequently this is done under extreme time pressure, which does not allow for the complete collection and appraisal of data and information. Thus a person responsible for an area often does not have time to ensure that the best principles of management or supervision are being followed. In addition, he may be so involved in his area that it is difficult for him to realise performance is not as good as it should be. If office work audits are carried out periodically, they can identify areas where improvements can be made. There are two major questions concerning the office work audit: the first is who should undertake it; the second how it should be undertaken.

Who should undertake the audit?
It has already been mentioned that the local manager is unlikely to have the time or to be the most objective person to undertake a management audit of his area; in the latter respect it may turn out to be a self-justifying exercise. The alternatives are to use somebody from another area of the entity or to bring in a complete outsider. Jeffrey Ridley suggests that the internal audit function can contribute to the office audit, noting that 'Modern internal auditors see themselves as part of that management audit'.[19] The cost of an outsider is likely to be high so any potential benefits must be considered before incurring such a cost. The higher cost of using outsiders comes about partly because they are unlikely to be familiar with the entity they are appraising and so will need time to familiarise themselves with the situation.[20] Another problem in using outside consultants is that they may not have an ongoing role to follow through the implementation of any recommendations they make. However, the obvious advantages of using a complete outsider are: one can be selected with expertise in the area to be audited; he will have a knowledge of the techniques of scientific management, especially as related to cost reduction, including O & M and value analysis; and he will be able to make a more objective appraisal.

The stages in an office management audit
There are a number of basic stages in an office management audit, which may involve all of the office work or only a part of it. These stages apply whether or not the area has previously been subjected to an office audit. They are: to become familiar with the work of the entity and of the area being audited; to ascertain the objectives of the entity and of the area undergoing audit; to find out about the organisational structure and any organisational procedures that exist; to ask how decisions and plans are made and about the control techniques applied; and to look at the way the work is being done, consider more effective alternatives, and make recommendations about changes if appropriate.

Finding out about the entity and its environment involves collecting information on the products it manufactures or services it provides and, in the case of private-sector organisations the markets that it operates in, or for the public sector the social or infrastructure services it is associated with. The ownership and control of the entity and the technical or technological expertise it has developed must be determined. The resources available in terms of capital, equipment and personnel (the 3 Ms – money, machines and men) in the area under study need to be examined in detail. However, if office audits are undertaken on an ongoing basis, much of this information will already be available.

The objectives of the entity and especially of the area under study must be known since the management audit will ask whether these are being achieved. All too frequently organisations, especially smaller ones, are not too clear about their objectives. Objectives can be divided into strategic, administrative and operational ones. *Strategic* objectives are the overall long-term objectives. For the enterprise in the private sector these will concern aspects of such things as profit, sales and growth; for the public-sector entity they will include the provision of services in the most effective way with the resources allocated for that purpose, i.e. the value-for-money approach. The *administrative* objectives involve producing an organisational structure to maximise potential performance. The *operational* objectives are short-term and concern the achievement of the entity's strategic objectives.

Information on *organisational structure and procedures* must be obtained. Sometimes the former will be found in the organisational chart for the entity and the area under review. Although such charts will show formal lines of responsibility and authority and provide information on who reports to whom, they will not show any informal relationships. If there are procedural manuals or job descriptions it will be useful to obtain these and see that the skills required for the work are matched to the people doing the jobs. A change in the allocation of work or the need for some training may be indicated. It is also important to consider whether the procedures laid down in the organisational manuals are the most efficient, and if so whether they are being followed.

It is important to compare the short- and long-term decision-making and planning procedures available. How budget plans are made must also be examined, especially the allocations of financial resources between expenditure on premises, equipment and staff, and the subsequent distribution to the various tasks undertaken. It is necessary to monitor the effects of any decisions to see whether they have been satisfactory.

Once the preliminary considerations are dealt with the person undertaking the office work audit can move to more fundamental issues and examine *the way in which the work is done*, following the procedures and techniques used in O & M. Then it can be asked whether more effective and efficient ways of doing the work are possible, and so *alternative methods* are looked for. From these the feasible cost-effective alternatives will be considered. *Recommendations* can then be made as to how the work should be completed in the future, with senior management deciding whether to implement the recommendations of the office audit, and if so how. As with O & M, any recommendation implemented must be monitored.

Conclusions

Because of the substantial resources most entities employ in the processing of office work, control has become extremely important. This chapter started by looking at some aspects of financial control in the office. It then moved on to look at quality control and how errors can be reduced, especially through systems which discipline the worker to do the job correctly. Finally, three areas which are closely related – the investigation of office work, O & M and the office audit – were examined.

Questions and discussion problems

1. During the next budget period the office manager has been asked to submit plans for his department which show a cut in his budget of 10 per cent in real terms. Explain the likely effects of such cuts and consider areas in which adjustments could be made to enable such a budget reduction. In your answer carefully evaluate the respective merits of across-the-board cuts and the alternative of reducing selected activities.

2. A small branch office has its financial activities controlled through an expenses budget. Describe how such a budget for a branch office would be established, and how the expenditure of this cost centre would be controlled throughout the budget period.

3. You have just changed jobs and become the manager of an office. You find that no budget is provided for your area of responsibility. Write a report which details the advantages of using a system of budgetary control for an office and in this briefly suggest a budgeting system for your office. (NB: Marks will be given for the form and style of the report.)

4. (a) On auditing a company's insurance policies you find that the insurance on the contents of two similar branch offices is quite different. One is under-insured, whereas the other is over-insured. Explain the advantages and/or disadvantages of such situations.

    (b) The person responsible for arranging an organisation's insurance has recently been approached by an insurance broker who has offered to deal with insurance matters on the company's behalf. What are likely to be the advantages and disadvantages of the use of such a broker's services?

5. Define and discuss the following insurance principles, giving appropriate examples to illustrate their application:
    (a) Under- and over-insurance.
    (b) Insurable interest.
    (c) Utmost good faith.
    (d) Contribution.

(e) Indemnity and benefit policies.

6. Frequently, peak-load periods are found to be associated with particular aspects of office work. These may arise over the short (daily, weekly or monthly) or longer (quarterly or annual) period. Selecting one particular peak-load influence for each of the short and the long periods, explain the problems associated with these and suggest ways in which they can be minimised.

7. Write a report on the major areas in an office which might benefit from a cost reduction exercise. In your report explain why you have selected the areas given and why it may be possible to make cost reductions within them. (NB: Marks will be given for the form and style of the report.)

8. (a) Define work measurement and explain fully its value to the office.
   (b) Describe three major techniques of work measurement and how they are applied.

9. A major goal in office management today is to obtain increased white-collar efficiency and effectiveness through office automation. How is this goal achieved?

10. What is organisation and methods? List the stages in an O & M assignment and explain how each of these is pursued.

11. What points need to be borne in mind when measuring office work? Briefly describe three methods of measuring office work.

12. 'Frequently when method improvement is used with the aim of reducing the amount of fatigue office employees face, they merely end up with a higher work-load than before. Therefore the objective is negated.' Discuss this statement and the problems that it highlights.

13. You are to advise an organisation on the establishment of an Integrated Management Information System (IMIS). This system is to cover all aspects of the firm's information requirements. What will you consider when designing and implementing IMIS?

7
Office technology

Information technology

The first six chapters of this book require a postscript about the likely impact of information technology (IT) on the processing efficiency and effectiveness of office work, which in the context of this book can best be described as office technology (OT), especially since this will gain force over the next few years. Of the numerous phrases in common usage today to describe the modern office – 'The electronic office', 'The paperless office',[1] 'The peopleless office', 'The office of the future', 'Tomorrow's office', 'The office of the 21st century' or something similar – the vogue seems to favour the idea that enshrines these titles as 'The automated office'. What does this concept cover and what are the developments related to it likely to be? The automated office refers to the application of information technology[2] to office work.

Graham Carr states that 'The term "information technology" was coined to describe the phenomenon created by the convergence of the technologies associated with computing, communications and office systems.' He continues, 'Thus information technology cuts across traditional organisational boundaries and has an impact on all aspects of information handling whether in the form of data, text, image or voice. The universal nature of information technology means that almost all occupational groups will be affected but none more than those who deal with paper-based information – the office worker.'[3] Rod Montgomerie defines information technology as 'The handling of vocal, pictorial, textual and numerical information by means of microelectronics based on a combination of computing and telecommunications'.[4] Office work has always had to adapt to the changing environment, both economic and social, and in the future will have to react to this even faster as the pace of change continues to accelerate. Roger Henderson writes, 'Very few people can now be unaware that office work is likely to be transformed over the next few years by the introduction of information technology at the work place. What remains in doubt, however, is the impact this will have on the design of offices and their management.'[5] An article in *Administrator*, the journal of the Institute of Chartered Secretaries and Administrators, states, 'The high productivity office of the future will be one in which the traditional manual support functions, such as business analysis and projections, and time and resources management, are automated in conjunction with operational tasks such as the reporting of meetings and budgetary control.'[6]

The two processing components of Rod Montgomerie's definition of information technology are computer power and communications – and some predictions can be made about these. As seen in this book the information processing needs of an entity will depend upon its organisational structure, style of management and any statutory requirements to produce information. The orientation may be towards decentralisation, or centralisation with the resultant bureaucracy. Future managers will require more information than their predecessors as they develop management skills based upon the use of increased levels of information. So the manager of the future is likely to be more innovative and pro-active in relation to the new technology rather than be re-active, and will use forward- rather than backward-looking information to help him in his tasks. In decision-making the problems on hand and the planning and controlling of operations will use information provided by supporting technology, the production of this lending itself to office automation. Thus the application of the technology of the various processing units to office work will extend it from being merely transaction-based to becoming much more of a support system. Whereas in the early stages of the development of computer power it was used to process standardised information, as for the payroll, this will be consolidated and expanded. Where initially a processing system was developed to fit the technology, this is now being reversed through the advent of smaller and less costly machines with more power – which has enabled *distributed processing* to become more common. When a system is designed today the question of what meets the user's needs is the foremost one, i.e. it will be user and not supplier driven. However, to get the maximum benefit from distributed processing there must be some co-ordination of the units within an enterprise, especially in the standardisation of equipment and procedures. For there is little progress to be made if each area adopts disparate systems; and there must be compatibility in order to avoid an unnecessary duplication of data bases.

Another development will be the weakening of the concept of the office as a building at a specific location. The evolution of communication technology indicates that the people processing the information and those using it, wherever they may be, can be linked together. These developments mean that management will be provided with a better service, since more accurate information will be available in greater quantities and on a more timely basis – although there will be a danger that with greater capacity for producing information, it will not be sufficiently sifted for relevancy. All in all it is more likely that things will be done better, rather than changes being made in the objectives of an information system and basic concepts used. Another benefit is that the resources saved offer the choices of: (a) reducing staff; (b) enabling them to do more; or (c) improving the quality of the work or service.

Developments in the new technology

Much of the technology required for office automation has already been developed and is in use, although new advances will certainly be achieved. One of the developments will be that more desk-top terminals will be made available, especially to managers. The software packages will become increasingly 'user friendly' and will offer greater flexibility. The development of local area networks (LANs) will not be the only improvement in internal communications, for there will also be internal telex and facsimile information transfer systems.

At the moment, when data bases are established the way of entering information is generally through keying in. However, optical character readers (OCR) to read and enter text in printed form are developing apace and will save the chore and cost of having to rekey information already available as text. Voice entry recognition is also developing and entry by speaking to the equipment will no doubt become a real possibility; the technology in this field still has to overcome the problem of recognising imprecise speech and the different accents with which a language is spoken. So until this system is perfected managers will still have to learn keyboard skills. Other developments will include icons[7] and touch screens. Ergonomics will become a more important consideration in the design of desk-top consoles to allow comfort at the workplace and reduce the glare of the VDU, and in the design of the office generally.

Organisations' data bases are already able to plug into commercial data bases and use their information, and this facility will grow as the latter become more extensive and specialised, perhaps accessed on a licensing basis. For example, mailing lists and information on the products of an industry can be obtained through access to outside viewdata or videotex banks of information, provided by such agencies as British Telecom through its public data system Prestel.[8]

Much of the system will be on-line with automatic data entry (ADE). There is already electronic mail, on-line ordering in shops and stores, booking at theatres and electronic banking. For example, viewdata systems are used by stores such as Debenham's, where executives are linked into the group's computer network through which the stock position can be checked and orders placed, and senior executives can interrogate the system to find out about the previous day's performance while at home. Thus the use of interactive data bases will grow.

The electronic storage of information has progressed from the development of magnetic tape housed in cassettes and cartridges, which provide a relatively cheap form of storage; through the magnetic disc, which has increased storage capacity, high access speeds, and a substantially lower cost; to the flexible or floppy disc, which has brought random access capabilities within the reach of the microcomputer. Then the hard disc, which is a fixed, sealed system with even greater storage space, came along. Currently there is the development of optical discs to provide digital optical storage, which could be a revolutionary step since these introduce non-magnetic technology.[9] These hold greater quantities of information more cheaply by etching it on to the disc with a laser, to be read by laser; when perfected this will offer many advantages. However, at the moment they cannot erase and amend information so are suitable only for 'write once – read many' (WORM) situations, such as storing information from the *Encyclopaedia Britannica* or the *Oxford English Dictionary*. Nevertheless, it is inevitable that once in use they will be developed for greater flexibility.

David Orr notes that 'Efficient, economic communication facilities are a vital ingredient in successful business practice'. He continues, 'Computer technology and the application of the ubiquitous microprocessor have already transformed office work-stations, and even the smallest organisations can find it worthwhile to invest in a mini-computer or word processor.' So 'The next few years will be more a process of consolidation, when the problems to be solved will be not so much the type of equipment that is available, but more the ways that machine can be linked to machine, and office linked to office.'[10]

Telecommunication networks will develop the use of facilities to divert calls from one number to another, to queue calls trying to access the system, and to introduce voice dialling. Cellular radio will be further developed and its coverage and use extended, with hand versions becoming available to enable the executive to maintain contact with his office wherever he may be. The use of station message data recording (SMDR) will grow, as will the development of cable and satellite facilities. The application of the cordless telephone will develop and the telephone will house personal telephone directories and speaker systems for conferencing to enable more than one person to hear and join in a conversation. Telephone exchanges will have computer-based memory facilities.

Introducing the new technology

There are strong economic arguments for introducing an information processing network, especially since unit labour costs are increasing while the cost of the technology in real terms is decreasing. Experience has shown that the application of the new technology tends to come in 'bottom up' – i.e. in its introduction the system is rarely designed on an overall basis for the entity as a whole; rather it is the lower levels of an organisation that start to introduce such things as word processors and electronic filing. These usually replace rather than displace old equipment. If in the process some employees are found to have less to do, they are deployed elsewhere or it is left to natural wastage to reduce overall staffing levels. The approach also tends to be an add-on modular one, gradually building on the foundations laid at lower levels. The major danger in this evolutionary initiation of the new technology is that the equipment introduced into different sections of an entity may not be compatible; thus possible benefits of standardisation can be lost. One of the major benefits which may come from office automation is that the information gathering and creation processes may form the basis for a group resource which, through the development of LANs, means that: the passing of paper will be reduced; the duplication of records will be minimised, for when information is pooled the amount of copying will decrease; and the amount of space required for the office function will at least be contained, even if not effectively reduced. With the establishment of networks, management can have immediate access to the entity's data bank through direct interrogation.

When office automation arrives, structural changes are likely to be required as the corporate standardisation of office work processes and processing takes place. The focal point of contact will probably be centralised, and the major consideration will be who manages the resources. A possible result of change is that the numbers in a manager's span of control will increase and so produce organisations which flatter management structures. Questions about the number of stations to be hooked up in a multi-user network will have to be answered, especially in order to determine its size and the response speeds required. A decision also has to be made as to where the stations will be situated. The ability of the network to expand, its ease of use and the costs of establishing and operating it will all come into the analysis. It is also important that the system is dynamic, user friendly, based on standardised solutions and yet flexible enough to deal with the processing problems particular to each of the organisation's areas. And *as the information technology aspect of management services develops user support facilities, the question of whether to charge out this shared resource has to be faced.[11]

Roger Henderson says that if current trends continue, 'The next generation of computerisation will not affect numbers of office employees so much as the work they actually do'.[12] If so, staff and management training programmes will be necessary, especially for the various aspects of the information network. Even training techniques will change, with much of the training likely to be carried out through the use of interactive videos and computer-based training (CBT) packages which allow people to be trained at their own pace.[13]

These developments may mean that there will be industrial relations and behavioural problems. Laurie Mullins writes:

> The impact of information technology will demand new patterns of work organisation. It will affect the formation and structure of groups, and the nature of individual jobs. There will be a movement away from large scale centralised organisation to smaller working units . . . Individuals may work more on their own, from their personal work stations or even from their own homes . . . There will be changes in the nature of supervision and in the traditional hierarchical structure of jobs and responsibilities . . . Failure to

match technological change to the concomitant human and social considerations means that staff may become resentful, suspicious and defensive.[14]

Other changes likely to occur: the structure of the working day may alter and the data base and network will be open 24 hours a day, seven days a week, although employees may well work shorter hours than they do now; or more people will work from their homes. According to Sir George Jefferson, 'Convergence between communications and computing is already making the office of the future a reality. There is no doubt that the technology is there to transfer many of the office functions to the home, and the high-speed links are technically available to link different homes throughout the country.'[15]

In the introduction of information technology, Roger Henderson says that 'Immediate and total change is not the practical answer; evolution must happen at a manageable rate'. He continues that the administrator should have started to think through a progressive programme for introducing automation; he must consider the cost implications, and identify and quantify the benefits that it will bring. Then he must develop a long-term strategy to carry out the changes, with a step-by-step approach for the introduction of automation together with a parallel programme for office reorganisation.[16] Another writer, Neville Osrin, suggests that 'Holistic planning of the office environment coupled with very strong corporate commitment points us solidly in the direction of worker effectiveness'. He continues, 'That holistic overview defines a problem with four distinct dimensions: Technology and Computers; Facilities and Furniture; Work Processes; and Social and People Concerns.'[17] Holistic is another name for the systems approach, and it can be seen that taking this approach has much to offer in the introduction of information technology for office work processing.

The manager and data banks and networks

Research has shown that a manager's time tends to be divided among three main areas: attending meetings, communicating on the telephone and writing documents. If the manager is to gain the fullest possible benefit from the introduction of information technology into his organisation, he will need a change in attitude, especially in relation to who keys the entries into the system. Barry Barker, Secretary of the Institute of Chartered Secretaries and Administrators, writes that 'The more general effect of the IT revolution is to remove specialists (particularly of the numerate variety) and provide management with a vast array of tweakable data requiring interpretation and analysis – not by any professionally qualified advisor, but by the manager himself or herself'.[18] The manager will have a work-station hooked into a network which has facilities for word processing, electronic filing and access to outside viewdata systems, and he will be able to transmit data through the network's electronic messaging and facsimile systems. The system will also provide the manager with a desk-top diary.

Managers are likely to write many of their own communications, thus freeing secretaries for other work. All in all, the manager will take over that part of the secretary's job related to data entry and enquiry of the system. The secretary will not be made obsolete but will rather see a change in direction and job enhancement. Managers will have to develop new skills and work practices and will become more and more reliant on their work-station, through which the technology feeds them information. More time will be spent interpreting and analysing information at their fingertips rather than producing it, especially through its computational manipulation which will be done more or less automatically and instantly by the carefully programmed system. The manager will also acquire the skills which will enable him to develop and extend his own information system within the framework of his entity's network.

One benefit of the new technology is that the manager will be able to access the organisation's data base directly through its LAN. The advantage is that he will know exactly what he is looking for and will not have to go through a third party to whom he must explain his requirements. The use of portable versions of computers will become more common, and battery-driven ones, which will be no larger than today's bulky calculator, will provide the executive with computing power in different locations. Thus he will be able to send discs along to his organisation for processing or prepare his memos instantly if printer facilities are available. He will also have access to voice messaging and telephone conferencing facilities.

However, one needs to be wary of making it all sound too easy. For there are likely to be problems in the application and implementation of the new technology, and perhaps even in training for it.

It would be appropriate to conclude with a quotation from an address entitled 'Change or Fade Away', given by Sir Monty Finniston to the Registrars' Group, an important practising element of the Institute of Chartered Secretaries and Administrators, on 13 September 1982. He commenced his address by saying, 'A feature about good administration as defined by administrators is that their job is carried out in a routine fashion. Any disturbance externally or internally generated in the recognized practice is considered an intrusion upon the administrative machine.' Sir Monty concluded his address with the words, 'The unfortunate and damning feature of today's society is its resistance to change. What is wanted is a rational, which means intellectual, solution to the problem of what change induces.'[19]

Questions and discussion problems

1. 'Very few people can now be unaware that office work is likely to be transformed over the next few years by the introduction of information technology at the workplace. What remains in doubt, however, is the impact that this will have on the design of offices and their

management.' (From *Administrator*, June 1983.) Discuss the impact that information technology is likely to have on the future of:

(a) office design, considering both (i) existing offices, and (ii) new buildings; and

(b) the management of the office.

2. 'The office of the future will be both peopleless and paperless.' Comment on this statement.

3. 'Traditionally, "the office" is thought of as a room designated within an entity where typists and clerical workers carry out routine paper work.' Critically discuss this traditional concept of 'the office'.

4. Terms such as 'the electronic office', 'the paperless office', 'the peopleless office', and 'the office of the 21st century' conjure up a range of images in people's minds. Consider whether these terms are synonymous and critically evaluate the likely major effects of the concept on office work in the future.

5. Local networks are likely to become more prevalent in providing integrated office systems throughout an organisation. Discuss the effects of networking in the production of management information.

6. 'Because all office work concerns low-level, routine information and data processing, and as the use of the microcomputer continues to develop, eventually what have traditionally been clerical functions will become absorbed into an organisation's overall data-processing system.' Discuss this statement.

7. In an article entitled 'Tomorrow's Office' in the April 1980 issue of *Professional Administration*, it was stated that in essence there were four areas in which policy decisions about future developments had to be made. These were: equipment; techniques; training; and general awareness. Discuss these in relation to tomorrow's office.

8. 'The typist of the first half of the century and the keypunch operator of the third quarter are being replaced by data input specialists.' Do you agree with this statement? Assuming such a change is taking place, discuss the likely effects it will have on both the employer and employees.

9. While visiting another country you are asked to go along to an office which has no document copying facilities and to advise on the purchase of suitable machines. You know nothing whatsoever about the office you are about to visit. List the sort of questions that you would like answered before you offer any advice.

10. A contribution in the October 1981 issue of *Professional Administration* stated: 'Word processing is about the recording of text which, once recorded, can be revised, amended and re-typed as often as necessary.' Explain, in non-technical language, the principles behind word-processing equipment in relation to its advantages in the production of written communications.

11.   'Data base' is a term increasingly used in association with office work.
        (a) What does the term 'data base' mean?
        (b) Describe one aspect of a data base that would be useful in the
            efficient operation of the office.
12.   The microchip has increased the opportunities for automation in the
        office, one of which concerns word processing. Discuss the likely effect
        of this development on office organisation and procedures.
13.   You have just visited an office exhibition. Write a report to your
        superior which clearly indicates the major relevant developments in
        office efficiency, apart from computer-based equipment, that you
        would have seen at this exhibition.

Notes and references

Chapter 1

1. *The Concise Oxford Dictionary*, 7th edn (Oxford, The Clarendon Press, 1982), p. 242.
2. *Ibid.*, p. 514.
3. D. Longley and M. Shain, *Dictionary of Information Technology* (The Macmillan Press, 1982), p. 83.
4. *Ibid.*, p. 164
5. The *octopoid* industries are defined as those which have 'tentacles' in the form of wires, pipes or rails to distribute their products to the consumer – e.g. utilities such as electricity, gas and water, or railway and telephone networks. In the United Kingdom such industries are generally under public ownership or control.
6. *Broadening* capital structure occurs when a firm duplicates its capital assets, for example when a textile firm adds more spindles to its capacity which, although increasing its overall production, will not increase its productivity per unit of capital employed. *Deepening* capital structure is where an organisation replaces its old equipment with that using newer technology, thus causing productivity per unit of capital employed to increase – although in this case, overall production may or may not be increased depending upon the amount of new equipment installed to replace the old.
7. Marketing mix comprises everything associated with the marketing of a product, from the initial market research and product development, packaging and price, to the balance between personal selling effort and any advertising for the product.
8. G. R. Terry, *Office Management and Control*, 6th edn (Richard D. Irwin, 1970), p. 25.
9. *Ibid.*, p. 26.
10. A. Delgado, *The Enormous File: A Social History of the Office* (John Murray, 1979), p. 11.
11. H. W. Richardson, *Elements of Regional Economics* (Penguin Books, 1969), p. 80.
12. F. Eul, 'When is an Office not a Factory?', *Administrator* (November 1983), p. 6.
13. Rates are a form of property tax levied by local government authorities in the United Kingdom as the major source of their revenues. In an article 'On-site parking is the big attraction' by Christopher Mayer in the December 1982 issue of *Administrator*, Bernard Thorpe is quoted as saying 'The high level of commercial rates would seem to be playing a more important part in the decision-making process, and may encourage those firms who do not specifically need a city centre location to move out into the suburbs.'
14. S. Fothergill and G. Gudgin, 'The Shift to Small Towns', *Professional Administration* (September 1981), p. 6.
15. A case study on the relocation of the offices of a small publishing company will be found in R. Thomas, 'Office Relocation', *Professional Administration* (September 1981), p. 8.
16. For a fuller explanation of this approach see M. G. Harvey, 'Balancing facts against figures: framework for management decisions', *Certified Accountant* (July 1984).
17. It has become increasingly popular to refurbish existing office buildings in city centres where these have become outdated or if planning permission will not be given for an old, 'listed' building to be torn down and replaced with a new one. In 'The Practicalities of a Face-lift',

Administrator (June 1984), p. 23, Michael Foster says that refurbishment is 'The process of creating prime occupational space within existing buildings'.

18. *Office Workers' Survival Handbook* (BSSRS Publications, 1981), p. 101.
19. An article entitled 'The Stress Factor' by Valerie Ridgeway, appeared in *Administrator* (June 1985), p. 18.
20. B. Duke, 'The Shock of the New', *Administrator* (October 1983), p. 12.
21. A special feature on office planning can be found in the April 1982 issue of *Administrator*, pp. 17–23.
22. B. H. Walley, *Handbook of Office Management*, 2nd edn (Business Books, 1982), p. 47.
23. From 'Furniture for the Modern Office', *Administrator* (April 1982), p. 21.
24. *A Handbook of Management*, ed. Thomas Kempner (Penguin Books, 1976), p. 137.
25. R. G. Anderson, *A Dictionary of Management Terms* (Macdonald and Evans, 1983), p. 37.
26. Ergonomics goes much further than merely considering the seating arrangements of the word-processing operator. Fergus Hampton points out: 'If one is using terminals inefficiently, productivity will not be as high as could have been realised, errors will still be read from or entered into the screens, and so on. Terminal designs have some way to go yet in screen shades, colours and contrasts, keyboards could be better designed, but above all, the environment in which terminals are used has to change.' F. Hampton, 'Increase productivity with improved ergonomics', *Administrator* (March 1985), p. 13.

Chapter 2

1. H. R. Light, *The Nature of Management*, 3rd edn (Pitman, 1968), p. 1.
2. The conclusion of most is that the education of managers is beneficial. However, David Hussey points out that 'British managers usually lack high educational qualifications'. And although he continues that 'Some might argue that this does not matter, and one school of thought holds that experience is the thing', he nevertheless concludes that if an entity is to be successful, it is important to have well-trained managers.
3. There are many texts about the scientific aspects of management, especially as related to quantitative techniques. Two examples are: D. Heinze, *Management Science: Introductory Concepts and Applications* (South-Western Publishing, 1978), and T. W. McRae, *Analytical Management* (Wiley-Interscience, 1970).
4. For example, M. Armstrong, *How to be a Better Manager* (Kogan Page, 1983), has sections on: achieving results; appraising people; clear thinking; creative thinking; developing people; innovating; leadership; motivation; persuading; team building; and trouble-shooting.
5. There is also a distinction between the word 'organisation' and the term 'an organisation'. J. K. Galbraith writes that the most famous definition of an organisation is the one provided by Chester I. Barnard in *The Functions of the Executive* (Harvard University Press, 1958), p. 73, which holds it to be a 'system of consciously coordinated activities or forces of two or more persons'. See J. K. Galbraith, *The New Industrial State* (Penguin Books, 1967), p. 137.
6. R. G. Anderson, *A Dictionary of Management Terms* (Macdonald and Evans, 1983), p. 2.
7. *Ibid.*, p. 70.
8. *Ibid.*, p. 88.
9. H. A. Simon, *Administrative Behaviour*, 2nd edn (The Free Press, 1957), p. 159.
10. R. Falk, *The Business of Management* (Penguin Books, 1963), p. 15.
11. R. Stewart, *Managers and their Jobs* (Macmillan, 1967), pp. 98–99.
12. A useful book on planning is *The Planning Process* by W. H. Brickner and D. M. Cope (Winthrop Publishers, 1977).
13. Walley, *Handbook of Office Management*, p. 184.
14. The entity, of course, will be interested in its own overall image. See for example 'Polish up your Public Image' by Anthony Davis, *Administrator* (November 1984), pp. 18–19.
15. See 'Managing Time: Survival and Success' by Roger Black, *Administrator* (June 1981), p. 2.
16. For example, see *The Principles and Practice of Management*, 2nd edn, ed. E. F. L. Brech (Longmans, 1968), pp. 64–71.
17. In E. F. L. Brech, *Organisation: The Framework of Management* (Longmans, 1966), Brech suggests that a better term would be 'span of responsibility' (see p. 105).
18. For a discussion of this point see Brech (*ibid.*) pp. 103–8, with extracts from a paper by V. A. Graicunas entitled 'Relationships and Organisations' (International Management Institute,

March 1933), which introduced this principle of management. See also pp. 150–55 of Brech's book.
19. Harold Koontz and Cyril O'Donnell prefer this term. They write, 'In much of the literature of management, this is referred to as the "span of control". Despite the widespread use of this term, the authors prefer to use "span of management", since the span is one of management and not merely of control, here regarded as a basic function of management.' H. D. Koontz and C. J. O'Donnell, *Principles of Management*, 3rd edn (McGraw-Hill, 1964), p. 216.
20. L. A. Allen prefers the term 'span of supervision'. See L. A. Allen, *Management and Organisation* (McGraw-Hill, 1958).
21. An interesting case study on the centralisation of a firm's administrative services will be found in J. P. Anson, 'Whitebread's Plan for Centralised Administration', *Administrator* (May 1982), pp. 11–13.
22. O. S. Hiner, *Business Administration: An Introductory Study* (Longmans, 1969), p. 91.
23. For a discussion of this law see H. R. Pollard, *Developments in Management Thought* (Heinemann, 1974), p. 165.
24. This Act, which consolidated all the previous legislation on employment, has been slightly amended by the Employment Act 1980.
25. Reported in *Administrator* (February 1984), p. 21.
26. For example, Paul Stait writes 'If there is one outstanding reason for the UK's relatively poor economic performance, it is surely the poor quality of its managers'. P. Stait, 'Britain Requires Professional Management in Depth', *Administrator* (May 1983), p. 8.

Chapter 3

1. *Encyclopaedia Britannica* 1964, Vol. 20, p. 644a.
2. *Ibid.*, p. 644a.
3. K. Townsend and K. Townsend, *Choosing and Using a Word Processor* (Gower, 1981), p. 19.
4. As typewriter manufacturers work feverishly to make their machines act more like computers, certain word-processing software houses are equally tied up making computers behave more like typewriters. S. Lowe, *PC* (December 1985, Vol. 2, Issue 12), p. 82.
5. 'PROOF. This term refers to the printing, on hard copy, of a document or report, to allow inspection for errors and revisions. Where alterations are required, the proof reader (usually the originator) only needs to re-read the revised portions since unaltered script will be faithfully reproduced by this [word-processing] system. This contrasts with the non-word-processing environment, where all the script would have to be re-read to ensure a valid final copy.' A. V. J. Davies, *Word Processing for Modern Business* (Prentice Hall, 1984), p. 244.
6. A. Doswell, *Office Automation* (John Wiley, 1983), p. 216.
7. *Encyclopaedia Britannica* 1964, Vol. 20, p. 573.
8. J. Derrick and P. Oppenheim, *A Handbook of New Office Technology* (Kogan Page, 1982), p. 76.
9. J. Harnett, 'Catching on to the Copying Market', *Administrator* (April 1984), pp. 14–15.
10. J. Harnett, 'Progress in Reprographics', *Administrator* (June 1985), pp. 4–5.
11. J. Harnett, 'The Economics of In-house Copying', *Administrator* (June 1984), pp. 20–21.
12. F. C. Cox, *Reprographic Management Handbook*, 2nd edn (Business Books, 1979), p. 15.
13. J. Graeme, 'How Good is your Filing System?', *Professional Administration* (June 1981), p. 9.
14. 'A major fire, or loss of all the accounts on a computer can have a more lasting effect than the loss of all the cash held on your company's premises.' D. Wright, 'Document and Information Security', *Professional Administration* (March 1981), p. 8.
15. There is another aspect to security. Don Wright also points out that 'Organisations are becoming increasingly open to information leakage . . . Industrial Espionage is the fashionable name for theft of information . . . Your competitor can obtain information covertly if not actually overtly . . . Examples of covert methods are document theft, document copying, theft or photocopy of prototypes, eavesdropping . . . and finally through people. Any good security system should defeat the first three.' *Ibid.*, p. 8.
16. 'To guard against mistakes arising from ambiguity, subjects or names which may be requested in different ways should be cross referenced.' S. Feldman, *The Complete Desk Book* (Hamlyn, 1981), p. 75.
17. 'Filing cabinets, if we're honest about human frailty, are frequently stuffed with duplication and obsolete material that we have had no time to sort out. The up-to-date information

everyone's looking for is probably still draped across the filing tray, and will only be filed when it has reached the level of obsolescence that makes it useless.' L. Heigi, *The Electronic Office and You* (Gower, 1985), p. 74.

18. Some office managers are responsible for their entity's car fleet. A good summary of Tolley's 1984 survey of company car schemes is provided in 'The Driving Force Behind your Business', *Administrator* (January 1985), pp. 23–27.

19. See Statement of Standard Accounting Practice Number 21: *Accounting for Leases and Hire Purchase Contracts*, (Accounting Standards Committee, August 1984), where the distinction between operating and finance leases is made and their accounting treatment explained.

20. Technically, ownership does not pass until the last HP instalment has been paid, although under British law when an item is purchased using HP there are rights against repossession during the period of repayment.

21. In an article about whether to lease or buy a computer, Harry Scott makes some valuable points which are equally applicable to any form of office equipment. He says 'The decision whether to rent or buy comes down basically to two considerations: the use to which the equipment is to be put, and the financial priorities of the company itself.' H. Scott, 'To Buy or Not to Buy', *Administrator* (October 1984), p. 23.

22. Julie Harnett points out: 'It is estimated that around 12,000 companies have their own in-plant printing department in order to maintain control of print expenditure, and there is no reason to suppose that the advent of computers will diminish that number. On the contrary, the numbers are likely to increase as the need to disseminate computerized information in readable form becomes a vital part of good communication.' She goes on to explain how to go about setting up an in-plant printing department. J. Harnett, 'Profit from In-plant Print', *Administrator* (June 1985), pp. 3–4.

Chapter 4

1. L. Mullins, 'The Personnel Function – a Shared Responsibility', *Administrator* (May 1985), pp. 14–16.

2. See S. Fouracre, 'Do you Value your Staff Equally?', *Administrator* (February 1984), pp. 4–5.

3. Although not a recent book, *Productivity Agreements and Wage Systems* by D. T. B. North and G. L. Buckingham (Gower Press, 1969), has sections on: conducting a feasibility study for a productivity agreement; designing and developing the system; installing it; and the situation after the agreement.

4. The word 'staff' is generally used to define those employees who receive a salary, i.e. they are paid on a monthly basis, whereas the word 'worker' in this context is defined as those employees who receive their wage packet each week.

5. W. E. Beveridge, *Problem Solving Interviews* (George Allen and Unwin, 1968), p. 9.

6. The Employment Protection (Consolidation) Act 1978 states that in cases of dismissal the reason, or the principle reason, for the dismissal must be identified. Nevertheless, sometimes dismissal becomes necessary and has to be coped with; see, for example, J. Muir, 'Firing (or Coping with) Incompetent Employees', *Administrator* (June 1985), pp. 22–23.

7. Jonathan Sharpe says, 'It must be admitted that men's prejudices constitute the chief stumbling block to women's progress in the professional world'. J. Sharpe, 'Unfair to the Fair Sex', *Administrator* (October 1984), p. 29. However, there are a number of Acts and Regulations covering this area, including the Sex Discrimination Act 1975. This states that unless sex is a genuine occupational qualification, people are to be treated neither favourably nor unfavourably on the grounds of sex or marital status. Then the codes of the Commission for Racial Equality and of the Equal Opportunities Commission respectively lay down rules in relation to race and equal opportunities for all; see for example G. Janner, 'Are you too Discriminating?', *Administrator* (June 1984), p. 11.

8. J. A. Muir writes, 'Most people are ill when they say they are. On the other hand, there is much experience to suggest that giving "sickness" as the reason is not always a proper reflection of the situation. Some employees deliberately give sickness as a reason to cover another reason for the absence, including malingering, and sometimes sickness absence reflects a lack of will to meet minor indispositions.' J. A. Muir, 'If Absence does not Make the Heart Fonder', *Administrator* (June 1983), p. 15.

9. *Office Job Evaluation: Graded Framework* (The Institute of Administrative Management, 1976).

10. Roy Carter writes, 'Because of the critical nature of many hiring decisions, particularly for managerial posts and positions of special trust, the requirement for applicant screening often transcends the traditional taking-up of references and moves into the sphere of in-depth enquiry. Such methods are increasingly necessary, even vital.' R. Carter, 'Hiring . . . (or Pre-employment Vetting)', *Administrator* (June 1985), p. 20.
11. M. D. Dunnette, *Personnel Selection and Placement* (Tavistock Publications, 1966), p. 1.
12. J. M. Fraser, *Employment Interviewing*, 4th edn (Macdonald and Evans, 1966), p. 15.
13. M. Jinks, *Training* (Blandford Press, 1979), p. 1.
14. W. McGehee and P. W. Thayer, *Training in Business and Industry* (John Wiley and Sons, 1961), p. 256.
15. Alan Mumford writes: 'Winston Churchill is supposed to have said that he was always willing to learn, although he did not always like being taught', adding that he knows many managers who feel the same way; see A. Mumford, *Making Experience Pay* (McGraw-Hill, 1980), p. 1. This book has two chapters of special interest: Chapter 5, 'The self-directed learner', and Chapter 7, 'Opportunities to learn through job experience'.
16. 'The training or T-group is an approach to human relation training which, broadly speaking, provides participants with an opportunity to learn more about themselves and their impact on others and, in particular, to learn how to function more effectively in face-to-face situations. It attempts to facilitate this learning by bringing together a small group of people for the express purpose of studying their own behaviour as it occurs when they interact with the small group.' *T-Groups: A Survey of Research*, C. L. Cooper and I. L. Mangham, eds. (Wiley Interscience, 1971), p. v.
17. An excellent book for somebody who knows little about this area but would like to learn more is *Introduction to Behavioral Science for Business* by J. B. Kolasa (John Wiley and Sons, latest edn).
18. See E. Mayo, *The Human Problems of an Industrial Civilization* (Macmillan, 1933). In D. S. Pugh, D. J. Hickson and C. R. Hinings, *Writers on Organizations* (Penguin, 1971), the authors say that Elton Mayo (1880–1949) 'has often been called the founder of both the Human Relations movement and of industrial sociology'; see p. 126.
19. See A. H. Maslow, 'A Theory of Human Motivation', in *Management and Motivation*, V. H. Vroom and E. L. Deci, eds. (Penguin, 1970).
20. See F. Herzberg, B. Mausner and B. B. Snyderman, *The Motivation to Work* (Wiley, 1959).
21. R. Henderson, 'Health and Safety: The Legal Requirements', *Professional Administration* (March 1981), pp. 2–3.
22. V. Ridgeway, 'The Stress Factor', *Administrator* (June 1985), p. 18.
23. Administrators must realise that although the Offices, Shops and Railway Premises Acts 1963 required that accidents to employees be reported and records kept, the Notification of Accidents and Dangerous Occurrences Regulations 1980 extended these requirement to 'new entrant areas' such as advertising and market research, art galleries, education, entertainment, medical and dental services, museums, and religious organisations, among others. See B. Walsh, 'Accidents at Work', *Professional Administration* (March 1981), pp. 4–6.
24. In his book *Personality and Organization* (Harper and Row, 1957), Chris Argyris develops this theme.

Chapter 5

1. The Pocket Oxford Dictionary, 5th edn (Oxford University Press, 1969), p. 214.
2. *Ibid.*, p. 616.
3. *Ibid.*, p. 176.
4. 'Semantics is concerned with problems of relationships between words and things, especially those problems of making relationships stable and reliable enough for us to communicate with one another accurately on matters of fact and judgment.' R. Stamper, *Information in Business and Administrative Systems* (B. T. Batsford, 1973), p. 70.
5. A useful book for those who want to learn more about the basics of spoken and written communications is *Business Communications*, 4th edn by R. T. Chappell and W. L. Read (Macdonald and Evans, 1979).
6.   I keep six honest serving-men
     (They taught me all I knew);
     Their names are What and Why and When

And How and Where and Who.
R. Kipling, 'The Elephant's Child', *Just-So Stories*.
7. A. Cox, 'Putting your Phone to Good Account', *Administrator* (June 1983), p. 12.
8. 'If a company wants to set up a training or sales meeting between representatives of its offices in various locations, whether in the same country or elsewhere in the world, it is possible to line up with all these different locations on one telephone call.' B. Goodman, 'Liberalizing the Networks', *Administrator* (October 1985), p. 20.
9. An advance on audio-conferencing is video-conferencing or tele-conferencing. Lyn Heigi writes that it is '. . . another way of avoiding physical travel while transmitting information (words *and* pictures this time) between locations'. L. Heigi, *The Electronic Office and You* (Gower, 1985), p. 68.
10. 'With such a [facsimile] machine it is possible to send a page of A4 down the telephone line in as little as 20 seconds to anywhere in the world, as long as there is a compatible machine at the other end. The machines can be programmed to send the text at some later time, so as to take advantage of different time zones and cheaper rates.' Goodman, *op. cit.*
11. Goodman, *op. cit.*
12. S. Connell and I. A. Galbraith, *The Electronic Mail Handbook* (Century Publishing, 1982), p. 9.
13. J. Sharpe, 'Writing Practice makes Letter Perfect', *Administrator* (February 1983), p. 13.
14. J. Sharpe, 'Reading is the Key to Good Letter Writing', *Administrator* (April 1983), p. 26.

Chapter 6

1. *Organisation and Methods*, 2nd edn, ed. G. E. Milward (Macmillan, 1967), p. 223.
2. C. A. Horn, 'Who's Working in Your Office?', *Administrator* (October 1983), pp. 13–14.
3. C. Vecchi, 'Covering the Market', *Administrator* (February 1984), p. 9.
4. *Everyman's Dictionary of Economics*, compiled by A. Seldon and F. G. Pennance (J. M. Dent and Sons, 1965).
5. *A Handbook of Management*, ed. T. Kempner (Penguin Books, 1976).
6. 'Not everyone is honest, as we know only too well these days. Yet fidelity insurance is not exactly booming, as many managements look upon it as a luxury cover. But the potential loss is frightening.' J. Vann, 'Taking Cover against Fraud', *Administrator* (May 1984), p. 23.
7. John Gaselee says, 'The commercial risks involved in running a vehicle fleet can be considerable.' He suggests ways in which vehicle insurance costs can be controlled in 'Fleet Motor Insurance', *Professional Administration* (April 1981), p. 10.
8. Martin Roffey points out, 'The likelihood of a client instituting claims procedures against his professional advisor was, until quite recently, very remote.' He continues, 'Attitudes have changed . . . and now everybody appears to be out for all they can get.' M. Roffey, 'Professional Negligence: Inoculate against "Litigation Fever"', *Administrator* (January 1982), pp. 3 and 5.
9. 'Travel Insurance for the Business Man', *Administrator* (February 1982), p. 17, and J. Vann, 'What's your Policy on Overseas Travel?', *Administrator* (December 1984), p. 16, discuss various aspects of travel insurance for the business man.
10. *Measuring Office Work* by L. H. Bunker (Pitman, 1964) is a useful, short, readable book on the subject.
11. British Standards Institute, BS 3138.
12. *A Handbook of Mangement*, ed. T. Kempner (Penguin Books, 1976), p. 278.
13. T. J. Bentley, *Practical Cost Reduction* (McGraw-Hill, 1980), p. 135.
14. D. Zerdin, 'Expenses: Cards Cut Cash Handling Costs', *Administrator* (April 1983), p. 18.
15. T. G. Rose, *The Management Audit*, 3rd edn (Gee and Co., 1961), p. 39.
16. R. A. Lindberg and T. Cohn, *Operations Audit* (American Management Association, 1972), p. 122.
17. F. Finch, *A Concise Encyclopedia of Management Techniques* (Heinemann, 1976).
18. From an unpublished paper 'Value for Money Update', presented by David Bishop to 'Update for Accountants' organised by the Certified Accountants Educational Trust at the University of Lancaster, September 1985.
19. J. Ridley, 'Internal Audit Managers feel the Need to Belong', *Administrator* (February 1983), pp. 16–17.

20. The entity's external auditors could be asked to undertake the management audit of office work, with the advantages that they are already familiar with the work of the organisation and have a continuing role; thus they can monitor the implementation of any recommendations made. However, it is suggested that the carrying out of an office audit may be incompatible with their role as financial auditors, and they may find it difficult to be completely objective in this second role since they will probably have helped to design the systems they audit.

Chapter 7

1. Writing about the developments in document copying, Julie Harnett points out that 'The "paperless office" we hear so much about is quite obviously a myth, not least because computers are the main culprits for its proliferation'. J. Harnett, 'Catching on to the Copying Market', *Administrator* (April 1984), p. 15.
2. The Institute of Chartered Secretaries and Administrators' International Conference *Impact 85*, held in London from 21 to 23 May 1985, took as its theme, *Managing Information Technology*. A full report of the proceedings of this conference, including extracts from papers, will be found in the July/August 1985 issue of *Administrator*.
3. J. G. Carr, *Information Technology and the Accountant* (Summary and Conclusions) (Gower Publishing, 1985), p. 13.
4. R. Montgomerie, 'The electronic village', *The Information Revolution, An Accountancy Age Review* (July 1984), p. 10.
5. R. Henderson, 'Will the Information Boom Wreck your Office?', *Administrator* (June 1983), p. 16.
6. 'The Future of Automated Information', *Administrator* (March 1982), p. 19.
7. In lieu of software operating instructions in the form of words and figures, icons have been developed which give the instructions as pictures. This is said to make the system more user friendly.
8. For a discussion on videotex see J. Simms, 'Cheap and Friendly', *Administrator* (October 1984), pp. 12–14.
9. For a more detailed description of this technology, see J. Williams, 'The Laser Lights the Way', *Administrator* (November 1983).
10. D. Orr, 'Putting Fibre in the Business Diet', *Administrator* (December 1982), p. 7.
11. For example, see B. V. Piggott, 'Internal Charging for Computer Services', *Administrator* (June 1982), p. 17.
12. R. Henderson, 'Are you Prepared to Face the Information Technology Revolution?', *Administrator* (January 1983), pp. 15 and 17.
13. For example, the Chartered Accountants Educational Trust/Plato Financial Series of CBT.
14. L. Mullins, 'Information Technology – the Human Factor', *Administrator* (September 1985), p. 6.
15. G. Jefferson, 'End of the Monopoly Game', *Administrator* (March 1984), p. 6.
16. *Ibid.*, p. 15.
17. N. Osrin, 'Preparing for the Office of the Future', *Administrator* (October 1985).
18. B. Barker, 'IT and the Institute', *Administrator* (July/August 1985).
19. This address is reported in the November 1982 issue of *Administrator*.

Index

259